Maker Innovations Series

Jump start your path to discovery with the Apress Maker Innovations series! From the basics of electricity and components through to the most advanced options in robotics and Machine Learning, you'll forge a path to building ingenious hardware and controlling it with cutting-edge software. All while gaining new skills and experience with common toolsets you can take to new projects or even into a whole new career.

The Apress Maker Innovations series offers projects-based learning, while keeping theory and best processes front and center. So you get hands-on experience while also learning the terms of the trade and how entrepreneurs, inventors, and engineers think through creating and executing hardware projects. You can learn to design circuits, program AI, create IoT systems for your home or even city, and so much more!

Whether you're a beginning hobbyist or a seasoned entrepreneur working out of your basement or garage, you'll scale up your skillset to become a hardware design and engineering pro. And often using low-cost and open-source software such as the Raspberry Pi, Arduino, PIC microcontroller, and Robot Operating System (ROS). Programmers and software engineers have great opportunities to learn, too, as many projects and control environments are based in popular languages and operating systems, such as Python and Linux.

If you want to build a robot, set up a smart home, tackle assembling a weather-ready meteorology system, or create a brand-new circuit using breadboards and circuit design software, this series has all that and more! Written by creative and seasoned Makers, every book in the series tackles both tested and leading-edge approaches and technologies for bringing your visions and projects to life.

More information about this series at https://link.springer.com/bookseries/17311.

Industrial Vision Systems with Raspberry Pi

Build and Design Vision products Using Python and OpenCV

K. Mohaideen Abdul Kadhar
G. Anand

Apress®

Industrial Vision Systems with Raspberry Pi: Build and Design Vision products Using Python and OpenCV

K. Mohaideen Abdul Kadhar
Centre for Computational Imaging and
Machine Vision, Dept of Electronics &
Communication, Sri Eshwar College of Engineering,
Coimbatore, Tamil Nadu, India

G. Anand
ML Analyst
Vismaya Infotech Solutions
Trivandrum, Kerala, India

ISBN-13 (pbk): 979-8-8688-0096-2
https://doi.org/10.1007/979-8-8688-0097-9

ISBN-13 (electronic): 979-8-8688-0097-9

Managing Director, Apress Media LLC: Welmoed Spahr
Acquisitions Editor: Miriam Haidara
Development Editor: James Markham
Editorial Project Manager: Jessica Vakili

Cover designed by eStudioCalamar

Distributed to the book trade worldwide by Springer Science+Business Media New York, 1 New York Plaza, Suite 4600, New York, NY 10004-1562, USA. Phone 1-800-SPRINGER, fax (201) 348-4505, e-mail orders-ny@springer-sbm.com, or visit www.springeronline.com. Apress Media, LLC is a California LLC and the sole member (owner) is Springer Science + Business Media Finance Inc (SSBM Finance Inc). SSBM Finance Inc is a **Delaware** corporation.

For information on translations, please e-mail booktranslations@springernature.com; for reprint, paperback, or audio rights, please e-mail bookpermissions@springernature.com.

Apress titles may be purchased in bulk for academic, corporate, or promotional use. eBook versions and licenses are also available for most titles. For more information, reference our Print and eBook Bulk Sales web page at http://www.apress.com/bulk-sales.

Any source code or other supplementary material referenced by the author in this book is available to readers on GitHub. For more detailed information, please visit https://www.apress.com/gp/services/source-code.

If disposing of this product, please recycle the paper

To my dear father,
Your unwavering support, unconditional love, and wisdom
have been my guiding light. Even though you are no lon-
ger with us, your presence is felt in every page of this book.
Thank you for believing in me and inspiring me to pursue
my dreams. This book is dedicated to you, with all my love.

Forever in my heart,
—Dr. K. Mohaideen Abdul Kadhar

To my parents, who have always stood by me and whose
steadfast love and guidance have brightened every chapter
of my life's journey. I will forever be grateful for all that you
have done and continue to do for me.

—G. Anand

Table of Contents

About the Authors

 **Dr. K. Mohaideen Abdul Kadhar** completed his undergraduate degree in Electronics and Communication Engineering in 2005 and his M.Tech with a specialization in Control and Instrumentation in 2009. In 2015, he obtained a Ph.D. in Control System Design using evolutionary algorithms. He has more than 16 years of experience in teaching and research. His areas of interest include computer vision, image processing, data science, optimization techniques, controller design, Python programming, working with Raspberry Pi boards and edge AI. He is currently developing customized industrial vision systems for various industrial requirements. He has been a consultant for several industries in developing machine vision systems for industrial applications, a master trainer, and delivered workshops on computer vision, image processing, optimization techniques, control system, data science, and Python programming.

G. Anand completed his undergraduate degree in Electronics and Communication Engineering in 2008 and his postgraduate degree (M.E.) in Communication Systems in 2011. He has more than 11 years of experience in teaching and research and one year of industrial experience. His areas of interest include signal processing, image processing, vision systems, Python programming, data science, and machine learning. He has also delivered workshops on signal processing, image processing, and Python programming. He is currently working as an ML Analyst at Vismaya Infotech Solutions.

About the Technical Reviewer

Farzin Asadi received his B.Sc. in Electronics Engineering, his M.Sc. in Control Engineering, and his Ph.D. in Mechatronics Engineering. Currently, he is with the Department of Electrical and Electronics Engineering at the Maltepe University, Istanbul, Turkey. Dr. Asadi has published over 40 international papers and 25 books. He is on the editorial board of seven scientific journals as well. His research interests include switching converters, control theory, robust control of power electronics converters, and robotics.

Acknowledgments

I am deeply grateful to my parents and family for their unwavering support and encouragement throughout this journey. Their belief in me has been my strength.

I would like to express my heartfelt gratitude to my wife Mrs. M. Jashima Parveen for her endless patience, incredible support, and understanding throughout this journey. Her unwavering belief in me, even when I doubted myself, has been my pillar of strength. Her patience, love, and encouragement have been instrumental in making this book a reality. I am truly blessed to have her by my side.

I would like to express my sincere thanks to the principal and management of Sri Eshwar College of Engineering for their continuous support and encouragement. In particular, I would like to thank Principal Dr. Sudha Mohanram for her visionary leadership and unwavering support in developing the advanced research center "Computational Imaging and Machine Vision." Her continuous support, guidance, encouragement, and belief in my strength have been instrumental in making this book a reality. Her dedication to fostering a culture of innovation and excellence has been truly inspiring.

I would like to extend my heartfelt thanks to my coauthor, G. Anand, for his invaluable contributions to this book. His expertise, dedication, and insights have enriched the content and quality of this work. Collaborating with him has been a rewarding experience, and I am grateful for his partnership throughout this journey.

My sincere thanks to the Apress team, especially Shobana Srinivasan, James Markham and Jessica Vakili for their patience and support makes to write quality contents of this book.

—K. Mohaideen Abdul Kadhar

ACKNOWLEDGMENTS

I thank the almighty for blessing me with this wonderful opportunity to share my knowledge. I thank my parents and my sister for their endless love, support, and encouragement.

I am grateful to my company Vismaya Infotech Solutions for allowing me to pursue this project while continuing my responsibilities within the organization. I am thankful to the management for fostering a culture of growth and empowerment providing opportunities for both personal and professional development.

I am deeply indebted to my coauthor Dr. K. Mohaideen Abdul Kadhar for continuously encouraging and pushing me to bring out the best in me. His constant guidance and domain expertise have helped me a great deal in developing quality content for this book. I am filled with gratitude to have worked alongside him in this journey.

I would like to express my sincere thanks to Shobana Srinivasan from the Apress team for being patient with us and ensuring that the project stayed on track despite some unanticipated delays from our end.

Finally, I'd like to extend my thanks to the James Markham and Jessica Vakili for their timely and valuable comments that have helped us to deliver quality content.

—G. Anand

Introduction

In recent years, there has been a significant demand for vision systems in industries due to their noninvasive nature in inspecting product quality. Industrial vision systems can be developed for various applications such as identifying surface defects and faults, verifying component orientation and measurements, and more. Modern image processing techniques like image segmentation, thresholding, contours, feature extraction, object detection, image analysis, and frame analysis can be utilized to create real-time vision systems for quality checks in industries.

This book demonstrates the implementation of industrial vision systems in real time using Raspberry Pi. It is designed to be helpful for graduate students, research scholars, and entry-level vision engineers. The book begins with an introductory chapter that provides readers with an overview of such systems. The second chapter introduces readers to Raspberry Pi hardware, guiding them through OS installation and camera setup with practical demonstrations in Python software. Chapter 3 helps readers learn and practice essential Python libraries for handling images and videos.

Chapter 4 covers the challenges involved in developing standard industrial vision systems, including the choice of cameras, their placement, and required lighting conditions. Chapter 5 provides a detailed overview of fundamental image processing techniques, starting with basic concepts like image properties and types, and progressing to advanced image operations like filtering, morphological operations, and thresholding.

Chapter 6 is dedicated to graphical user interface, offering readers a hands-on experience in developing interactive user interfaces for vision systems using various widgets offered by the Python tkinter library. Chapter 7 introduces readers to prominent image features like SIFT, SURF, and FAST and demonstrates how they can be extracted from raw images to be used for applications like recognition, segmentation, and matching.

Chapter 8 discusses image segmentation techniques, which are crucial for most vision systems, introducing readers to commonly used segmentation techniques for partitioning images into objects or segments. Chapter 9 focuses on optical character recognition (OCR) systems, providing readers with an opportunity to develop such systems using pre-trained APIs from leading cloud service providers and available Python libraries.

Chapter 10 discusses machine learning algorithms, which have seen rapid growth due to advancements in computing capacity and memory specifications. It provides a quick introduction to traditional machine learning algorithms followed by a detailed discussion on neural networks, especially convolutional neural networks (CNN) that is commonly used in image and video-based applications.

In the final chapter, Chapter 11, readers are given a hands-on experience in developing end-to-end standard industrial vision systems with the Raspberry Pi board using the knowledge accumulated throughout the book.

CHAPTER 1

Introduction to Industrial Vision Systems

Modern manufacturing relies on industrial vision systems, which give machines the ability to see and understand their surroundings with previously unheard-of efficiency and precision. These cutting-edge technologies revolutionize quality control and automation processes by converting raw data into insights that can be put into practice. A thorough introduction to industrial vision systems, this book can be considered as a comprehensive guide for students, scholars, and professionals just starting out in the field of computer vision. This book provides both theoretical insights and practical implementation, as it carefully examines the diverse components and cutting-edge techniques essential to vision systems. Readers will get practical experience creating reliable vision systems for industrial use, with an emphasis on using the flexible Raspberry Pi board and Python programming. By the end of this journey, readers will possess the knowledge and capabilities necessary to design and develop efficient vision systems, paving the way for novel ideas and breakthroughs in the area of industrial automation.

© K. Mohaideen Abdul Kadhar and G. Anand 2024
K. Mohaideen Abdul Kadhar and G. Anand, *Industrial Vision Systems with Raspberry Pi*,
Maker Innovations Series, https://doi.org/10.1007/979-8-8688-0097-9_1

Introduction to Computer Vision

The prospect of developing a computer vision system was originally conceived in the late 1960s by universities spearheading the field of artificial intelligence at that time. The basic idea, initially, was to imitate the human vision system. The students pursuing this field were given summer projects to build a vision system by simply attaching a camera to a computer and programming it to describe "what it saw." Further studies made in the following years laid the foundation of many of the existing vision system algorithms such as edge detection, image segmentation, object representation, motion estimation, etc.

Image processing systems usually involve the acquisition, processing, and analysis of images to extract information, whereas a vision system additionally involves the understanding of the images and making decisions based on the knowledge. As per the definition provided by IBM, "Computer vision is a field of artificial intelligence (AI) that enables computers and systems to derive meaningful information from digital images, videos and other visual inputs—and take actions or make recommendations based on that information."

It is not a wise idea to try mimicking human vision every time a vision system needs to be developed. To understand this, let's draw out some of the stark differences between the human vision system and a simple computer vision system. In human vision system, the image acquisition is done using the eyes and the image processing is carried out using the brain, whereas in computer system, the acquisition of images is done with the help of cameras and the processing is carried out using computers that are aided by image processing software. The degree of human vision is limited, as the head cannot be turned beyond a certain limit, and the perception of images also varies with respect to the field of vision. The computer vision system, on the other hand, can be built to provide uniform vision across 360 degrees.

The images in the human vision system are carried by nerve impulses from the retina of the eye to the brain where they are processed, whereas the images in the computer vision system are carried by electric impulses. The most important difference in terms of the performance of the two systems is that the human vision system is trained by a lifetime of context that enables humans to perceive a lot of information regarding a scene, such as the types of objects present, the distance in which they are present, if they are moving or stationary, the speed of a moving object, etc., in a split second. On the other hand, the computer vision system developed for a particular application needs to be trained only with respect to the context of that application that enables the system to perform particular tasks relatively quickly compared to human vision.

Over the years, computer vision has found a lot of applications across various domains. For instance, a lot of imaging techniques are currently used in the field of medicine to diagnose as well as gather information on a number of ailments. Computer vision has naturally found its way into biometric recognition where a number of imaging techniques, ranging from simple thumbprints to face images, are used to verify the authenticity of persons. Another area where computer vision has been gaining prominence is the military where a number of sensors including imaging sensors are used to sweep over a particular area and learn a lot of information that can be helpful in making timely strategic decisions. One more interesting application of computer vision system is the development of autonomous vehicles, ranging from simple cars or trucks to advanced technologies like UAVs and rovers for space exploration that learn from the images of the scene in front of them to make real-time split-second decisions that can be used to perform maneuvering or even more complicated tasks. The industrial sector is another domain that is deeply impacted by computer vision techniques in the recent times with a goal of driving efficiency and precision. By utilizing computer vision, industrial vision systems may transform manufacturing processes and guarantee unmatched quality and operational performance. Let us delve a little into these industrial vision systems to get us started on our journey.

Industrial Vision Systems

With drastic advancements in technology over the past few decades, industries have gone through a number of revolutions that have completely transformed the manufacturing process. Currently, we are in the fourth industrial revolution which is shortly named as Industry 4.0. The idea behind this technology is to enable an automation-driven operation using a network of sensors that are capable of gathering data across the industry, communicate with each other to share data, and monitor each other without human intervention. The main constituents of Industry 4.0 are cyber-physical systems, Internet of Things (IoT), cloud computing, and cognitive computing. This book covers the process of incorporating a vision system to meet specific industrial needs. Starting with the hardware and software required for the implementation, the book goes on to cover core algorithms involved in industrial applications, such as object detection and recognition, and provides specific case studies with respect to real-time systems for production line.

Before delving into much more detail about the industrial vision system, let us try to understand the requirements of and challenges in implementing a computer vision system. A vision system is basically composed of two parts: image acquisition and image processing and analysis. The acquisition system consists of all the hardware required to capture the image of an object of interest with respect to the application. Irrespective of the environment in which the system is implemented, we could build a highly reliable and accurate system if we are able to acquire a uniformly illuminated and clear image of the object in question. Firstly, we need to select a camera or imaging sensor that is well suited for the application for which the vision system is to be built. Second, we need to ensure that either the environment, in which the system is to be used, is well lit or the camera/sensor that we select is able to provide reasonably good images under variable lighting conditions. In case of indoor applications with fixed conditions, setting up of some light source to uniformly illuminate the field of vision could do a great deal in improving the efficiency of the system. The positioning of both the light source and camera/sensor would also play a crucial role in determining the accuracy of the processing algorithm in the next stage.

The image captured using a camera/sensor is sent to a processor or computer equipped with the appropriate tool/software needed to analyze the image. Numerous software packages have been developed over years that are able to work with computers as well as specialized processors. One such package we will be discussing a lot in this book is the OpenCV, which stands for Open Source Computer Vision Library, released in the year 2000. It is basically an open source software with a collection of programming functions developed mainly for computer vision. OpenCV is written in the programming language C++ with language bindings in other programming languages like Python, Java, and MATLAB. It can run on desktop operating systems like Windows, Linux, macOS, etc., and on mobile operating systems like Android, iOS, etc. It can also be installed on specialized operating systems of single-board computers such as the Raspberry Pi OS for Raspberry Pi boards. There are plenty of applications for OpenCV like facial recognition, gesture recognition, human-computer interface (HCI), object detection, augmented reality, etc. *Raspberry Pi board is a good choice for implementing vision-based applications at the edge to perform automated tasks. This book explores a wide range of Raspberry Pi topics starting from the hardware details to building stand- alone computer vision tasks for industrial applications.*

Raspberry Pi is a series of small single-board computers developed by the Raspberry Pi Foundation in association with an American semiconductor manufacturer Broadcom. Originally developed for teaching purposes, this board gained more popularity than expected and later went through a series of upgrades to cater to a wide range of domains such as computer vision, robotics, localized cloud, etc. It supports a number of operating systems depending on the nature of application for which the board is to be used. The primary OS provided by the Raspberry Pi Foundation is the Raspberry Pi OS, previously named as Raspbian OS, which is a Unix-like operating system based on Debian Linux distribution. It comes with a default integrated development environment (IDE) for Python which can be utilized for implementing our vision system using the OpenCV package. The Raspberry Pi board provides a dedicated interface to connect with the camera, and Raspberry Pi camera modules are also available that are compatible with all the Raspberry Pi models. The Pi board also provides USB ports for which USB webcams can also be interfaced.

The manufacturing industries usually have a production line followed by an assembly line. The production line in a manufacturing industry is basically a line of machines and workers along which a product moves while it is being produced. For example, a production line may involve processes like molding, packaging, painting, dying, etc. The parts or components coming out of various production lines are usually passed to an assembly line where they are assembled or configured in a series of steps to get a final product.

Quality control is an essential part of a production line as it helps to meet customer expectations and ensure satisfaction, maintain a strong brand reputation to stay competitive, reduce cost by minimizing defects, and comply with standards and regulations. Most industries employ inline quality control wherein multiple inspection points are incorporated across the production line. These points often employ people to manually inspect the quality of the product with respect to various standards or specifications, identify any noncompliant or defective product, and isolate them from the production line or the assembly line. But humans are often prone to a number of shortcomings such as biased views, error-prone judgments, and limited speed/efficiency. This is an area where a vision system can be used effectively to minimize human intervention and improve the speed, accuracy, and efficiency of the process. Therefore, we can think of industrial vision systems as automated systems using computer vision to inspect, monitor, and control industrial processes. These systems perform tasks such as product inspection, quality control, and process monitoring.

Industrial vision uses AI and machine vision techniques to automate various industrial processes in an optimal way. This involves the use of camera, lighting, and image processing techniques to inspect and analyze the products or materials at the various inspection points and make decisions based on the collected data. Through this automation of processes, industrial vision systems can help to increase productivity, reduce costs and human errors, and improve quality. These industrial vision systems are used in a number of industries like manufacturing, agriculture, healthcare, logistics and warehousing, consumer goods, etc.

With considerable advancements in computing hardware as well as the associated software, there have been substantial improvements with respect to the capabilities of industrial vision systems. On one hand, we have been witnessing a rapid development of different kinds of digital cameras with varying capabilities, and on the other hand, the consistent increase in the computational capabilities of processors has led to the widespread adoption of machine learning and AI techniques to implement vision systems. Other developments that have greatly aided industrial vision systems include 3D imaging to inspect products from multiple angles, increased automations such as robots and conveyors, enhanced real-time capabilities, and increased ease of use due to the relatively user-friendly software and interfaces. Due to these advancements, the industrial vision systems of recent times can perform a wide range of complex tasks such as object tracking, object recognition, pattern matching, defect detection, etc. Furthermore, these systems are being integrated with other automation technologies like robotic controllers and conveyors to create futuristic production lines.

Steps Involved in Industrial Vision Systems

Though the exact components of an industrial vision system may vary with respect to the nature of the application and requirements, the generalized steps shown in Figure 1-1 are involved as far as the processing of images are concerned.

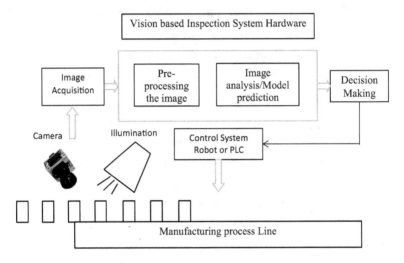

Figure 1-1. *Industrial vision system*

- Image Acquisition: This block is responsible for capturing the images from the industrial environment which can be achieved with the help of cameras or other image acquisition devices. An important aspect in this step is to ensure the product under inspection is uniformly illuminated to get good-quality images. The quality of the image is very crucial for achieving better efficiency with respect to the remaining process.

- Preprocessing: This step mainly involves the enhancement of the captured images to improve their quality via various means such as noise reduction, deblurring, brightness and contrast correction, etc.

- Image Analysis/Model Prediction: The preprocessed images are then analyzed in this block to obtain information such as the type of object, dimension, classification into defective or not, etc., which can then be used to make decisions and direct a robotic controller to perform certain actions or simply provide alerts based on certain criteria. This analysis could be done by designing a learning model that is trained using a large dataset of images to differentiate between good and defective products.

- Control System Robot or PLC: The decision obtained from the analysis can then be used to activate a robotic arm to perform certain operations. For instance, if a defective product is detected in the analysis stage, then a robotic arm can be activated to isolate that product from proceeding further down the line.

Summary

This chapter has provided a peek into the word of industrial vision systems where we discussed the following topics:

- A gentle introduction to computer vision systems touching upon its history, relevancy with human vision, and its applications

- Introduction to industrial vision systems, its requirements and unique challenges, various components, and possible applications

- Breakdown of the steps involved in developing an industrial vision system

With this fundamental knowledge of what an industrial vision system entails, we will now start exploring the concepts in more detail. In the next chapter, we will learn and get accustomed to the Raspberry Pi board which we will be using later to develop standalone vision systems for industrial applications. Followed by this, we will get accustomed to the OpenCV package offered by Python library and then go on to discuss the challenges in implementation of vision systems in the next two chapters. We will learn the fundamentals of image processing techniques that are crucial for implementation of vision systems and then learn to develop user-friendly graphical user interfaces (GUI) in the next two chapters. Once these basic concepts are covered, then we will start discussing advanced techniques like feature extraction, image segmentation, OCR, and deep learning algorithms in the next four chapters. Finally, we will conclude with real-time implementation of vision system for some generic industrial use cases in the last chapter.

Having gone through a brief introduction of the industrial vision system, the rest of the chapters in the book will discuss each aspect of the tools and techniques involved in building an operational industrial vision system. In Chapter 2, we will go through a brief introduction to Raspberry Pi boards followed by the procedures involved in installing an operating system, setting up the environment, and interfacing a camera with the board. Chapter 3 will give us a general idea of the OpenCV package provided by the Python community. We will start the unit with simple introduction to Python programming. Then we will go through a detailed description about NumPy arrays which is very important since the images are treated as numerical arrays while working with different image processing techniques. Finally, we will discuss about the OpenCV package and the functions it provides to read and visualize images in Python. Chapter 4 will cover the different challenges in implementing a vision system like the lighting requirements, camera angles, etc. Chapter 5 will be dedicated entirely to image processing where we will discuss a wide range of algorithms and techniques related to the processing of images and the numerous functions provided by the OpenCV package to implement those techniques. Chapter 6 will be about the different features in images and the techniques available to extract those features from a given image. Chapter 7 will focus on image segmentation for extracting a particular object from a given image which is a formidable technique that can be utilized for vision system. Another growing technique that is finding more and more usage in recent times is the optical character recognition (OCR) which can be used to identify the text or numbers in mechanical parts like shaft, gears, bearings, etc. Chapter 8 will be completely committed to OCR techniques. Machine learning algorithms can prove to be handy in increasing the accuracy of the vision system by a great deal, and hence, Chapter 9 will cover the various learning algorithms that find predominance in vision systems. The final chapter of the book will be the application of all the techniques learned from the previous chapters for real-time case studies.

CHAPTER 2

Getting Started with Raspberry Pi

Raspberry Pi is a series of small credit-card-sized single-board computers developed by the Raspberry Pi Foundation in London. These minicomputers are portable and less expensive and provide interoperability with other hardware such as monitor, keyboard, and mouse, thereby effectively converting it as a low-cost PC. Originally developed for educational purposes, these boards became more popular as a multifunctional device and went on to find applications across various domains such as robotics, network management, weather monitoring, etc. It also turned into a favorite gadget for people with computer or electronics background to develop hobby projects. This chapter starts with a brief introduction about the components of the Raspberry Pi hardware to give the readers a feel of its capabilities. Then, it delves into the installation of the Raspberry Pi OS along with the OpenCV library followed by the configuration of the board for remote access. The chapter ends with a demonstration of interfacing a camera to the Pi board that would enable us to capture images or videos in real time.

© K. Mohaideen Abdul Kadhar and G. Anand 2024
K. Mohaideen Abdul Kadhar and G. Anand, *Industrial Vision Systems with Raspberry Pi*,
Maker Innovations Series, https://doi.org/10.1007/979-8-8688-0097-9_2

Raspberry Pi Boards and Pin Details

The working of a Raspberry Pi board is pretty straightforward. It comes with an onboard processor and a SDRAM similar to an average computer but without any internal memory and additional peripherals. In order to work with the board, we need to insert an external SD card, with the operating system installed, into the space provided on the board. Once the OS is set up, the Raspberry Pi can be interfaced with input devices like mouse or keyboard and output device such as computer monitors or HDMI TV, thereby converting it as a PC that can be programmed to perform various operations. Additionally, the Raspberry Pi board provides a number of general-purpose input/output (GPIO) pins that can be used to interface various devices such as sensors, LEDs, motors, etc. The pin details of the board as provided in the official Raspberry Pi documentation[1] are illustrated in Figure 2-1.

The current Raspberry boards available in the market provides a 40-pin GPIO header comprising of 4 voltage pins (two 5V pins and two 3.3V pins), 8 ground pins (which are unconfigurable), 2 ID EEPROM (designated as GPIO pins 0 and 1 but reserved for advanced use), and 26 GPIO pins. A GPIO designated as an input pin can be read as high (3.3V) or low (0V). Similarly, a GPIO pin designated as an output pin can be set to high (3.3V) or low (0V). Any of these GPIO pins can be designated as input or output pin using software and can be used for a range of purposes.

---

[1] www.raspberrypi.com/documentation/computers/raspberry-pi.html

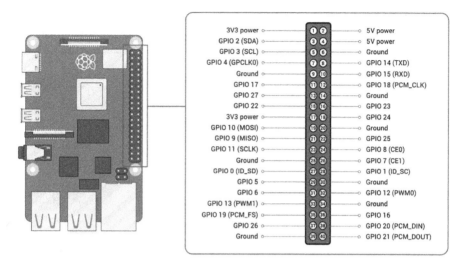

Figure 2-1. *Raspberry Pi GPIO pin diagram*

The first Raspberry Pi board was released in the year 2012. Since then, the Raspberry Pi series has gone through a lot of changes. Each stage of evolution came with something new that was embraced at once by the Pi community. Table 2-1 shows the changes in features across the different models of Raspberry Pi released over the years.

15

Table 2-1. *Various models of Raspberry Pi and their features*

Model	Ethernet	Wi-Fi	GPIO pins	Bluetooth	CPU	RAM
Raspberry Pi 1 B	Yes	No	26	No	700MHz ARM1176JZF-S	256/512 MB
Raspberry Pi 1 A	No	No	26	No	700MHz ARM1176JZF-S	256 MB
Raspberry Pi 1 B+	Yes	No	40	No	700MHz ARM1176JZF-S	512 MB
Raspberry Pi 1 A+	No	No	40	No	700MHz ARM1176JZF-S	512 MB
Raspberry Pi 2	Yes	No	40	No	900 MHz 32-bit / 64-bit quad-core ARM Cortex-A7	1 GB
Raspberry Pi Zero	No	No	40	No	1GHz ARM1176JZF-S	512 MB
Raspberry Pi 3 B	Yes	Yes	40	4.1 BLE	1.2 GHz 64-bit quad-core ARM Cortex-A53	1 GB
Raspberry Pi Zero (W/WH)	No	Yes	40	4.1 BLE	1GHz ARM1176JZF-S	512 MB
Raspberry Pi 3 B+	Yes	Yes	40	4.2 BLE	1.4 GHz Quad Core ARM Cortex-A53	1 GB
Raspberry Pi 3 A+	No	Yes	40	4.2 BLE	1.4 GHz Quad Core ARM Cortex-A53	512 MB
Raspberry Pi 4 B	Yes	Yes	40	5.0 BLE	1.5GHz or 1.8GHz Quad Core ARM Cortex-A72	1, 2, 4, or 8 GB

In addition to the features provided in Table 2-1, Raspberry Pi boards provide additional capabilities like multiple USB ports, HDMI ports, 3.5mm audio jack, and on-chip graphics processing unit (GPU). All these provisions make the Pi boards much desired across multiple application domains. Let's see how to install an operating system (OS) to this minicomputer that would get us started.

Installing OS

Now that we have a basic understanding of the hardware features supported by the different versions of Raspberry Pi boards, it's time to see how to interface the board with I/O devices, install the operating system, and use the board as a PC. We'll need a computer monitor, keyboard and mouse, the Raspberry Pi power supply, and an SD card (a minimum of 8GB microSD card is recommended).

A software called "Raspberry Pi Imager" is recommended by the Raspberry Pi community to install an operating system to your SD card. Another SD card-based installer named NOOBS (New Out Of the Box Software) was previously used widely, but the Raspberry Pi community no longer recommends or supports using NOOBS. Use the following steps to install the Raspberry Pi OS in the SD card.

1. Download the latest version of Raspberry Pi Imager in a PC, and install it.

2. Connect the SD card to the PC using an SD card reader.

3. Open the Raspberry Pi Imager tool, and choose the required OS from the list provided. A number of operating systems are available in a drop-down list, of which the "Raspberry Pi OS" is developed by the Pi community. We can also choose other OS depending upon our requirements or expertise.

4. Under the Storage drop-down menu, select the SD
    card that we have connected to the PC as shown in
    Figure 2-2.

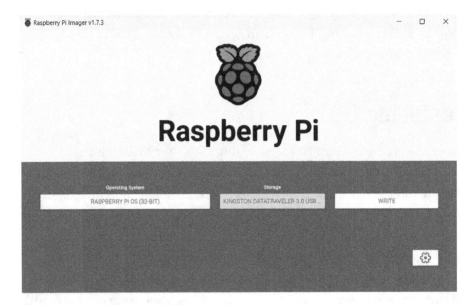

Figure 2-2. Raspberry Pi installation window

5. Review the OS and Storage selections, and click
    on the "Write" button to begin writing data to the
    SD card.

Once the writing process is completed, we can remove the SD card
and insert it into our Raspberry Pi board. We can then connect a computer
monitor to the HDMI port of the board. If the monitor has VGA support
instead of HDMI, we can use a VGA to HDMI converter to connect it to
the HDMI port of the board. Following this, we can connect a keyboard
and mouse to the Pi board using the available USB ports. If needed, we
can connect a speaker to the 3.5mm audio jack provided on the board.
The keyboard, mouse, and speaker can also be connected via bluetooth

provided that all those devices as well as our Pi board have bluetooth support. After connecting all the I/O devices, we can go ahead and power up the board.

When the Raspberry Pi boots up for the first time, it will take us to a configuration wizard that will allow us to set up our Raspberry Pi. The wizard will first allow us to configure international settings and our time zone information, following which we will be prompted to create a user account where we can choose our username and password. Note that some old versions of the OS may require us to go with a default username of "pi." After creating our user account, we can configure our screen (like reducing the size of the desktop) and our wireless network. Once the wireless network is configured, the Raspberry Pi board will have access to the Internet. Sometimes, we will be prompted to update our OS to the latest version once we are connected to the Internet. In this case, we can go ahead with the update following which we will be prompted to reboot the Raspberry Pi. Now the board will boot into the Raspberry Pi OS which will have an easy-to-navigate interface like other operating systems such as Windows and Linux.

Installing OpenCV on Raspberry Pi

OpenCV is a powerful open source library for real-time computer vision that can be used to implement advanced image processing tasks such as object detection, motion tracking, etc. Using this OpenCV package along with Python programming, we can acquire images from a camera interfaced to the Raspberry Pi board and perform real-time machine vision tasks. Let us start by looking at how to install the OpenCV package and its dependencies in our Pi board.

Before proceeding with the installation, we need to perform some prerequisite operations in the Raspberry Pi OS. First, open the terminal and type *sudo raspi-config.* This will open the Raspberry Pi Software

Configuration Tool where we need to go to *Advanced Options* and select *Expand Filesystem.* This will ask us to reboot the system. This step is being taken primarily to ensure that there is no shortage of space on the system we are working on. After rebooting, we need to update and upgrade our system by typing *sudo apt-get update && sudo apt-get upgrade* in the terminal. This is done to fetch and install the latest updates for each outdated package and dependency on our system.

The next step is to install a package called CMake. CMake is an open source software that is used for packaging and installation of software by using a compiler-independent method. To install CMake, we will first install a different package management tool called snap. The difference between the snap and apt package management is that snap includes everything required to run an application, including its dependencies, whereas the dependencies have to be deployed as separate packages in case of apt. The snap package can be installed using the terminal command *sudo apt install snapd.* Once the installation is complete, we can go ahead and install the CMake package using the terminal command *sudo snap install cmake –classic.* If this command throws an error, go to "Preferences" and click "Raspberry Pi Configuration." In the resulting window, go to "Performance," and ensure that the "GPU Memory" is set to at least 256. This will probably clear the error and install CMake successfully.

Next, we will install Python 3 development headers using the terminal command *sudo apt-get install python3-dev.* Some of the Pi boards come with Python 3 installed by default. In this case, the above command will show the version that is already installed, instead of installing a new copy again. Once the installation of Python is done, we will download the source code packages of OpenCV and compile it using CMake. The OpenCV zip file can be downloaded from GitHub using the following terminal command:

```
wget -O opencv.zip https://github.com/opencv/opencv/
archive/4.0.0.zip
```

This will download the entire zip file to our Raspberry Pi. After this we need to download the OpenCV contrib zip file which has an extended library that is extremely important for our entire OpenCV to work. These are pre-built packages for Python and can be downloaded using the following terminal command:

```
wget -O opencv_contrib.zip https://github.com/opencv/opencv_
contrib/archive/4.0.0.zip
```

We should now unzip both the zip files using the terminal command *unzip opencv.zip* and *unzip opencv_contrib.zip*, respectively. Both the folders are now unzipped and ready to use. The next step will be to install the Python library called *numpy* which provides support for working with multidimensional arrays and matrices. Since images are represented as an array of numbers (we will discuss more about this in Chapter 5), OpenCV requires *numpy* library support to perform most of the image processing tasks. This library can be downloaded using the terminal command *pip install numpy*. Note that this pip package is already downloaded along with our Python package.

We already have two unzipped folders or directories named "opencv-4.0.0" and "opencv_contrib-4.0.0" in our home directory. In order to compile the OpenCV library, we need to create a new directory called "build" inside the "opencv-4.0.0" directory which can be done using the following terminal commands.

```
cd ~/opencv-4.0.0
mkdir build
cd build
```

Now that we have navigated into the "build" folder in our terminal window, the next important step will be to run CMake for OpenCV. This is where we can configure how OpenCV has to be compiled. Type the following lines in the terminal window:

```
cmake -D CMAKE_BUILD_TYPE=RELEASE \
     -D CMAKE_INSTALL_PREFIX=/usr/local \
     -D OPENCV_EXTRA_MODULES_PATH=~/opencv_contrib-4.0.0/
     modules \
     -D ENABLE_NEON=ON \
     -D ENABLE_VFPV3=ON \
     -D BUILD_TESTS=OFF \
     -D WITH_TBB=OFF \
     -D INSTALL_PYTHON_EXAMPLES=OFF \
     -D BUILD_EXAMPLES=OFF ..
```

Once the configuration is completed, we should see the text "Configuration done" and "Generating done" messages. In case of any errors, ensure that the proper path is typed in and that the two unzipped directories are present in the home directory path. Finally, type the terminal command *make -j4*. This will make use of all the four cores of our Raspberry Pi to compile everything and start running OpenCV. This will take roughly around 30 minutes to complete. If the process is interrupted and ends up showing an error, then try the command *make -j1* which will use a single core. Though this takes a lot of time, it is much more stable. Before testing the OpenCV, let us install another simple library using the terminal command *sudo apt-get install libopencv-devpython-opencv.*

We can check if the library was added successfully by running the command *import cv2 within* the Python interface. We can either do this in an IDE (Raspberry Pi comes with a default Python IDE named Thonny) or in the terminal window itself. In the terminal window, type Python and press enter. This will take us to a Python interface with the >>> symbol. Now, type *import cv2* next to the symbol and hit enter. If the library is successfully imported, it will not show any message, and we will see the >>> symbol in the next line. Now we can use all the functions available in the OpenCV to perform image processing tasks. But in case of an unsuccessful installation, we will get a "ModuleNotFoundError," and we will need to identify where we went wrong with the installation.

Remote Access with Raspberry Pi

While implementing industrial vision systems based on Raspberry Pi, it is common practice to use multiple Pi boards at different points, all of them connected to a local network. In this case, we might need to connect with each board remotely without individually connecting them to a monitor. For instance, we may need to view some information from the Pi board, or we may need to access some data (like images, videos, etc.) stored in the SD card connected to the board. In such cases, remote access could save a lot of trouble rather than personally accessing each board by connecting it to a monitor, keyboard, and mouse.

Any device that is connected to a local area network (LAN) will be assigned an IP address. So, we'll need to know the IP address of the Raspberry Pi board for connecting to it from another machine in the network. There are two methods used mostly to make this connection. The first method is the Secure Shell (SSH) protocol using which we can access the command line (terminal) of our Raspberry Pi board, and the second method is the Virtual Network Computing (VNC) which allows us to control the desktop interface of one computer from another computer. Before getting into the details of the two methods, let us first discuss some of the methods that can be used to get the IP address of the Raspberry Pi board.

The simplest method to find the IP address of our Raspberry Pi is to connect a display to the board, boot into the OS, open the terminal window, and type the command *hostname –I.* This will reveal the IP address of the Raspberry Pi. As we discussed earlier, when we have an industrial vision system with multiple Pi boards, this method will become cumbersome. Another method to accomplish this is by accessing the list of devices connected to the router of a LAN. Routers usually come with their IP address and credentials printed on it. In some cases, the credentials would be provided in the paperwork accompanying the router. For instance, if the IP address of our router is 192.168.1.1, then we can

23

navigate to *https://192.168.1.1* in our browser and login using the given credentials. Now, we can browse through the list of connected devices and get the IP address of our Pi board from there.

We can also use mDNS to reach our Raspberry Pi board since multicast DNS is supported out-of-the-box by Avahi service on Raspberry Pi OS. We can reach the Raspberry Pi from another device connected to the LAN, provided it supports mDNS, by using the hostname of the Pi board and the ".local" suffix. In most cases, the default hostname on a fresh Raspberry Pi OS installation is "raspberrypi". So, by default, any Raspberry Pi running Raspberry Pi OS responds to the command *ping raspberrypi.local.* If we change the system hostname of the Raspberry Pi, we can use that new hostname along with the ".local" suffix. If the Raspberry Pi is reachable, then the ping will show its IP address as follows:

```
PING raspberrypi.local (192.168.1.131): 56 data bytes
        64 bytes from 192.168.1.131: icmp_seq=0 ttl=255
        time=2.618 ms
```

One more way to get the IP address of our Raspberry Pi is to use the nmap command. The nmap (Network Mapper) command is a free, open source tool for network discovery, available for different OS like Windows, Linux, and macOS. To install nmap on windows, visit the nmap. org download page. To use the nmap command to scan the devices on our network, we need to know the subnet we are connected to. First we need to find our own IP address. For instance, go to the Control Panel on Windows, then click "View network connections" under "Network and Sharing Center," select the active network connection, and click "View status of this connection" to view the IP address. Once we have the IP address of our computer, we can scan the whole subnet for other devices. For example, if the IP address of our computer is 192.168.1.3, then the subnet range will be 192.168.1.0/24. We can then use the nmap command *nmap –sn 192.168.1.0/24* which will ping scan all the IP addresses to see if they respond and the response from each device shows the hostname and

IP address. We can look out for the hostname of our Raspberry Pi (default hostname is "raspberrypi" as mentioned earlier) in this list and get its IP address.

There are other ways of getting the IP address of the Pi board, which the readers are free to explore on their own. Once we have the IP address, we can access our Raspberry Pi using either the SSH protocol or the VNC. Let us discuss both these options in detail.

Secure Shell (SSH) Protocol

As mentioned earlier, this protocol can be used to access the command line of a Raspberry Pi remotely from another device on the same network. First, we need to ensure that the Raspberry Pi is properly set up and connected to our local network. Then we need to enable the SSH server in the Raspberry Pi OS. This can be done in two ways: launch "Raspberry Pi Configuration" from the "Preferences menu," navigate to the "Interfaces" tab, and select "Enabled" next to SSH, or enter *sudo raspi-config* in the terminal window, select "Interfacing Options," navigate to and select SSH, choose yes, and select OK.

Once this is done, we can now use SSH to connect to our Raspberry Pi from a Windows 10 system that is using October 2018 update or later (this is essential in order to use SSH without the need for any third-party clients). We need to open the command window on our computer and run the command *ssh pi@<IP>*, replacing <IP> with the IP address of the Raspberry Pi. When we connect for the first time, we may see a security/ authenticity warning, where we can simply type "yes" to continue. Next, we will be prompted for the pi login where we need to type the password and hit enter (the default password on Raspberry Pi OS is "raspberry," but it is highly recommended to change the default password while configuring the OS initially). We should now be able to see the Raspberry Pi prompt: *pi@raspberrypi ~ $*. This implies that we are connected to the Raspberry Pi remotely and we can start executing commands.

Virtual Network Computing (VNC)

VNC is a graphical desktop sharing system that allows us to control the desktop interface of one computer by running a VNC Server on it, from another computer running a VNC viewer. The purpose of the VNC viewer is to transmit either the keystroke or the mouse/touch events to the VNC Server and receive updates to the screen in return. Putting it simply, the desktop of the Raspberry Pi will be visible inside a window on our own computer enabling us to control it as if we are working on the Raspberry Pi itself.

The first step to accomplish this is to install VNC on our Raspberry Pi which can be done using the Terminal command *sudo apt install real-vnc-vncserver real-vnc-vncviewer.* Once the installation is complete, the VNC Server can be enabled by running the terminal command *sudo raspi-config,* navigating to "Interfacing Options," scrolling down, selecting "VNC," and clicking "Yes." The next step is to connect to the Raspberry Pi, and there are two ways of doing this.

The first method is to establish a direct connection with our Raspberry Pi which requires us to be joined to the same private local network as our Pi board. We just need to download the VNC viewer in the device that will be used to take control over the Pi board (for best result we should use the compatible app from RealVNC) and enter the Raspberry Pi's private IP address into the VNC viewer.

The second method is to establish a cloud connection with our Raspberry Pi. Cloud connections offer the advantages of convenience and end-to-end encryption. This method is highly recommended if we want to connect to our Raspberry Pi over the Internet. Another advantage of using this method is that we don't need to know the IP address of our Raspberry Pi. First, we need to sign up for a RealVNC account. Then, we need to sign into the VNC Server on our Raspberry Pi using our RealVNC account credentials. Next, we will download the compatible VNC viewer app from

RealVNC in the device we will be using to take control and then sign in to the VNC viewer using the same RealVNC account credentials and then click to connect to our Raspberry Pi.

To complete the direct or cloud connection, we must authenticate to VNC Server. If we are trying to establish a connection from the compatible VNC Viewer app from RealVNC, we need to enter the username and password that we normally use to log in to our user account on the Raspberry Pi. But, if we're connecting from a non-RealVNC viewer app, we'll need to downgrade VNC Server's authentication scheme, specify a password that is unique to VNC server, and then use that instead. To accomplish this, we need to open the VNC Server dialog on our Raspberry Pi, select Menu ➤ Options ➤ Security, and choose "VNC password" from the "Authentication" dropdown.

Interfacing a Camera with Raspberry Pi

The most crucial part of building a vision system based on Raspberry Pi is to interface a camera with the Pi board. There are two ways for doing this: using a dedicated Raspberry Pi-compatible camera module or the most common USB webcam. In this section, we will discuss both these options in detail.

Using a compatible camera module:

One of the advantages of the Raspberry Pi board is that it comes with a dedicated Camera Serial Interface (CSI), as shown in Figure 2-3, to which we can attach the PiCamera module which is also developed by the Raspberry Pi foundation. There are several official Pi camera modules developed over the years starting with the original 5-megapixel model released in 2013 to the 12-megapixel camera module 3 released in 2023. These camera modules come with a flex cable that connects with the CSI interface.

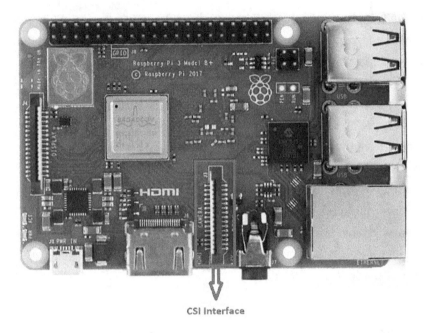

CSI Interface

Figure 2-3. *Camera Serial Interface in Raspberry Pi*

To connect the camera module, gently pull up on the CSI port's plastic clip and insert the flex cable from the camera module into the port. Ensure that the connectors at the bottom of the cable are facing the contacts in the port while inserting. Next, boot the Raspberry Pi and go to the "Raspberry Pi Configuration" in the "Preferences" menu. Select the "Interfaces" tab, enable the camera, and then reboot the Raspberry Pi.

There are two ways to control the camera module. The first method is to use the command line. Open the terminal window and run the following command to take a still picture: *raspistill -o Desktop/img.jpg.* This will open a camera preview for 5 seconds, then take a picture and save it in the path provided by us in the command (in our case, the picture is stored with the filename "img.jpg" in the desktop). In a similar way, we can record a video using the terminal command *raspivid -o Desktop/vid.h264.*

The second method is to use a Python library named *picamera* to control the camera module. To install the library in our Raspberry Pi, open the terminal window, and type the command *sudo apt-get install python-picamera*. Once the installation is done, the next step is to open a Python 3 editor, such as Thonny Python IDE that comes by default with the Raspberry Pi OS. In the editor, open a new file and save it using a filename with ".py" extension. Then, enter the following code in the file and execute it to get a camera preview.

```
from picamera import PiCamera
from time import sleep
camera = PiCamera()
camera.start_preview()
sleep(5)
camera.capture('/home/pi/Desktop/img.jpg')
camera.stop_preview()
```

The first two lines of the code are used to import the modules necessary to run the code. Here, we have imported the PiCamera module and sleep module. The third line of the code uses the PiCamera module to create a camera object that can be used to preview or Ucapture images. In the fourth line of code, we start a preview of the camera. As the camera is activated to sense the light levels, it needs some time to adjust to the lighting conditions. So we use the sleep module in the fifth line of code to delay the execution of the code for 5 seconds after starting the preview. Then, the capture function from the camera object is used to capture an image and store it in the desktop. The last line of the code is used to stop the preview. If our preview is upside down, we can use the line *camera.rotation = 180* next to the creation of the camera object (third line in our code). Also, we can use the start_recording() and stop_recording() function instead of the capture() function to record videos instead of capturing still images.

Using a USB camera:

As the Raspberry Pi board supports multiple USB ports, it is easier to set up multiple USB cameras. Let's see how to set up and use a single USB webcam in Raspberry Pi. First, plugin the camera to a USB port, and check if it is recognized by the Raspberry Pi by running the command *lsusb* in the terminal window. This command lists all the USB devices connected to the Raspberry Pi, and it should list the name of our camera if it has been successfully detected.

To control the camera from the terminal window, we need packages like "fswebcam" and "ffmpeg." The "fswebcam" is a simple webcam app used to capture images and save them as PNG or JPEG files, whereas the "ffmpeg" is a collection of libraries used to process multimedia files such as audio, video, etc. These packages can be installed from the Terminal window using the following commands:

```
sudo apt install fswebcam
sudo apt install ffmpeg
```

We can use the following command to capture an image with a certain resolution. The "-r" field is used to specify the desired resolution. The image captured using fswebcam usually has a banner denoting the timestamp showing the time at which the image is captured. So we use the "--no-banner" to remove the banner and get a plain image. Finally, we specify the path, filename, and format for the image to be saved.

```
fswebcam -r 1280x720 --no-banner /images/image1.jpg
```

In a similar way, we can use the following command to record a video using ffmpeg command. It has specifications for both audio and video. For instance, we are capturing audio from pulseaudio sound server and encode it to lossless raw PCM with 2 audio channels (stereo). As for the video, we grab a video stream from X11 at a frame rate of 25fps and a resolution of 1366x768 from the primary display (:0.0) and encode it to lossless h264 using libx264. The resulting stream will be saved as output.mkv.

```
ffmpeg -f alsa -ac 2 -i pulse -f x11grab -r 25 -s 1366x768 -i
:0.0 -vcodec libx264 \
-preset ultrafast -crf 0 -threads 0 -acodec pcm_s161e -y
output.mkv
```

To control the webcam with Python, we can use the OpenCV library. The following lines of code are used to create an infinite loop to capture the video and show it on our screen until we press a specified character key from the keyboard that will break the loop and stop the video.

```
import cv2
webcam = cv2.VideoCapture(0):
while True:
        ret, img = webcam.read()
        cv2.imshow('video',img)
        key = cv2.waitKey(1)
        if key == ord("x"):
              break
webcam.release()
cv2.destroyAllWindows()
```

The first line is used to import the OpenCV library modules. The VideoCapture(0) function is used to create an object named "webcam" to return the video from the first webcam on your Raspberry Pi. The "while True:" condition is an infinite loop to create an endless display of video on our display. The read() function is used to capture a frame from the "webcam" object, and imshow() function from the OpenCV module is used to display the image. The waitKey() function from the OpenCV module is used to wait for 1ms to detect any key stroke from the user. The ord() function is used to convert the character "x" to its corresponding

Unicode value. We use an if condition to check whether the key "x" is pressed and break the loop if the key is pressed. Once we break out of the loop, the "webcam" object is released and all windows opened while executing the program (like the window opened to display the video) are closed using the destroyAllWindows() function.

Summary

In this chapter, we have discussed about the following topics:

- The basic hardware configurations and compatibilities of the Raspberry Pi board

- Installing an OS to the board with the help of a microSD card and the "Raspberri Pi Imager" tool

- Installing OpenCV library and its dependencies in the Raspberry Pi OS

- Configuring a remote connection to the Raspberry Pi board in two ways: Virtual Network Computing (VNC) and Secure Shell (SSH) protocol

- Connecting a PiCamera or a webcam to the Raspberry Pi board to capture real-time image or video

In the next chapter, we will discuss more about using OpenCV to read and write images, as well as videos, and display them using a visualization library in Python called Matplotlib.

CHAPTER 3

Python Libraries for Image Processing

In this chapter, we will get introduced to Python programming, which would set us up for the different concepts we will be learning throughout the book using Python. We will start with the different Python-based IDEs available for Raspberry Pi. Then, we will move on to work with a couple of widely used Python libraries numpy and PIL that are used widely with respect to image processing tasks. Next, we will see how to visualize (display) images using the Matplotlib library. Finally, we will see how to capture and save images as well as videos using the OpenCV library.

IDEs for Python in Raspberry Pi

There are a number of different integrated development environments (IDEs) available for working with Python programs in Raspberry Pi. We will discuss three of the most common IDEs, two of which are available by default in the Raspberry Pi OS (Thonny and Geany), and the third one is the default IDE downloaded along with a new installation of Python package (IDLE).

© K. Mohaideen Abdul Kadhar and G. Anand 2024
K. Mohaideen Abdul Kadhar and G. Anand, *Industrial Vision Systems with Raspberry Pi*,
Maker Innovations Series, https://doi.org/10.1007/979-8-8688-0097-9_3

Thonny

This is a default IDE that comes with Python 3.10 installed along with the Raspberry Pi OS. We can open it by navigating to the "Programming" drop-down menu under the main menu (Raspberry Pi Logo) and clicking "Thonny Python IDE." The IDE has a very simple interface, as shown in Figure 3-1, with two parts: the code editor is where we can type our code and the shell is where we can get inputs to our program, display outputs and errors, and execute simple lines of code. There are additional tabs that can be added to the default interface, and they are available in the "View" menu. For example, if we check the "Variables" option in the "View" menu, this will display the "Variables" tab to the right side of the interface where all the variables we create in our program and their respective values are displayed. Similarly, the readers are free to explore the other windows on their own.

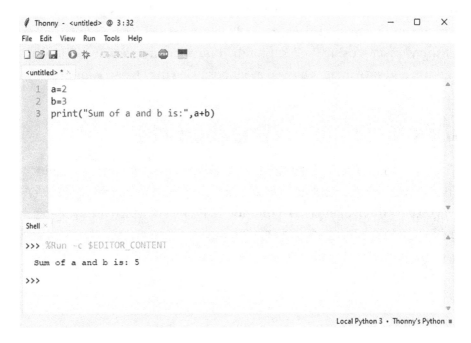

Figure 3-1. *Thonny IDE*

Geany

Geany is an open source lightweight IDE that is supported in many different operating systems such as Windows, Linux, MacOS, Raspberry, Pi OS, etc. This IDE is also installed by default along with the Raspberry Pi OS. This IDE supports multiple programming as well as markup languages such as C, C++, C#, Java, PHP, HTML, Python, Ruby, etc. The default interface of the Geany IDE is shown in Figure 3-2. As seen in the figure, the IDE opens with an empty untitled editor tab where we can type our code. The status tab shows the timestamp for every activity that has happened from the time we open Geany IDE. The Symbols tab will list all the symbols (variables) that we create in the program. Once we type the program in the editor, we can save it using the .py extension and execute the program by clicking "Execute" option in the "Build" drop-down menu or by pressing the F5 key in our keyboard. The output will be displayed in a separate command window.

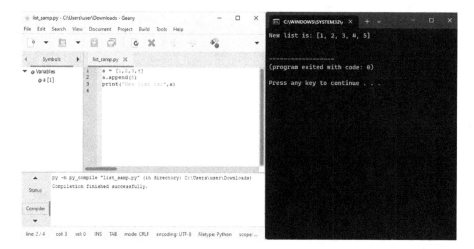

Figure 3-2. *Geany IDE*

IDLE

IDLE is a default IDE installed along with the Python package download from its official page. But in case of Raspberry Pi OS, Thonny is the default IDE for Python that comes with the OS. Since most Python programmers are accustomed to using IDLE in other OS environments, it would be comfortable for them to stick to the same IDE in Raspberry Pi OS as well. To install IDLE in Raspberry Pi OS, enter the following command in the Terminal window: *sudo apt-get install idle3.* The IDLE interface is shown in Figure 3-3. As we can see, the IDE opens to a shell window whose function is the same as the shell in Thonny IDE. To open an editor, go to "File" and click "New File." We can then type our complete code in the editor window, save the file using .py extension, and then execute the same.

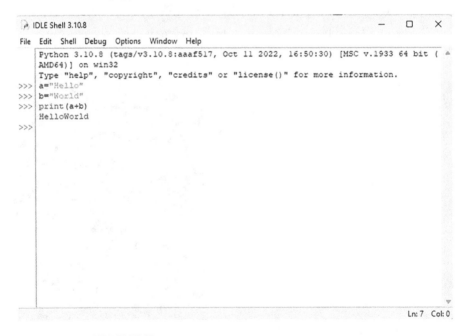

Figure 3-3. IDLE IDE

All the codes and demonstrations in this book are done using the default "IDLE" IDE. The readers are free to select an IDE of their choice as the choice of IDE will not affect the illustrated codes in the book. With the selection of a desired IDE, let us now proceed to understand the basic data types supported in Python.

Python Programming in Raspberry Pi

A complete discussion of all the basic concepts of Python programming is beyond the scope of this book. A simple introduction will be provided for some of the basic concepts, and it is left to the readers to further explore them. The first and foremost concepts that any Python programmer needs to be aware of are the different data types supported in Python. Figure 3-4 shows a classification of all the data types that are supported by Python.

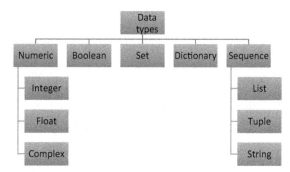

Figure 3-4. *Data types in Python*

There is not much to say about the numeric data types as most of us are familiar with them. The advantage in Python is that the data type is detected by default as soon as we assign a value to a variable. This is evident from the simple example shown as follows. The type() command displays the data type of the variable given to it. In Table 3-1, the output of the print statements is shown in the right column. Arithmetic operators and assignment operators can be used to perform mathematical operations with respect to these data types.

Table 3-1. *Illustration of numeric data types*

Code	Output
```# integer```	datatype of a is: <class 'int'>
```a=2```	datatype of b is: <class
```print("datatype of a```	'float'>
```is:",type(a))```	datatype of c is: <class
```# float```	'complex'>
```b=3.2```	
```print("datatype of b```	
```is:",type(b))```	
```# complex```	
```c=3+4j```	
```print("datatype of c```	
```is:",type(c))```	

The Boolean data type consists of just two values: true and false. This data type is mostly associated with conditional statements where conditional operators and logical operators applied on other data types result in a Boolean data type based on which a subset of code is executed. The set data type is an unordered collection of elements (of other data types) separated by commas written inside curly brackets. A unique feature of set is that it does not allow duplicate values. Set operations such as union, intersection, difference, and complement can be performed on these sets. Dictionaries are used to store data points as key-value pairs separated by commas written inside curly brackets. Each value in a dictionary can be accessed only with the help of its key. A simple example of these three data types is shown in Table 3-2.

Table 3-2. *Illustration of Boolean, set, and dictionary data types*

Code	Output
``# boolean
a=True
print("datatype of a
is:",type(a))
# set
b={1,2,1,3,2,4}
print("datatype of b
is:",type(b))
print("Values in set b:",b)
# dictionary
c={1:"Hello",2:"world"}
print("datatype of c
is:",type(c))
print("Value for key=2
is:",c[2])```	```datatype of a is: <class
'bool'>
datatype of b is: <class
'set'>
Values in set b: {1,2,3,4}
datatype of c is: <class
'dict'>
Value for key=2 is: world```

The list is an ordered, indexed, and mutable collection of elements (of any data type) separated by commas written inside square brackets. The indexing of a list starts from 0, and a particular element in a list can be accessed using its index. A number of list methods are provided by Python to perform operations like append, remove, sort, etc., which the readers can explore to get well versed with list operations. The tuple is similar to a list except for two changes: tuple is immutable (values cannot be changed), and the elements (of any data type) of the tuple are written inside parentheses. Similarly, the string is an immutable collection of alphanumeric characters written inside single or double quotes. The indexing of tuple and string is the same as that of list. Like lists, some predefined methods are available for tuples and strings as well which the readers can explore. Table 3-3 shows some simple examples for these sequence data types.

Table 3-3. Illustration of sequence data types

Code	Output
```# list a=[1,2.3,3+4j,[1,2,3],'hello'] print("datatype of a is:",type(a)) print("Firs value in a is:",a[0]) # set b=(1,3.1,[1,2,1]) print("datatype of b is:",type(b)) print("Second value in b is:",b[1]) # dictionary c="Take care" print("datatype of c is:",type(c)) print("Third character is:",c[2])```	```datatype of a is: <class 'list'> Firs value in a is: 1 datatype of b is: <class 'tuple'> Second value in b is: 3.1 datatype of c is: <class 'str'> Third character is: k```

Once we are accustomed to the different data types in Python, we can go for some advanced programming concepts like loop and control statements, functions, etc. Let us go through simple examples for the loop statement and function. The major loop and conditional statements are *if...else, for,* and *while* loops. The *if...else* statements are conditional statements that execute a set of code if a condition is satisfied and another set of code if the condition is not satisfied. The *if…else* conditional statement given in Table 3-4 checks which among the two given numbers is greater.

Table 3-4. *Illustration of if…else statement*

Code	Output

``
# if..else conditional statement 	
a=5
b=2
if a>b:
  print("a is greater than b")
else:
  print("a is less than b")
``
	a is greater than b

The *for* loop is used for iterating over a sequence (such as a list, tuple, string, set, or dictionary). The *for* loop can execute a set of statements, once for each item in the sequence. For example, the *for* loop in Table 3-5 performs the sum of numbers 1 to 5.

Table 3-5. *Illustration of for loop*

Code	Output

``
# for loop 	
x=0
a=[1,2,3,4,5]
for i in a:
  x=x+i
print("The sum is:",x)
``
	The sum is: 15

The *while* loop, on the other hand, can execute a set of statements repeatedly as long as a condition is true. The sum of numbers 1 to 5 can also be performed using a *while* loop using the code in Table 3-6.

Table 3-6. *Illustration of while loop*

Code	Output

``
# while loop 	
y=0
i=1
while i<6:
  y=y+i
  i+=1
print("The sum is:",y)
``
	The sum is: 15

Next, we will get a glimpse of Python functions. A function is a block of code that can perform a specific task and return a value. The purpose is to make a user-defined function for tasks that are repeated at different parts of a program and call the function instead of writing the same set of code over and over again. An example of a function that takes a list of numbers as input and returns the sum of elements in the list is given in Table 3-7.

Table 3-7. *Illustration of Python function*

Code	Output
``# define a function
def listsum(a):
s=0
for i in a:
s=s+i
return s
# call the function
x=listsum([1,2,3,4,5])
print("The sum is:",x)```	The sum is: 15

Now that we have been introduced to some of the fundamental concepts in Python programming, we will move on to discuss a couple of important libraries that + will come in handy while performing image processing tasks: NumPy and PIL.

NumPy

NumPy is a library used specifically for working with multidimensional arrays and matrices. Created by an American data scientist and businessman Travis Oliphant in the year 2005, NumPy offers a collection of functions that can be used to create as well as perform mathematical operations on arrays. The NumPy package can be installed in our Raspberry Pi OS using the terminal command *sudo apt-get install python3-numpy.* It is essential that we get comfortable with NumPy arrays, as the OpenCV library that we will be using to build our vision systems utilize the NumPy arrays to store and operate on the image data. This is not a surprise as images are stored in memory as a matrix of numbers also known as pixel values. So, let's dive in and get a feel of the different aspects of the NumPy library.

The NumPy package can be used to create an n-dimensional array using the array() function as shown in Table 3-8. We have used three functions here. The *ndim* function is used to get the number of dimensions in a given matrix. For instance, if we have a 3 x 3 matrix, the number of dimensions is 2 which implies that it is a 2D matrix. The shape function is used to get the number of entities with respect to each dimension. Considering the same 3x3 matrix, the shape function would yield the result (3,3) which implies that it has 3 rows and 3 columns. The size function is used to get the total number of values in the given matrix. For a 3x3 matrix, the size is 9 which implies it has 9 values.

The NumPy library is first imported with a shorter alias name "np," and whenever we call the array function from the package, we can simply type np.array(). When we use only a single value inside the array function, it is then treated as a 0-D matrix. But when we go for higher dimensions, care must be taken with respect to how we use the square brackets for creating the arrays. It can be seen from Table 3-8 that a 1D array can be created by typing elements separated by commas within square brackets. A 2D array can be created by treating each row of values as a 1D array and putting those 1D arrays separated by commas inside another pair of square brackets. Likewise, a 3D array can be created by treating each matrix as a 2D array and putting those 2D arrays separated by commas inside another pair of square brackets.

Table 3-8. *Illustration of numpy arrays*

Code	Output
| ```
import numpy as np
#0D array
a=np.array(42)
print(a)
print("Number of dimensions:",a.ndim)
print("Shape of a:",a.shape)
print("Number of elements in a:",a.size)
``` | 42<br>Number of dimensions: 0<br>Shape of a: ()<br>Number of elements in<br>a: 1 |
| ```
#1D array
b=np.array([1,2,3])
print(b)
print("Size of b:",b.ndim)
print("Shape of a:",b.shape)
print("Number of elements in a:",b.size)
``` | [1 2 3]<br>Size of b: 1<br>Shape of a: (3,)<br>Number of elements in<br>a: 3 |
| ```
#2D array
c=np.array([[1,2,3],[4,5,6]])
print(c)
print("Number of dimensions:",c.ndim)
print("Shape of a:",c.shape)
print("Number of elements in a:",c.size)
``` | [[1 2 3]<br>[4 5 6]]<br>Number of dimensions: 2<br>Shape of a: (2, 3)<br>Number of elements in<br>a: 6 |
| ```
#3D array
d=np.array([[[1,2,3],[4,5,6]],
[[6,5,4],[3,2,1]]])
print(d)
print("Number of dimensions:",d.ndim)
print("Shape of a:",d.shape)
print("Number of elements in a:",
d.size)
``` | [[[1 2 3]<br>[4 5 6]]<br><br>[[6 5 4]<br>[3 2 1]]]<br>Number of dimensions: 3<br>Shape of a: (2, 2, 3)<br>Number of elements in<br>a: 12 |

The indexing in NumPy arrays is similar to that of lists except the fact that there may be more than one index value depending upon the number of dimensions in the array. For example, consider a 3x3 matrix stored in a variable "a". a[2,2] denotes the value of the array a at the intersection of the 3rd row and 3rd column (since the index starts from 0). The above indexing is illustrated in the following table.

	0	1	2
0	1	2	3
1	4	5	6
2	7	8	9

As we can see, the number 9 at the intersection of the 3rd row, 3rd column has a row index of 2 and a column index of 2. We can also slice an array using the format "start:end+1" with respect to any dimension. For instance, a[0:2,:] indicates that we take the values from all the columns in rows 1 and 2 alone. If we don't provide a value for "start," then the start value is assumed as "0" by default (so we can also write :2 instead of 0:2), and if we don't provide a value for "end+1," then the values up to the last row or column are taken. The following table would clearly illustrate this example.

	0	1	2
0	1	2	3
1	4	5	6
2	7	8	9

Let us consider another example to get the hang of how the indexing works. This time we would type the code to perform the operation as illustrated in Table 3-9.

Table 3-9. *Illustration of array indexing*

Code	Output
| ```
import numpy as np
a=np.
array([[1,2,3],[4,5,6],[7,8,9]])
print(a)
``` | ```
[[1 2 3]
 [4 5 6]
 [7 8 9]]
``` |
| ```
print("Middle value of the
matrix:",a[1,1])
``` | ```
Middle value of the
matrix: 5
``` |
| `print(a[:2,:2])` | ```
[[1 2]
 [4 5]]
``` |
| `print(a[1:,1:])` | ```
[[5 6]
 [8 9]]
``` |

There are numerous functions provided by the NumPy library that could be very handy in performing various operations on arrays. Again, it would be beyond the scope of the book to discuss all of those functions. A few of those functions and their descriptions are listed in Table 3-10 which the readers can explore themselves.

Table 3-10. *NumPy library functions for array operations*

Function	Description
sum()	Returns the sum of array elements over the specified axis
add()	Returns the element-wise addition of two arrays
subtract()	Returns the element-wise subtraction of two arrays
sqrt()	Returns the element-wise square root of an array
multiply()	Returns the element-wise multiplication of two arrays
matmul()	Returns the matrix multiplication of two arrays
copy()	Creates a copy of the original array; changes made to one will not affect the other
view()	Creates a view of the original array; changes made to one will affect the other
reshape()	Changes the shape of the original array
concatenate()	Merges two arrays along a specified axis
array_split()	Splits an array into multiple parts
where()	Searches an array for a certain value and returns the indexes that get a match
sort()	Sorts the array along a specified axis

With this foundation of fundamental Python concepts, let us now move on to two commonly used Python libraries for working with images.

Python Imaging Library(PIL)

PIL stands for Python Imaging Library which is a free, open source library for Python that can help us to work with different image file formats. PIL was discontinued in the year 2011 and does not support Python 3. Later on, a new library called Pillow was built on top of PIL which provides support for Python 3 and can run on all operating systems. A wide variety of image file formats are supported by Pillow such as jpeg, png, bmp, gif, tif, etc. We can perform various operations on the images such as filtering, blurring, resizing, cropping, adding a watermark, etc. This library can be installed in our Raspberry Pi OS using the terminal command *sudo apt-get install pillow.*

To read and display an image, we can use the open() and show() functions in the Pillow library, respectively. The filename of the image along with the path name should be specified inside the open() function which would then read the image and create an object with the name that we provide. Then, the object name must be given to the show() function to display the image. We can then use instance attributes to get more details about the image such as format, size, and mode. The format attribute tells us the type of the image such as jpeg, png, bmp, etc. The size attribute gives us a 2-tuple which contains the width and height of the image in pixels. The mode attribute gives the names of the bands in the image like "L" for grayscale images, "RGB" for true color images, etc. The code given in Table 3-11 illustrates all these functions and attributes.

Table 3-11. *Reading and displaying an image using PIL*

Code	Output

```from PIL import Image```
```a=Image.open("C:/Users/User/```
```Pictures/Lenna.png")```
```a.show()```

```print("Format of a is:",a.```
```format)```
```print("Size of a is:", a.size)```
```print("a belongs to```
```category:",a.mode)```
	```Format of a is: PNG```
	```Size of a is: (512, 512)```
	```a belongs to category: RGB```

We can see that the image is a png file. The size of the image is 512,512 which implies that it is 512 pixels wide and 512 pixels high and it belongs to the category of RGB images. Pillow library provides a number of functions to perform various image processing tasks. We will see a few of them in action, and the rest of them are left to the readers to explore.

The crop() function can be used to get a sub-rectangle region from the given image. The boundary of the sub-rectangle region is specified by a 4-tuple with coordinates specified in the template: "crop(left, upper, right, lower)". In other words, we specify the row and column number for the pixel in the top-left corner of the sub-rectangle followed by the row and column number for the pixel in the bottom-left corner. This operation is illustrated in Table 3-12.

Table 3-12. *Cropping an image in PIL*

Code	Output
```python from PIL import Image a=Image.open("C:/Users/User/ Pictures/Lenna.png") a.show() ```	
```python # size of the image in pixels w,h=a.size b=a.crop((w/2, h/2, 2*w/2, 2*h/2)) b.show() ```	

Pillow offers a few functions that can be used for performing geometric transformations. For instance, the resize() function, illustrated in Table 3-13, can be used to change the size of the image where we need to specify the number of rows and columns required inside the function.

Table 3-13. *Resizing an image in PIL*

Code	Output

```from PIL import Image```
 ```a=Image.open("C:/Users/User/```
 ```Pictures/Lenna.png")```
 ```a.show()```

```b=a.resize((150,150))``` ```b.show()```	

The rotate() function, illustrated in Table 3-14, can be used to rotate the image in counterclockwise direction where we need to specify the angle (in degrees) inside the function.

Table 3-14. *Rotating an image in PIL*

Code	Output

``python
from PIL import Image
a=Image.open("C:/Users/User/
Pictures/Lenna.png")
a.show()
``

``python
b=a.rotate((45))
b.show()
``

The transpose() function, illustrated in Table 3-15, can be used to perform different transformations like flipping an image horizontally or vertically, and it can also be used for rotating the image. We need to specify the required operation in the predefined template inside the function. For example, to flip the image vertically, the function will be defined as "transpose(Image.Transpose.FLIP_LEFT_RIGHT)".

Table 3-15. *Flipping an image in PIL*

Code	Output

``python
from PIL import Image
a=Image.open("C:/Users/User/
Pictures/Lenna.png")
a.show()
``

``python
b=a.transpose(Image.FLIP_LEFT_
RIGHT)
b.show()
``

We can also perform color transformation using the convert() method where we need to specify the required format inside the function. For instance, to convert the image into a grayscale format, the function will be defined as "convert("L")". The filter() function can be used to perform different types of filtering such as blur, contour, smooth, sharp, etc. We need to specify the type of filter inside the function in the predefined format. For instance, to apply a blurring filter to the image, the function will be defined as "filter(ImageFilter.BLUR)". These functions are illustrated in Table 3-16.

Table 3-16. *Color transformation and filtering of an image in PIL*

Code	Output
```from PIL import Image a=Image.open("C:/Users/User/ Pictures/Lenna.png") a.show()```	
```# colour transform b=a.convert("L") b.show()```	

(*continued*)

Table 3-16. (*continued*)

Code	Output

``
# filtering the image 	
c=a.filter(ImageFilter.BLUR)
c.show()
``

Let us now see how a visualization library named "*Matplotlib*" can be used to create a grid-based display of multiple images in a single window.

Visualizing Images Using Matplotlib

Matplotlib is an open source plotting library for Python programming that can be used to create static, animated, and interactive visualizations in Python. The Matplotlib library offers a number of advantages which make it a popular choice among plotting libraries in Python. Some of the advantages are listed as follows:

- Provides publication-level quality plots

- Provides customization option with respect to visual style and layout

- Ability to export plots to many file formats

- Provides MATLAB-like interface

One of the significant features of the Matplotlib library is the ability to create subplots which helps to visualize multiple plots in a single window. The subplot option basically divides the figure window into multiple grids and enables the users to display different visuals in each grid. The format for creating subplots is "subplot(*nrows,ncols,index*)" where *nrows* indicate the number of rows, *ncols* the number of cols, and *index* the grid number (numbered in a zigzag manner). For instance, "subplot(2,2,x)" divides the window into two rows and two columns, and x is replaced by the grid number where we need to display our visual. This process is illustrated in Figure 3-5.

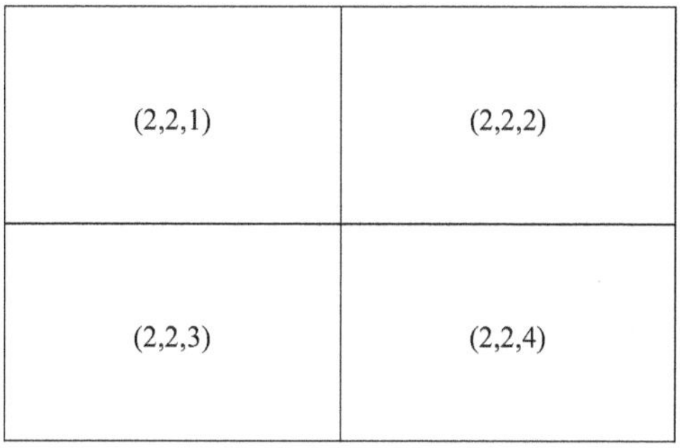

(2,2,1)	(2,2,2)
(2,2,3)	(2,2,4)

Figure 3-5. *Grid format for subplots in Matplotlib*

The imshow() function is used to visualize images using the Matplotlib library where we need to pass the variable holding the image to the function. In the previous section, we have discussed a number of functions provided by the Pillow library. Now we will apply those functions to our image and display the output images using subplots. Further, we can use the title() functions to give a title to each subplot where we need to pass the title of the image in single or double quotes to the function. Finally, the show() function should be used at the end to display the figure window. Without providing this function, no visual would be produced.

The following code illustrates the application of the image processing functions. The comment lines in the code make it easier for the readers to follow. The figure following the code shows the output of these functions visualized in subplots. The code as follows and Figure 3-6 illustrate the subplots with the image processing functions we discussed so far.

```python
from PIL import Image, ImageFilter
import matplotlib.pyplot as plt
a=Image.open("C:/Users/user/Pictures/Lenna.png")
plt.subplot(221)
plt.imshow(a)
plt.title('Original Image')
# flip image
b=a.transpose(Image.FLIP_LEFT_RIGHT)
plt.subplot(222)
plt.imshow(b)
plt.title('Flipped Image')
# colour transform
c=a.convert("L")
plt.subplot(223)
plt.imshow(c)
plt.title('Grayscake Image')
# filtering the image
d=a.filter(ImageFilter.BLUR)
plt.subplot(224)
plt.imshow(d)
plt.title('Blurred Image')
plt.show()
```

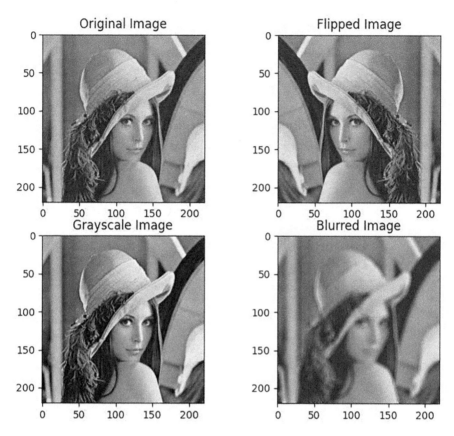

Figure 3-6. *Illustration of subplots*

Read and Write Images Using OpenCV

We have already discussed how to read and display images using libraries like Pillow and Matplotlib. In this session, we will see how to do the same using the OpenCV library. In some cases, we would want to save the images obtained after performing certain operations. So, we will also see how to write images into a file directory. Similar to Pillow, the OpenCV library also supports a number of image file formats such as png, bmp, jpeg, tif, etc.

The imread() function can be used to read an image. The filename along with the pathname should be provided to the function as was the case in the Pillow library. The imshow() function can be used to display the image. Two parameters need to be passed to the imshow() function: a title for the display window and the name of the object(variable) containing the image. The imwrite() function can be used to save an image to a selected location. The pathname/filename and the object name(variable) containing the image are passed to the function. The following code and Figure 3-7 clearly demonstrate all these functions.

```
import cv2
a=cv2.imread("C:/Users/User/Pictures/Lenna.png")
cv2.imshow("Lenna_image",a)
cv2.imwrite("C:/Users/User/Documents/Lenna_new.jpg",a)
```

Figure 3-7. *Illustration of Lenna Image displayed using OpenCV*

Image Properties in OpenCV

There is an important difference between the variables created by reading an image using the PIL package (i.e., using Image.open command) and the OpenCV package (i.e., using cv2.imread command). The variable "a" created by reading the "Lenna" image using the PIL package is of the data type "PngImageFile." This data type does not support the indexing of the pixels in the image, thereby making it difficult to manipulate the pixel values using mathematical operations manually. The only way to process the pixels using the PIL package is to use predefined commands available with the package like crop(),resize(), etc., as we discussed earlier.

The variable "a" created by reading the "Lenna" image using the OpenCV package is of the data type "ndarray." Therefore, the individual pixels can be accessed by indexing, and the different functions available with the numpy package can be applied to this variable. For instance, the shape() command applied to the variable "a" with the "Lenna" image will result in the tuple (512, 512, 3), which indicates that the variable is a 3D array with 3 different matrices of size 512 x 512 corresponding to the three color channels blue, green, and red.

This brings us to another stark difference between the image type in reading with PIL and OpenCV package. The color images of "png," "jpeg," and most other related file extensions are basically composed of these three color channels blue(B), green(G), and red(R). The PIL package uses the RGB channel ordering, whereas the OpenCV package uses the BGR channel ordering. The imshow() command in the OpenCV package changes the ordering to RGB and then displays the image. But if we use the *imshow* function in Matplotlib package, it will display the image with the same BGR channel ordering.

Since the image is made of three color channels, each pixel in the image is composed of three values corresponding to the three colors. Technically, this implies that the color of each pixel is obtained by a mixture of different shades (intensities) of the three basic colors blue, green, and red. As the variable containing the image in OpenCV implementation is a numpy array, the pixel values can be accessed using the normal array indices that we discussed earlier in this chapter. For instance, the first pixel in the "Lenna" image (matrix) stored in the variable "a" can be obtained using the index a[1,1,:] which means that we access the values at the intersection of the first row and first column from all three color channels.

Another difference is that the size function in PIL and OpenCV provide different values. In PIL, the size function for the variable "a" containing the "Lenna" image produces the tuple (512, 512) which is basically the dimension of the 2D image. The third dimension, number of color channels, is not displayed at the output, whereas the shape function from numpy can be used to display it in case of OpenCV. The size function in

OpenCV provides the total number of pixels in the image which is nothing but the product of the three values in the tuple obtained from the shape function, that is, 512 x 512 x 3 = 786432 pixels. All these properties we discussed above are illustrated using the code in Table 3-17 and the figure following the code. Figure 3-8 shows the difference caused by the channel ordering in these two different packages.

Table 3-17. *Image properties in PIL and OpenCV*

Code	Output
| ```
import cv2
import matplotlib.pyplot as plt
from PIL import Image
# PIL implementaion
a=Image.open("C:/Users/User/
Pictures/Lenna.png")
print(type(a))
print(a.size)
plt.subplot(211)
plt.imshow(a)
plt.title('Lenna Image read
with PIL package')
# OpenCV implementaion
b=cv2.imread("C:/Users/User/
Pictures/Lenna.png")
print(type(b))
print(b.shape)
print(b.size)
plt.subplot(212)
plt.imshow(b)
plt.title('Lenna image read
with OpenCV package')
plt.show()
``` | <class ' PIL. PngImagePlugin. PngImageFile '> (512, 512)<br><br><br><br><br><br><br><br><br><br><br><br><br>&lt;class 'numpy.ndarray'&gt;<br>(512, 512, 3)<br>786432 |
```

Figure 3-8. *Lenna Image from PIL and OpenCV displayed using Matplotlib*

Conversion Between Image Data Types

While working with images, we often find the necessity to change the data type of the images with respect to the specific requirements for each application. For instance, we have seen from the illustration in the previous section that the *imshow* function in the Matplotlib package displays the image read using OpenCV package in BGR channel ordering. Therefore, it is necessary to convert the BGR image to RGB image in order to display the color image properly. This can be achieved by using the OpenCV function cv2.cvtColor which takes the variable containing the input image and the function for type of conversion as parameters.

The conversion from BGR image to RGB image can be obtained by providing the function cv2.COLOR_BGR2RGB as a parameter to the cvtColor function. Similarly, the function for converting the BGR image to a 2D grayscale image is cv2.COLOR_BGR2GRAY. The conversion to binary image, on the other hand, is done using threshold operation with the cv2. threshold function. This function takes four parameters: the variable containing the grayscale input image, the threshold value, the maximum value (which is 255 in case of grayscale image), and the thresholding method. The two commonly used thresholding methods are binary thresholding and OTSU thresholding. We will discuss these two types in Chapter 5 of this book, whereas we will illustrate the binary thresholding with the cv2.THRESH_BINARY function in the following code. Figure 3-9 shows the different image conversions discussed above. It can be observed that the color map function "gray" has to be provided along with the image variable in the *imshow* function for displaying single-channel images like grayscale and binary images. The readers are encouraged to explore the other image conversions from the OpenCV documentation.

```
import cv2
import matplotlib.pyplot as plt
a=cv2.imread("C:/Users/Lenovo/Pictures/Lenna.png")
plt.subplot(221)
plt.imshow(a)
plt.title('Original BGR image')
b=cv2.cvtColor(a, cv2.COLOR_BGR2RGB)
plt.subplot(222)
plt.imshow(b)
```

```
plt.title('RGB image')
c=cv2.cvtColor(a, cv2.COLOR_BGR2GRAY)
plt.subplot(223)
plt.imshow(c,cmap='gray')
plt.title('Grayscale image')
d=cv2.threshold(c,127,255,cv2.THRESH_BINARY)[1]
plt.subplot(224)
plt.imshow(d,cmap='gray')
plt.title('Binary image')
plt.show()
```

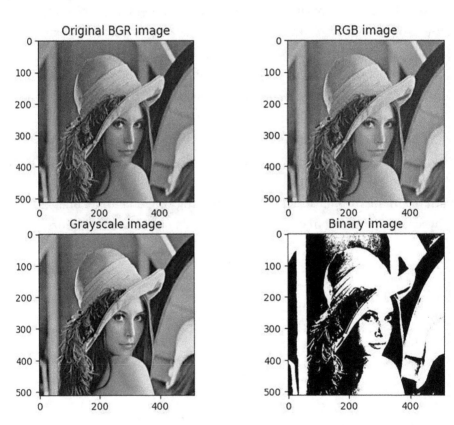

Figure 3-9. *Image data type conversions*

Basic Image Operations in OpenCV

The basic image operations like cropping, resizing, rotating, flipping, and blurring can also be performed using OpenCV. We will have a brief discussion followed by an illustration for these processes in this section. The cropping of the image can simply be performed by the index-slicing that we discussed in the numpy array section earlier. The resizing operation can be performed using the resize() function in OpenCV. We have to provide the variable containing the input image, a tuple containing the size of the output array (i.e., number of rows and columns required in the output image), and the type of interpolation used for resizing operation. There are many different types of interpolation functions like AREA, LINEAR, CUBIC, etc. If the parameter is not provided, then the LINEAR interpolation is taken by default.

The rotate() function in OpenCV can be used to rotate a 2D array in multiples of 90 degrees. The variable containing the 2D input image and the function for rotation (e.g., ROTATE_90_CLOCKWISE) have to be given as parameters to the rotate() function. The flip() function in OpenCV can be used to flip the input image. The variable containing the input image and the axis around which the image is to be flipped (0 for x-axis and 1 for y-axis) are to be given as parameters to the function. The blur() function can be used to blur the input image. The blurring operation is basically performed by applying a smoothing filter (low pass filter) to the input image which involves performing a convolution of the image with a kernel (mask) matrix. The details of the filtering operation would be discussed in detail in Chapter 5. The size of the kernel matrix in the form of a tuple must be given as a parameter to the blur() function along with the variable containing the input image. All these operations are illustrated in the following code, and the corresponding results are displayed in Figure 3-10. Since the color information is not necessary for these operations, the original image is initially converted to a grayscale image and then subjected to all the above operations.

```python
import cv2
import matplotlib.pyplot as plt
# read the input Lenna image
img=cv2.imread("/content/Lenna.png",0) # read the image as
grayscale
# perform image operations using opencv
cropped_image = img[0:320, 0:320]
resized_image = cv2.resize(img, (256, 256))
rotated_image = cv2.rotate(img, cv2.ROTATE_90_CLOCKWISE)
clipped_image = cv2.flip(img, 1)
blurred_image = cv2.blur(img, (3,3))
# diplay the images
plt.subplot(231)
plt.imshow(img, cmap='gray')
plt.title('Original Image')
plt.subplot(232)
plt.imshow(cropped_image,cmap='gray')
plt.title('Cropped Image')
plt.subplot(233)
plt.imshow(resized_image, cmap='gray')
plt.title('Resized Image')
plt.subplot(234)
plt.imshow(rotated_image,cmap='gray')
plt.title('Rotated Image')
plt.subplot(235)
plt.imshow(clipped_image,cmap='gray')
plt.title('Clipped Image')
plt.subplot(236)
plt.imshow(blurred_image,cmap='gray')
plt.title('Blurred Image')
plt.show()
```

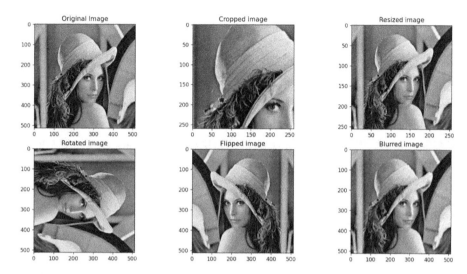

Figure 3-10. *Image operations*

Capturing the Video Using OpenCV

In this section, we will see how to capture video using OpenCV and save the video in a desired location. The first step is to create an object for capturing video using the VideoCapture(0) class as we have seen in the previous chapter. Then, we need to create an object for writing the captured video using the VideoWriter() class. We need to provide four parameters to this Writer class. The first one is the pathname and filename to which the video is to be saved. The second one is a 4-character code for the codec used to compress the frames. There are many different options such as H264, MPG1, WMVA, XVID, etc. We can use the function VideoWriter_fourcc to set the desired codec. The third parameter is the desired frame rate of the video. The last parameter is a tuple consisting of the size (resolution) of the video frame.

The next step will be to capture the frames using the read() method of the object created for video capture and then save the frames to the output video using the write() method of the object created for writing the captured video. These two operations would be carried out in an infinite loop which can be terminated by a specified keystroke as we discussed in the previous chapter. Once the loop is terminated, we can destroy all windows and release both the Capture and Writer objects. We can also use the imshow() function to display the frames that we are recording. The following code summarizes the entire process behind capturing and saving a video using OpenCV.

```python
import cv2
vid=cv2.VideoCapture(0)
filename = "C:/Users/User/Pictures/out.mp4"
codec = cv2.VideoWriter_fourcc('H','2','6','4')
framerate = 30
resolution = (640,480)
vid_out =cv2.VideoWriter(filename,codec,framerate,resolution)
while(True):
    ret,frame=vid.read()
    vid_out.write(frame)
    cv2.imshow('frame',frame)
    key = cv2.waitKey(1)
    if key == ord("x"):
        break
vid.release()
vid_out.release()
cv2.destroyAllWindows()
```

Video Transformations

In most applications, the video frames need to be transformed before analyzing them for information. The image operations discussed in the previous section can be applied to the frames of the video captured in real time. For instance, if the color information is not important, then the frames can be converted to a grayscale image prior to further processing. The following code illustrates three different operations applied to the video frames in real time. Initially, the captured frames are converted to grayscale images. Next, the grayscale images are cropped to a smaller size. The cropping operation is normally performed to capture the area of interest. In this illustration, the height and width of a frame are used to create the indices for cropping the image array. Note that the double forward slash (//) operator is used for division which indicates integer division since the array indices must be integers. Finally, a blurring operation is used to smoothen the frames.

```python
import cv2
vid=cv2.VideoCapture(0)
framerate = 30
resolution = (640,480)
while(True):
    ret,frame=vid.read()
    gray = cv2.cvtColor(frame, cv2.COLOR_BGR2GRAY)
    h=gray.shape[0]
    w=gray.shape[1]
    gaussianblur = cv2.GaussianBlur(gray[h//2:3*h//2,
    w//2:3*w//2], (5, 5), 0)
    cv2.imshow('blur',gaussianblur)
    key = cv2.waitKey(1)
    if key == ord("x"):
        break
vid.release()
cv2.destroyAllWindows()
```

Summary

The following are the topics we covered in this chapter:

- Integrated development environments (IDEs) that can be used in Raspberry Pi OS

- Fundamental concepts of Python programming such as data types, loops and conditional statements, numpy arrays, and functions

- Basic image operations using Python Imaging Library (PIL)

- Displaying images in a grid with the help of *Matplotlib* package

- Understanding image data types and properties with OpenCV

- Capturing and transforming video frames using OpenCV

In the next chapter, we will discuss the various challenges involved in setting up and calibrating vision systems for industrial vision systems.

Challenges in Machine Vision System

Implementing machine vision systems can be challenging due to various factors. One of the challenges is the need for accurate calibration and alignment of cameras and sensors to ensure precise image capture. Additionally, the complexity of processing large amounts of visual data in real time requires powerful computational resources and efficient algorithms. Furthermore, integrating machine vision systems into existing manufacturing industry infrastructure may require significant investment in hardware and software upgrades. The challenges with implementing machine vision systems can be categorized as technical, environmental, integration, performance, and human factors. In this chapter, we'll look more closely at these challenges.

Technical Challenges

One of the major technical challenges is the complexity of hardware and software integration. Integrating machine vision systems into existing infrastructure in the industry often involves connecting cameras and

K. Mohaideen Abdul Kadhar and G. Anand, *Industrial Vision Systems with Raspberry Pi*, Maker Innovations Series, https://doi.org/10.1007/979-8-8688-0097-9_4

sensors to existing networks and systems, which can be a complex task requiring expertise in both hardware and software. Additionally, ensuring compatibility between different hardware components and software platforms can be challenging, as they may have different protocols or requirements. However, there are instances where software integration can be relatively straightforward. For example, if the hardware and software are from the same manufacturer and designed to work together seamlessly, integration may be a smooth process with minimal challenges. Additionally, if the software being integrated is open source and widely supported, it may have pre-built connectors and libraries that simplify the integration process. This book uses the Python environment for implementing vision system concepts for industries. Python is an open source programming language that is widely used because of its simplicity and readability, which make it easier for developers to understand and modify code. Additionally, Python has a vast ecosystem of libraries and frameworks for computer vision that provide ready-made solutions for various tasks, saving time and effort in board implementation. A wide variety of cameras and boards compatible with the Python environment for building machine vision system products are available. Moreover, we have used a Raspberry Pi for implementing the machine vision system concepts in real time, which reduces the technical challenges and minimizes the cost of machine vision system product development.

Selecting and Optimizing Suitable Algorithms for Image Processing

Selection and optimization of suitable algorithms for image processing is another crucial aspect of integrating machine vision systems. This involves identifying the specific image processing tasks that need to be performed and selecting algorithms that can efficiently and accurately handle those tasks. Furthermore, optimizing these algorithms to meet the specific requirements of the application is essential for achieving desired results in terms of speed, accuracy, and reliability. For example, in a quality control application for a manufacturing process, machine vision systems can be used to identify defects on products. The specific image processing task in this case would be to detect and classify different types of defects, such as scratches or dents. To accomplish this, algorithms like edge detection and pattern recognition can be selected and optimized to accurately identify and classify these defects in real time.

Selecting a Camera Model

Ensuring accurate and reliable image capture and analysis is crucial for the success of the quality control application. This can be achieved by using high-resolution cameras and implementing robust lighting conditions to capture clear and detailed images of the products. Additionally, regular calibration and maintenance of the machine vision systems are necessary to ensure consistent and precise defect detection results. For example, in a manufacturing plant producing electronic components, machine vision systems can be used to inspect printed circuit boards (PCBs) for defects such as soldering errors or missing components. High-resolution cameras can capture detailed images of the PCBs, while carefully controlled lighting conditions ensure that any defects are clearly visible. Regular calibration and maintenance of the machine vision systems help to maintain their accuracy and reliability, ensuring that any defects are accurately identified and classified in real time.

Selection of camera model for machine vision systems is another crucial challenge for accurately acquiring images based on the different lighting conditions in the industry environment. Basically, three types of cameras are available, and they are (1) line cameras, (2) area scan camera, and (3) 3D cameras.

Line camera is a type of camera that captures images by scanning a single line at a time. It is commonly used for high-speed applications where continuous inspection is required, such as in production lines. The advantage of using a line camera is its ability to capture images at very high speeds, allowing for real-time defect detection and classification.

Area scan camera is another type of camera that captures images by scanning an entire area at once. It is commonly used for applications that require high-resolution images, such as in photography or document scanning. The advantage of using an area scan camera is its ability to capture detailed images with high clarity and accuracy.

Lastly, 3D cameras are a type of camera that captures depth information along with the visual data. They are commonly used in applications such as 3D modeling, virtual reality, and augmented reality.

Choosing the Right Area Scan Camera

There are various cameras available in the market with different characteristics with respect to color, resolution, shutter technology, and interfaces. For better understanding, a set of simple steps are proposed for selecting the suitable area scan camera based on the application. The reason for choosing area scan camera is that it is widely used in machine vision system products.

Step 1: Choose the color feature supported by the camera based on the application. For example, some industries manufacture metal-based products with only white, silver, or black colors. Hence, we can choose a monochrome camera instead of using color cameras. In some industries, like pharmacy, it is necessary to check the color variations in the bottles. At this time, the color camera can be chosen for the applications.

Step 2: Choosing the camera resolution: The camera resolution can be selected based on the minimum pixel required for displaying the object in detail. For example, for the bar code given in Figure 4-1, the Number of Minimum Pixels (NMP) required for displaying a bar line is 5, the Object

Detail Size (ODS) is 0.2mm (approximately), and the Object Size (OS) is 55mm (this can be set by the user, or based on trial-and-error method, the user can choose the length). The resolution can be calculated using the following formula (4.1).

a) Barcode Image   b) Single barcode image

Figure 4-1. *Image of the barline figure*

$$\text{Resolution} = (\text{NMP} \times \text{OS})/\text{ODS} \qquad \qquad \dots (4.1)$$

where NMP – Number of Minimum Pixels required for object detail

OS – Object Size

ODS – Object Detail Size

In our case, Resolution = (5x55)/0.2 = 1375 resolution horizontal

Hence, based on this value, the suitable megapixel camera can be chosen for this application from Table 4-1. Select the resolution of the camera, which provides clear information about the image.

Table 4-1. *Camera selection based on resolution*

Sl.no	MPx	Width	Height	Aspect Ratio
1	0.1	320	240	4:3
2	0.3	640	480	16:9
3	0.5	800	600	4:3
4	0.9	1280	720	5:4
5	1.2	1280	960	4:3
6	1.3	1280	1024	16:9
7	1.9	1600	1200	4:3
8	2.1	1920	1080	4:3
9	3.1	2048	1536	4:3

Environmental Challenges in Machine Vision System

Dealing with dynamic and unpredictable environments provides a realistic representation of the objects being inspected, allowing for more accurate analysis and decision-making. Additionally, images captured in real-time environments can also account for dynamic changes in lighting conditions, ensuring that machine vision systems can adapt and continue to function effectively. This is particularly important in industries such as manufacturing and quality control, where consistency and precision are crucial. The variability of illumination conditions in machine vision systems can have a substantial impact on image quality. Lighting is an important aspect in influencing image data quality and dependability for tasks such as object recognition, defect detection, and measurement. Here are some significant factors for how lighting conditions affect image quality in machine vision systems:

- Uniformity of Illumination: Uneven lighting can cause shadows and highlights on objects within the field of view. This can make it difficult for machine vision algorithms to accurately identify and analyze objects. To mitigate this, uniform illumination across the entire field of view is essential.

- Intensity and Brightness: Varying light intensity levels can affect the overall brightness of an image. Images that are too dark or too bright may result in the loss of critical details and information. Adjusting the lighting intensity to an optimal level is crucial for maintaining image quality.

- Direction of Lighting: The angle and direction of lighting can impact the visibility of certain features or surface irregularities on objects. Specular reflections, for instance, can occur when light is directed at certain angles, making it challenging to capture clear images. Choosing the right lighting angle is critical for minimizing such issues.

- Strobe Lighting vs. Continuous Lighting: Strobe lighting can freeze fast-moving objects, reducing motion blur, while continuous lighting provides a consistent source of illumination. The choice between these two lighting methods depends on the specific requirements of the machine vision application.

- Wavelength and Spectral Characteristics: Some applications require specific wavelengths of light to highlight certain features or materials. For example,

79

ultraviolet (UV) lighting can reveal certain types of defects that are not visible in the visible spectrum. Understanding the spectral characteristics of the lighting and the object is essential.

- Dynamic Lighting Conditions: Changes in ambient lighting conditions, such as natural light from windows or fluctuations in room lighting, can introduce variations in image quality. To mitigate this, controlled environments with consistent lighting or adaptive lighting systems that can adjust to changing conditions may be necessary.

- Glare and Reflections: Strong light sources or reflective surfaces can create glare and reflections that obscure image details. The use of polarized lighting or filters can help reduce these issues by minimizing unwanted reflections.

- Noise and Image Artifacts: Inadequate lighting conditions can lead to increased image noise, which can affect the accuracy of image analysis. Noise reduction techniques, such as image filtering or sensor settings adjustment, may be required.

- Calibration and Monitoring: Regular calibration and monitoring of the lighting system are essential to ensure that it continues to provide consistent and optimal illumination for machine vision applications.

This shows that lighting conditions play a critical role in machine vision systems, and understanding how various factors affect image quality is essential for achieving accurate and reliable results. Properly designed and controlled lighting systems can help mitigate the challenges posed by variability in lighting conditions and enhance the performance of machine vision applications. Figure 4-2 shows the effect of varying lighting conditions on an object in a real-time environment.

Figure 4-2. *Images captured under different lighting conditions from real-time environments*

Integration Challenges

Compatibility with existing systems and technologies includes compatibility with existing systems and equipment, such as conveyors or robotics, to seamlessly incorporate the machine vision system into the production line. Integration also involves ensuring that the machine vision system can effectively communicate and share data with other components of the production process, such as quality control databases or inventory management systems. Additionally, integration challenges may involve training and educating personnel on how to effectively use and interpret the data provided by the machine vision system. For example, in a manufacturing plant, a machine vision system can be integrated into the assembly line to inspect and verify the accuracy of components being assembled. The system can capture images of each component and compare them against a database of reference images to detect any defects or variations. The machine vision system can then communicate this information to the quality control database, triggering alerts or initiating corrective actions if necessary. Training and educating personnel on how to interpret the data provided by the machine vision system is crucial for effective decision-making.

Incorporating a machine vision system seamlessly into the overall workflow requires careful planning and coordination with various departments. This may involve conducting thorough assessments of existing processes and identifying areas where the system can be integrated without disrupting productivity. Additionally, regular maintenance and calibration of the machine vision system is essential to ensure accurate and reliable results over time. Furthermore, training employees on how to effectively use the machine vision system is necessary to maximize its potential. This includes educating them on how to interpret and analyze the data generated by the system, as well as troubleshooting any issues that may arise. By investing time and resources into the proper implementation and maintenance of a machine vision system, businesses can enhance their decision-making capabilities and gain a competitive edge in their domain. For example, in the manufacturing industry, a company could implement a machine vision system to automatically inspect and detect defects in their products. This system could analyze the shape, color, and size of each product to ensure they meet quality standards. By training employees on how to interpret the data generated by the machine vision system, they can quickly identify and address any quality issues, reducing production errors and improving overall efficiency.

One of the challenges of integrating a machine vision system with other sensors and data sources for comprehensive analysis is the compatibility of different technologies and data formats. It can be a complex task to merge data from various sources and ensure that they are synchronized in real time. Additionally, different sensors may have varying levels of accuracy and reliability, which can affect the overall accuracy of the analysis. Therefore, careful calibration and synchronization of these sensors are necessary to achieve reliable and accurate results. For example, in a smart city project, data from various sources such as traffic cameras, air quality sensors, and weather stations need to be integrated for comprehensive analysis. The challenge lies in harmonizing the different data formats and ensuring that the information is synchronized in real time. Additionally, the accuracy and reliability of each sensor may vary, so calibrating and synchronizing them properly becomes crucial to obtain reliable insights about traffic patterns, pollution levels, and weather conditions for effective urban planning.

Performance Challenges

The following performance problems of machine vision systems are critical for satisfying the user or customer:

- Real-time processing and response require the identification of potential limitations and obstacles that may arise when implementing the machine vision system in terms of performance, such as handling large volumes of data or dealing with complex product variations.

- Developing strategies to optimize the performance of the machine vision system, such as improving image processing algorithms or enhancing hardware capabilities, to ensure accurate and efficient defect detection.

- Evaluating the effectiveness of the machine vision system in reducing production errors and improving overall efficiency by conducting regular performance assessments and analyzing relevant metrics.

- Handling large volumes of data and ensuring scalability in implementing machine learning techniques to continuously improve the machine vision system's defect detection capabilities and adapt to new production challenges and variations.

- Collaborating with cross-functional teams to gather feedback and insights to further enhance the machine vision system's performance and address any issues or limitations.

- Regularly updating and maintaining the machine vision system to ensure it remains up-to-date with industry standards and technological advancements. For example, in a manufacturing setting, machine learning techniques can be used to continuously analyze and learn from images of defective products, allowing the machine vision system to identify and classify defects with higher accuracy over time. This enables the system to adapt and improve its defect detection capabilities as it encounters.

Human Factors Challenges

One of the common challenges associated with the human factor in maintaining a machine vision system is ensuring that the operators are adequately trained to interpret and understand the system's output. This includes providing training on how to accurately analyze and classify defective product images, as well as understanding the limitations of the system. Additionally, there may be challenges in effectively integrating the machine vision system with other human-operated processes, such as quality control inspections or decision-making processes. This requires clear communication and collaboration between the machine vision system and human operators to optimize its performance and ensure seamless integration within the workflow.

Furthermore, regular maintenance and calibration of the machine vision system is crucial to maintain its accuracy and reliability. This includes regular cleaning of lenses, proper lighting conditions, and periodic adjustments to ensure consistent performance. It is also important to regularly update the software and algorithms used by the system to keep up with changing defect patterns and improve its ability to accurately classify defects. Overall, a well-implemented machine vision system can greatly enhance the efficiency and accuracy of defect analysis, but it is essential to acknowledge and address its limitations and work toward continuous improvement.

Summary

This chapter provides information about challenges in implementing machine vision systems in terms of regular maintenance and calibration that should be performed to ensure its continued accuracy and reliability. This includes

- Cleaning the lenses and sensors

- Checking for any hardware malfunctions

- Calibrating the system for optimal performance

- Choosing the proper illumination used to acquire the images with minimum loss which provides great improvements in decision-making

- Providing proper training to operators and technicians who will be using and maintaining the system is crucial to maximize its benefits

By consistently investing in the system and addressing its shortcomings, an organization can achieve the best possible results and ensure the ongoing success of their defect analysis process. In the next chapter, we will discuss various commonly used image processing techniques using OpenCV.

CHAPTER 5

Image Processing Using OpenCV

A number of image processing techniques with varying levels of complexities are used in a number of applications like medical imaging, multimedia processing, computer vision, etc. OpenCV provides a huge collection of algorithms and functions that can help us to do a wide range of image processing operations such as filtering, edge detection, object detection, segmentation, and more. In this chapter, we will begin by exploring the various properties and types of images along with the various noises that could affect the images. Then, we will go on to explore various processing techniques like image enhancement methods, image filtering techniques for edge detection, morphological operations, thresholding techniques, blob detection, and contour detection.

Image Acquisition

Image acquisition is the first and foremost part of any vision system. It is the process of capturing images using hardware such as cameras or other imaging sensors. Several factors decide the quality of the captured images like the type of device used for acquisition, the resolution of the acquired images, the lighting conditions, etc. In case of digital photography, the

© K. Mohaideen Abdul Kadhar and G. Anand 2024
K. Mohaideen Abdul Kadhar and G. Anand, *Industrial Vision Systems with Raspberry Pi*,
Maker Innovations Series, https://doi.org/10.1007/979-8-8688-0097-9_5

acquisition process begins the moment the light enters the camera lens and hits the image sensor, which in turn captures the light and converts it into a digital signal that can be processed by the camera's software.

There are two main categories of digital image sensors: the charge-coupled device (CCD) sensors and the complementary metal oxide semiconductor (CMOS) sensors. The quality of the acquired image is affected by the type of sensor used in our camera. For instance, the CCD sensors are more sensitive to light, and hence, they can produce high-quality images, but they consume more power and are more expensive. On the other hand, CMOS sensors are much cheaper and consume less power compared to CCD sensors, but they produce low-quality images with more noise.

The resolution of an image is also a dominant factor in influencing the quality. High-resolution images will contain more pixels that results in a sharper and more detailed image. However, the increased number of pixels would require more storage space as well as processing power. Another important factor affecting the quality of an image is the lighting conditions prevalent at the time of image acquisition. Poor lighting conditions can result in underexposed, overexposed, or blurry images that may lead to more complexity during further processing. Therefore, there needs to be some control with respect to the lighting conditions while capturing images. This can be achieved by either adjusting the camera settings or using external lighting sources.

The vision systems used in industries are often subjected to adverse environments. Hence, it is essential to build a robust and reliable system that can perform convincingly in these conditions. By optimizing the abovementioned factors, it is possible to capture high-quality images which in turn can provide accurate results.

Image and Its Properties

An image is a visual representation of something like an object, a person, or a scene. Image is stored in computers as an array of elements called pixels where the pixels are represented as binary numbers. A pixel, short for pixel element, refers to a single point or a smallest unit of digital image that can be displayed in a rectangular grid on a digital display. A digital image may be represented mathematically as a two-dimensional function f(x,y), where x and y are called the spatial coordinates, and the amplitude "f" at any pair of coordinates (x,y) is called the intensity of the image at that point, where the coordinates and intensity values are all finite, discrete quantities. Images have several inherent properties that determines how they are perceived. These properties are listed as follows.

Resolution

Resolution refers to the number of pixels that the image is made up of. In simpler terms, resolution describes the level of detail in an image. For instance, higher the resolution, the sharper and more detailed the images will appear. In case of digital images, image resolution is often measured as a pixel count. More generally, image resolution is described in PPI (pixels per inch) or DPI (dots per inch) which represents how many pixels are displayed per inch of an image. For example, a 300 ppi image would be made of 300 pixels in every square inch of the image. A higher resolution implies that there are more pixels per inch(PPI) which result in a high-quality image with much more details. But the increase in pixels would also increase the storage requirements. In other words, high-resolution images would require more storage space, and it may take longer to load.

Aspect Ratio

Aspect ratio is the relationship between the height and width of an image. It essentially determines the shape of an image and can affect how the image is displayed or printed. The aspect ratio is usually written with two numbers separated by a colon. When we say that the aspect ratio of an image is w:h, then the image is "w" units wide and "h" units high. For examples, a square image has an aspect ratio of 1:1 as the width and height are equal. Other common aspect ratios are 4:3 (standard television) and 16:9 (widescreen television).

Color Depth

Color depth refers to the maximum number of colors that could be represented in an image. It is also called as bit depth since it represents the number of bits that define the color of each pixel. For instance, a pixel with a depth of 1 bit have two values: black and white. More the bit depth, more the colors that an image can contain, and more accurate the color representation is. For example, an 8-bit image can contain up to $2^8 = 256$ colors, and a 24-bit image can contain $2^{24} = 16,777,216$ colors (approximately 16 million). We would discuss about these different images in the upcoming sections. Despite the number of colors an image contains, the image displayed on to a screen is limited by the number of colors supported by the monitor. For example, an 8-bit monitor can support 256 colors per channel.

Image Size

The size of an image, also called its dimensions or pixel dimensions, is given in pixels in the format "width x height". In other words, it gives the number of pixels used to represent the image along the horizontal and vertical direction in a display. For instance, the Lenna image we used in the previous chapters has a dimension of 512 x 512 which implies that the image is represented using 512 pixels both horizontally and vertically. The image size can also be determined by multiplying both height and width (in inches) by the dpi. For example, the pixel dimensions of a 4 x 6-inch photograph scanned at 300 dpi is 1200 x 1800 (4x300=1200 and 6x300=1800).

Image File Formats

The file format of an image determines how the image is saved and stored on a computer or other device. There are a number of file formats that are optimized for different uses such as web display, printing, or editing. Some of the popular image file formats are JPEG, PNG, BMP, GIF, etc.

Noise

Image noise generally refers to the random variations in the brightness or color information in digital images that are not part of the original scene or object photographed. There are number of factors that cause these noises like the quality of the camera sensor, the camera setting used, the amount of available light, and so on. Depending on the causes and characteristics, several different types of noises can occur in an image. These noises can be removed or minimized by using filtering techniques which we would discuss later in this chapter. Some of the common types of noises are discussed as follows.

Gaussian Noise

This is the most common type of noise that occurs in most images during acquisition. The major cause of this type of noise is the variations in the level of illumination. It is called Gaussian noise because it has a probability distribution function (pdf) equal to that of normal distribution, which is also known as Gaussian distribution. It is additive in nature, independent at each pixel, and does not depend on the signal intensity. It appears in the image as a fine, grainy pattern spread across the entire image. Figure 5-1 illustrates the effect of a nut image affected by Gaussian noise with mean=0 and standard deviation=10. For better viewing, we will show a grayscale version of the nut image rather than the RGB image. We will discuss about these types of images under image types in the next section.

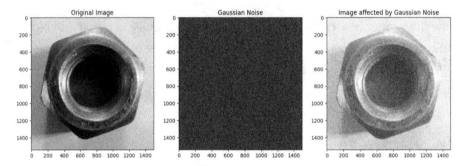

Figure 5-1. Illustration of image affected by Gaussian noise

Salt and Pepper Noise

The salt and pepper noise, also called as impulse noise, appears as black and white dots scattered throughout the image. More precisely, the black dots that appear in the brighter regions of the image are called pepper noise, and the white dots that appear in the darker areas of the image are called salt noise. These two kinds of noises are randomly distributed across the image and may highly affect processes like edge detection, image restoration, etc. There are a number of causes for this type of error such as analog-to-digital converter errors, bit error occurring in transmission, etc. Figure 5-2 illustrates the effect of salt and pepper noise on the nut image.

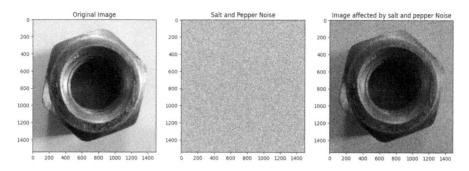

Figure 5-2. *Illustration of image affected by salt and pepper noise*

Speckle Noise

Speckle noise is a granular noise texture that degrades the quality of an image by appearing as a grainy pattern in the image. This type of noise mostly occurs in synthetic aperture radar (SAR) images, medical ultrasound images, holographic images, etc. Speckle noise can be generated artificially by multiplying the pixels of the image with random noise values. Like the Gaussian noise, the speckle noise is also statistically independent of the signal, but the difference is that the speckle noise is multiplicative whereas Gaussian noise is additive. Figure 5-3 illustrates the effect of speckle noise on the nut image.

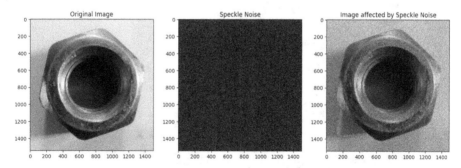

Figure 5-3. *Illustration of image affected by speckle noise*

Types of Images

Based on the bit depth, that is, the color information in an image and the number of bits used to represent a pixel, the image can be categorized as follows.

Binary Images

These are images that take only two possible pixel values. A pixel value of 0 denotes black color, and a pixel value of 1 denotes white color. These images are also called as black and white images or 1-bit images since a single bit is sufficient to represent the pixel values as they can take only either of the two values 0 and 1. We would use the same nut image to illustrate the different types of images in this section. Figure 5-4 shows the black and white version of the nut image. The matrix to the right shows the pixel values corresponding to the rectangular area highlighted by the red box in the image. We can see that the region of pixels with value 0 is dark (black) and the region of pixels with value 1 is bright (white). The transition between the black and white regions provides a sense of edge between the two regions.

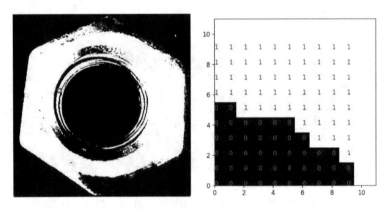

Figure 5-4. *Illustration of binary image*

Grayscale Images

Grayscale images are those images that are composed exclusively of shades of gray. These images are also called as monochrome images or 8-bit images as each pixel in this image is represented using 8 bits. This implies that there are $2^8 = 256$ possible values for a pixel. The values range from 0 to 255 where a pixel with value 0 is a black pixel and a pixel with value 255 is a white pixel. The values in between represent the different levels of intensities in moving from the dark region toward the bright region providing different shades of gray. Figure 5-5 shows the grayscale version of the nut image and the matrix of pixel values corresponding to the rectangular area highlighted by the red box in the image. We can see that the pixel values corresponding to the dark region of the rectangle are less than the values corresponding to the bright region.

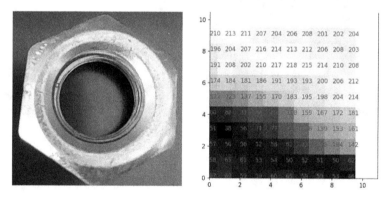

Figure 5-5. *Illustration of grayscale image*

Color Images

Color images are basically composed of three bands of monochrome (grayscale) image data where each band of data corresponds to a different color. In other words, the color image stores the gray-level information in each spectral band (color band). Each pixel in the image will be represented by three values corresponding to each color band, and each of these values is represented using 8 bits. Therefore, the number of bits required to represent a pixel value is 3x8=24 bits. The most common color bands used in the majority of the color images are red, green, and blue. These images are also called RGB images or 24-bit images. Figure 5-6 shows the true color version of the nut image. We can see that there are three bands of monochrome pixel values corresponding to the three colors. Each value represents the intensity of the corresponding color, and together the different combination of these colors results in the generation of colors in the image.

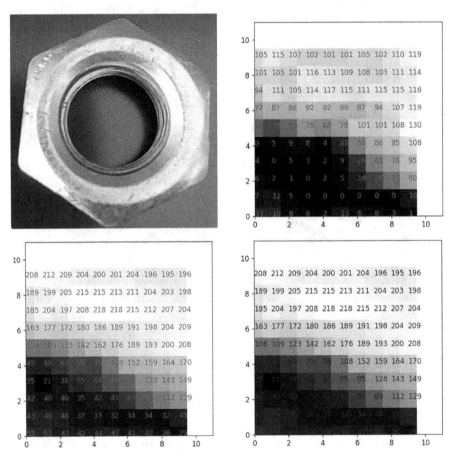

Figure 5-6. *Illustration of a color image*

Resizing the Images

The idea behind resizing of images is to modify the dimensions of the image while preserving its aspect ratio. Image resizing is essential for a number of purposes like storage, display, and transmission of images. For example, if there are constraints placed on the display size by the resolution of the display device, then we need to resize the image to accommodate the display capabilities. Likewise, if there is a constraint on the bandwidth of a communication channel, we may need to use smaller image sizes for faster transmission. Resizing is common in machine learning as well. For instance, we may want to reduce the size of the images before training as larger images tend to increase the memory and computation requirements which in turn slow down the training process. Moreover, the raw images collected for our dataset may have different sizes, and hence, they should be resized to have the same dimensions as most deep learning model architectures may require input images of the same size.

There are two popular ways of resizing images in spatial domain, namely, scaling up and scaling down. As the name suggests, scaling up is the process of increasing the size of an image that would require reconstruction of the image, whereas scaling down is the process of reducing the size of an image that would require resampling of the pixels. These resizing operations are carried out by a process called interpolation that works by estimating values at unknown points using known data. There are a number of interpolation techniques available, and detailing of all those techniques is beyond the scope of the book. Some of the most commonly used interpolation techniques are nearest neighbor, bilinear, bicubic, and Lanczos interpolations. The readers can explore the principle behind each of these techniques on their own volition.

Another important thing that we must be aware of is that different libraries come up with different implementations of these techniques thereby producing different quality of resized images. In this section, we would go through the illustration of the resizing operation using the two popular image processing libraries in Python, Pillow and OpenCV. The readers can try out other available packages like TensorFlow, PyTorch, etc., and decide which library offers better quality of resizing. So, we will use our nut image, apply different resizing techniques, and compare the results of Pillow and OpenCV libraries. The following code illustrates the process for resizing the image to half its size, that is, scaling down to 128x128. It can be seen from Figure 5-7 that the results for the same process vary with respect to the type of library used.

```python
import cv2
from PIL import Image
import matplotlib.pyplot as plt
import numpy as np
# Pillow library methods
img=Image.open("C:/Users/user/Pictures/Nut.jpg")
imgn = img.resize((128,128),Image.NEAREST)
imgbl = img.resize((128,128),Image.BILINEAR)
imgbc = img.resize((128,128),Image.BICUBIC)
imgl= img.resize((128,128),Image.LANCZOS)
plt.subplot(2,4,1)
plt.imshow(imgn)
plt.title('Nearest Neighbor_PIL')
plt.subplot(2,4,2)
plt.imshow(imgbl)
plt.title('bilinear_PIL')
plt.subplot(2,4,3)
plt.imshow(imgbc)
plt.title('bicubic_PIL')
plt.subplot(2,4,4)
plt.imshow(imgn)
plt.title('Lanczos_PIL')
# OpenCV library methods
```

```
img1 = cv2.imread("C:/Users/user/Pictures/ Nut.jpg")
img1 = cv2.cvtColor(img1, cv2.COLOR_BGR2RGB)
imgn1 = cv2.resize(img1,(128,128),cv2.INTER_NEAREST)
imgbl1 = cv2.resize(img1,(128,128),cv2.INTER_LINEAR)
imgbc1= cv2.resize(img1,(128,128),cv2.INTER_CUBIC)
imgl1= cv2.resize(img1,(128,128),cv2.INTER_LANCZOS4)
plt.subplot(2,4,5)
plt.imshow(imgn1)
plt.title('Nearest Neighbor_OpenCV')
plt.subplot(2,4,6)
plt.imshow(imgbl1)
plt.title('bilinear_OpenCV')
plt.subplot(2,4,7)
plt.imshow(imgbc1)
plt.title('bicubic_OpenCV')
plt.subplot(2,4,8)
plt.imshow(imgn1)
plt.title('Lanczos_OpenCV')
plt.show()
```

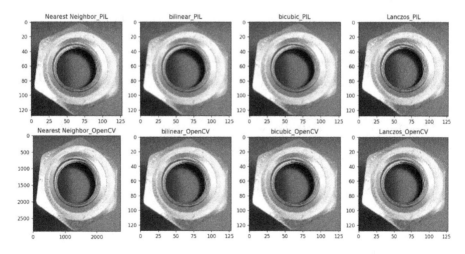

Figure 5-7. *Image resizing using different interpolation techniques*

Image Enhancement

The objective of image enhancement is to process an image so that
the result is much more suitable than the original image for a specific
application. It is a technique basically used to improve the visual quality
of the images. It is a crucial step for vision systems as the quality of the
image can have a significant impact on the outcome. Enhancement can
be considered as an umbrella term that includes a number of operations
such as removing blur, eliminating noise, increasing contrast, etc.
These enhancement operations can be done either in spatial domain
or frequency domain. The spatial domain techniques operate directly
on the pixels, whereas in frequency domain techniques, the frequency
information of the image is extracted using transformation techniques like
Fourier transform, and the enhancement operations are then done in the
frequency domain. We will focus only on the spatial domain operations.

The operation in spatial domain can be represented mathematically
as $g(x,y)=T[f(x,y)]$ where g is the output image, f is the input image, and
T is an operator on f defined over a neighborhood of (x,y). Based on this
neighborhood of pixels over which the operations are performed, the
spatial domain techniques can be further classified into two types, namely,
point operations and spatial operations. In point operations, the operator
is applied over a neighborhood of "1×1" which implies a single pixel. In
other words, the selected operator is applied independently over each
and every pixel in the image. Therefore, we can rewrite the mathematical
transformation function as $s=T(r)$, where T is a transformation technique
that maps a pixel value r to a pixel value s. On the contrary, spatial
operations are applied over a neighborhood of multiple pixels say "n×n".
Each pixel in the output image is obtained by applying an operator over
a neighborhood on "n×n" pixels in the input image. Filtering is one of

the most popular spatial operations which will be discussed in detail in the next section. So, we will discuss some of the point operations and its applications in this section.

Image Negatives

Assume that the given image has intensity levels in the range [0,L-1]. The negative of the image is obtained by using the transformation function *s=L-1-r*. For instance, if the input image is a grayscale image, then it will have intensity levels in the range [0,255]. Therefore, the negative of the grayscale image can be obtained by the function *s=255-r*. This function basically reverses the intensity levels of an image that makes it appear like a photographic negative. This function can be very useful especially in the field of medical image processing. The following Python code illustrates the negative operation on the nut image, and the resulting image is displayed together with the input image in Figure 5-8 to observe the difference caused by the operation.

```
Import cv2
import matplotlib.pyplot as plt
r=cv2.imread("C:/Users/user/Pictures/Nut.jpg",0)
s=255-r
plt.subplot(1,2,1)
plt.imshow(r,cmap='gray')
plt.title('Original Image')
plt.subplot(1,2,2)
plt.imshow(s,cmap='gray')
plt.title('Negative Image')
plt.show()
```

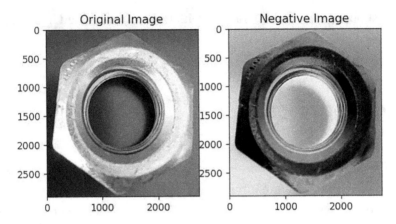

Figure 5-8. *Illustration of image negative*

Log Transformation

For an image with intensity levels in the range [0,L-1], the log transformation of the image can be obtained by the transformation function $s=clog(1+r)$. The log transformation is used to compress the dynamic range of an image with large variations in pixel values by expanding the range of low-intensity values while compressing the range of high-intensity values. The converse is true for the case of inverse log transformation. This transformation can be used when the dynamic range of an image exceeds the capability of a display device, thereby making it difficult for the display to faithfully reproduce the wide range of values. For the purpose of illustration, we will use the same nut image to see how this transformation affects the image (with c=1). We can see from Figure 5-9 that the dark regions have been enhanced implying an increase in the range of dark pixels.

```
import cv2
import matplotlib.pyplot as plt
import numpy as np
r=cv2.imread("C:/Users/user/Pictures/Nut.jpg",0)
```

```
s=np.log(1+r)  # c=1
plt.subplot(1,2,1)
plt.imshow(r,cmap='gray')
plt.title('Original Image')
plt.subplot(1,2,2)
plt.imshow(s,cmap='gray')
plt.title('Image after log transformation')
plt.show()
```

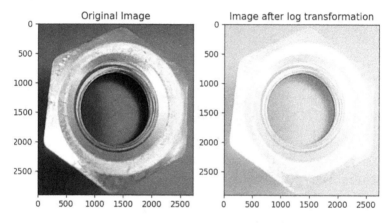

Figure 5-9. *Illustration of log transformation*

Power Law (Gamma) Transformation

The power law transformation is given by the mathematical expression $s=cr^\gamma$, where s and γ are positive constants. Similar to log transformation, the power law transformation also maps a narrow range of low-intensity input pixel values into a wider range of output values and the opposite for high-input pixel values. But, unlike log transformation, here we can control the levels of transformation by varying the value of gamma(γ). Hence, the power-level phenomenon is also called gamma correction.

Gamma correction can be used to compensate for undesired effects in displaying images, such as the bleaching effect or darkening of images, in different types of monitors with different display settings. The importance of this process can be understood by the fact that images available in the Internet would be accessed all over the world by different users using different types of display devices. Hence, gamma correction is important for the accurate display of images in different screens. The illustration of gamma correction for the nut image with different values of γ is demonstrated here (with c=1). We can see from Figure 5-10 that the image gets darker as we increase γ and lighter when we decrease γ.

```
import cv2
import numpy as np
import matplotlib.pyplot as plt
r = cv2.imread("C:/Users/user/Pictures/Nut.jpg",0)
gamma_corrected_1 = r**0.1   # gamma=0.1
gamma_corrected_2 = r**1.2   # gamma=1.2
gamma_corrected_3 = r**2.4   # gamma=2.4
plt.subplot(2,2,1)
plt.imshow(r,cmap='gray')
plt.title('Original Image')
plt.subplot(2,2,2)
plt.imshow(gamma_corrected_1,cmap='gray')
plt.title('Gamma = 0.1')
plt.subplot(2,2,3)
plt.imshow(gamma_corrected_2,cmap='gray')
plt.title('Gamma = 1.2')
plt.subplot(2,2,4)
plt.imshow(gamma_corrected_3,cmap='gray')
plt.title('Gamma = 2.4')
plt.show()
```

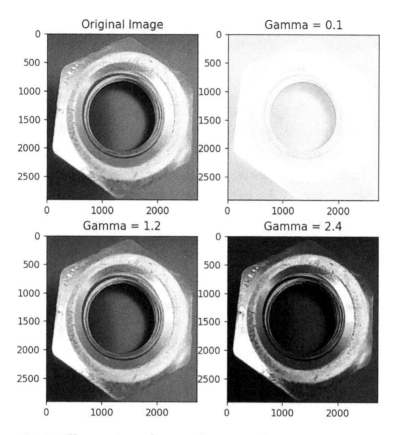

Figure 5-10. *Illustration of power law transformation*

Contrast Stretching

Contrast stretching is a part of functions called piecewise-linear transformation functions that are not entirely linear in nature. Contrast refers to the difference in luminance or color that makes an object distinguishable from other objects in a frame. Contrast of an image can be represented mathematically as

$$contrast = \frac{I_{max} - I_{min}}{I_{max} + I_{min}}$$

where I_{max} is the maximum possible intensity level and I_{min} is the minimum possible intensity level of the image. For example, a grayscale image has the maximum intensity value of $I_{max}=255$ and a minimum intensity value of $I_{min}=0$.

Contrast stretching process can be used to expand the range of intensity levels in an image in such a way that it covers the entire possible range of the camera or display. The mapping between the intensity levels of the input grayscale image and output image obtained from the contrast stretching process is shown in Figure 5-11 where the dotted line denotes the identity mapping for which the output image is equal to the input image and the solid line denotes the mapping for contrast stretching.

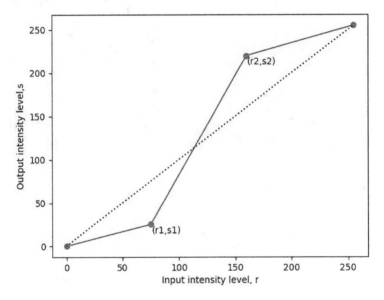

Figure 5-11. *Input-output pixel mapping for contrast stretching*

We have three lines of different slopes connected to each other rather than a single straight line or a nonlinear line, hence the name piecewise-linear transformation. The mapping corresponding to each line can be computed using the straight-line equation s=m*r+c, where m denotes the slope line and c denotes the intercept. As each of these lines has different slopes, we will have three different straight-line equations. The slope of the lines can be calculated using the slope triangle method. The mapping can be modified by changing the parameters (r_1, s_1) and (r_2, s_2). An important thing to note here is that when $r_1=s_1=0$ and $r_2=s_2=255$, then the function becomes equal to the straight dotted line. The following code illustrates this process with $(r_1, s_1) = (75, 25)$ and $(r_2, s_2) = (160, 220)$, and the resulting image is shown in Figure 5-12.

```
import cv2
import matplotlib.pyplot as plt
import numpy as np
r=cv2.imread("C:/Users/user/Pictures/Nut.jpg",0)
m=r.shape[0]
n=r.shape[1]
# enter the parameters
r1=75
s1= 25
r2=160
s2=220
# implement the straight lines
s=np.empty([m,n]) # initialize empty array for output image
for i in range(m):
    for j in range(n):
        if (0<=r[i,j] and r[i,j]<=r1):
            s[i,j]=(s1/r1)*r[i,j]
        elif (r1<r[i,j] and r[i,j]<=r2):
            s[i,j]=((s2-s1)/(r2-r1))*(r[i,j]-r1)+s1
        else:
            s[i,j]=((255-s2)/(255-r2))*(r[i,j]-r2)+s2

plt.subplot(1,2,1)
plt.imshow(r,cmap='gray')
plt.title('Original Image')
```

```
plt.subplot(1,2,2)
plt.imshow(s,cmap='gray')
plt.title('Image after contrast stretching')
plt.show()
```

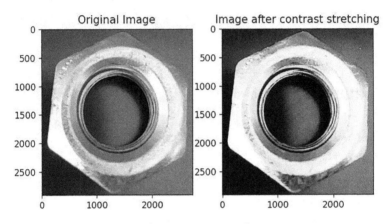

Figure 5-12. *Illustration of contrast stretching*

Edge Detection and Filtering Using OpenCV

Edge detection in image processing is a fundamental technique for finding the boundaries of objects in an image. The principle behind this operation is to detect discontinuities in brightness as the edges are marked by sudden changes in brightness. In computer vision, edge detection is often used in the preprocessing stage prior to further analysis like image segmentation, object recognition, object tracking, etc. The edge detection can be achieved by filtering the image in the spatial domain. Spatial filtering works by modifying the values of individual pixels based on their surrounding pixels. This is done by using a small matrix of numbers called a kernel or a mask. In addition to edge detection, spatial filtering can also be used for other applications such as noise removal. The edge detection filters are a type of spatial filters used to highlight the edges in an image by detecting the changes in intensity across neighboring pixels

When the kernel is centered on a pixel, the values of the pixels covered by the kernel and the values of the kernel are combined in some way to produce a new value for the center pixel. Basically, each value of the kernel is multiplied by the corresponding pixel value in the image over which it is placed on, and then all the multiplication results are then added to obtain the new value for the center pixel. The kernel is slid over the image to modify each pixel in the image. This combined operation of shift, multiply, and add is termed as convolution, and since this is done over a 2D image plane, it is also called 2D convolution. Let us look at some of the commonly used edge detection filters in this section.

Mean Filter

A mean filter is generally used to reduce noise in an image by averaging the pixel values in a small neighborhood surrounding each pixel in the image. The mean filter is implemented using a kernel that is a square matrix with odd number of rows like 3x3, 5x5, and 7x7, etc. When the center pixel of the kernel is positioned over the pixel being processed, the values of all pixels covered by the kernel are added, and the resulting sum is divided by the total number of pixels in the kernel to obtain the average. This average value is then used to replace the center pixel in the image covered by the kernel. The kernel is then slid over the image to perform the same operation over each and every pixel in the image. The effect of the mean filter is to smoothen the image which helps to reduce the high-frequency noise present in the image. Since the edges of the image correspond to high-frequency information, the edges can be blurred which in turn reduces the sharpness of the image.

This can be a drawback in applications that require edge preservation. One way to work around this blurring effect of the mean filter is to use a weighted mean filter, in which the kernel weights are chosen based on a predefined distribution such as the Gaussian distribution. The weighted mean filter assigns higher weight to the center of the kernel and lower weights as we move away from the center. This preserves the edges and reduces the blurring effect. The effect of mean filter and weighted mean filter on the grayscale nut image is illustrated in the following code. We can clearly observe the blurring of edges in the output of mean filter in Figure 5-13 which is then mitigated by the weighted Gaussian mean filter.

```
import cv2
import matplotlib.pyplot as plt
img = cv2.imread("C:/Users/user/Pictures/Nut.jpg",0)
new_img1 = cv2.blur(img,(7,7)) # (7,7) is the kernel size
new_img2 = cv2.GaussianBlur(img,(7,7),0)
plt.subplot(131)
plt.imshow(img,cmap='gray')
plt.title('Original Image')
plt.subplot(132)
plt.imshow(new_img1,cmap='gray')
plt.title('Output of mean filter')
plt.subplot(133)
plt.imshow(new_img2,cmap='gray')
plt.title('Output of weighted mean filter')
plt.show()
```

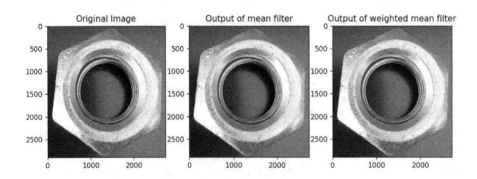

Figure 5-13. *Illustration of filtering with mean filter*

Median Filter

The idea behind median filter is pretty straightforward. When the kernel is placed over the image, the pixels covered by the kernel are sorted in ascending order, and the center pixel is replaced by the median value of the sorted list of pixels. The median filter can be quite handy in removing salt and pepper noise. We know that the intensity value of pepper noise is close to zero, whereas the intensity value of salt noise is close to 255. So, these noise values are at the two extremes of the intensity spectrum, and hence, they are naturally removed when we replace each pixel by the median value of the neighborhood covered by the kernel. This filtering process is illustrated in the following code using the nut image. We can clearly see the effectiveness of the median filter in improving the quality of the image affected by the salt and pepper noise in Figure 5-14.

```
import cv2
import numpy as np
import matplotlib.pyplot as plt
img = cv2.imread('C:/Users/user/Pictures/Nut.jpg',0)
# add salt and pepper noise
img_sn = img.copy()
prob=0.3
probs = np.random.random(img_sn.shape[:2])
img_sn[probs<(prob/2)] = 0
img_sn[probs>1-(prob/2)] = 255
# apply median filter
med = cv2.medianBlur(img_sn,3) # kernel size (3,3)
plt.subplot(131)
plt.imshow(img,cmap='gray')
plt.title('original image')
plt.subplot(132)
plt.imshow(img_sn,cmap='gray')
```

```
plt.title('Image affected by salt & pepper noise')
plt.subplot(133)
plt.imshow(med,cmap='gray')
plt.title('Noisy image filtered by median filter')
plt.show()
```

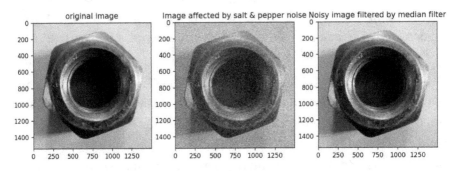

Figure 5-14. *Illustration of filtering with median filter*

Sobel Filter

Sobel filter is a popular edge detection algorithm that works by measuring the gradient of image intensity at each pixel within an image. It finds the edges by looking for smooth or abrupt intensity changes at each pixel and determining how likely that the pixel belongs to an edge. It also determines the direction in which the edge is likely to be oriented. The Sobel filter uses two 3x3 kernels, one each for the horizontal and vertical direction. The kernels are given as

Horizontal Kernel			Vertical Kernel		
-1	0	1	-1	-2	-1
-2	0	2	0	0	0
-1	0	1	1	2	1

Following are the steps involved in detecting edges using Sobel filter:

1. Convert the image to grayscale; there is no need for color information when we are just interested in detecting the edges.

2. Apply the horizontal Sobel kernel by convolving it with the image to get the horizontal gradient G_x.

3. Apply the vertical Sobel kernel by convolving it with the image to get the vertical gradient G_y.

4. Calculate the magnitude G of the gradient at each pixel using the formula:

$$G = \sqrt{G_x^2 + G_y^2}$$

5. Calculate the direction of the gradient using the formula:

$$\Theta = arctan\left(\frac{G_y}{G_x}\right)$$

6. Use a threshold value to obtain a binary image where values above the threshold are considered as edges.

The illustration of the Sobel filter with a real-world example will be given in the case study section following canny edge detection filter.

Canny Filter

Canny edge detector is a popular multistep algorithm used to detect the edges in a given digital image. Developed by John Canny in the year 1986, this algorithm has found widespread used in computer vision and image processing applications. Similar to Sobel filter, the Canny edge detection filter also works by detecting edges in an image based on the intensity gradient of the image. The algorithm consists of several steps:

1. Gaussian Smoothing: The image is first smoothed using Gaussian filter to reduce noise.

2. Gradient Calculation: The gradient magnitude and the direction for the smoothed image are then calculated using a Sobel operator.

3. Nonmaximum Suppression: This operation is performed to thin out the edges and reduce their width. This provides improved edge localization.

4. Double Thresholding: Two thresholds, a higher threshold and a lower threshold, are then applied to the image. If the gradient magnitude of a pixel is

    –   Above the high threshold, treat it as a strong edge pixel

    –   Between the high and low thresholds, treat it as a weak edge pixel

    –   Below the low threshold, treat it as a non-edge pixel

    This process helps to determine which edges to keep and which to discard thereby reducing false positives in the edge detection process.

5. Edge Tracking: Finally, edge tracking is done to connect the weak edges to the strong edges. This helps to produce more continuous and connected edges in the final image.

The sophisticated nature of the Canny edge detection algorithm helps to produce more accurate results as compared to Sobel filter. On the flip side, the Canny edge detector is a more computationally expensive algorithm. The illustration of Canny edge detector is provided in the following case study.

Case Study: Extracting the Edges of the Gear Teeth

The following Python code illustrates the process of detecting edges using Sobel and Canny filter on a gear image. Initially, we read the gear image and convert the same into a grayscale image. This grayscale image is then blurred using a Gaussian filter with a 3x3 kernel. A Sobel filter with a 3x3 kernel is applied to this image in the x and y direction to obtain the horizontal gradient and vertical gradient respectively. The *Sobel()* function in the OpenCV library is used to accomplish this. This function takes one other attribute *CV_64F* which is the parameter for output depth indicating that the output data type will be floating point numbers with a precision of 64 bits. Following this, we compute the magnitude and direction of the gradient at each pixel using the square root and arctan functions, respectively, as discussed in the theory behind Sobel filter. Finally, we apply a threshold to the gradient magnitude to get the binary image with edges as illustrated in Figure 5-15. For this, we convert every value in the gradient magnitude that is greater than the given threshold into 1 and other values to zero. We convert this resultant matrix to 8-bit unsigned integer from the previous floating point expression using the function *uint8()* from the numpy library so that the image could be converted to a format suitable for display. Finally, we multiply the matrix with 255, as 255 is the value of white pixels in a grayscale image, so that the edge pixels will be displayed in white.

115

The process is simply straightforward in the case of canny edge detection, as OpenCV offers a function *Canny()* that could easily detect the edges. This function takes the blurred image as the input along with two threshold values as we discussed in the theory behind Canny filter. The resulting image is shown next to the Sobel filter output in Figure 5-15 allowing us to compare the two images. It is quite clear by comparing the two images that the Canny edge detection algorithm produces thin and smooth edges as compared to Sobel algorithm. Another interesting aspect that can be noted from the figure is that the reflection of light in the area shown encircled in the original image creates an impression of an edge and the Canny edge detector is able to capture it better than the Sobel filter.

```python
import cv2
import matplotlib.pyplot as plt
import numpy as np
img=cv2.imread("C:/Users/user/Downloads/Gear.jpg")
# convert to grayscale image
grayimg=cv2.cvtColor(img,cv2.COLOR_BGR2GRAY)
# Smoothen the image
blurred=cv2.GaussianBlur(grayimg,(3,3),0)
# Apply Sobel Filter
# calculate x and y gradient
sobelx=cv2.Sobel(blurred,cv2.CV_64F,1,0,ksize=3)
sobely=cv2.Sobel(blurred,cv2.CV_64F,0,1,ksize=3)
# Calculate gradient magnitude and direction
grad_mag=np.sqrt(sobelx**2+sobely**2)
grad_dir=np.arctan(sobely,sobelx)
# Apply threshold to obtain binary image
threshold=120
s_edgeimg=np.uint8(grad_mag>threshold)*255
# Apply the Canny edge detector
```

```
c_edgeimg = cv2.Canny(blurred, 100, 200)
# Display grayscale image and edge image
plt.subplot(131)
plt.imshow(img)
plt.title('Original Image')
plt.subplot(132)
plt.imshow(s_edgeimg,cmap='gray')
plt.title('Sobel Edge Detection')
plt.subplot(133)
plt.imshow(c_edgeimg,cmap='gray')
plt.title('Canny Edge Detection')
plt.show()
```

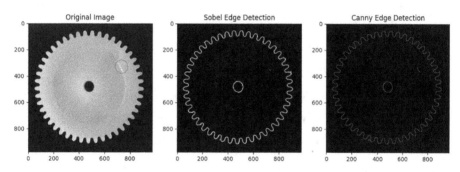

Figure 5-15. *Illustration of Sobel and Canny edge detection*

Morphological Operations with OpenCV

The term "morphology" refers to the form, shape, or structure. Therefore, morphological image processing involves a set of operations that process images based on their shape, size, and structure. These operations are well suited for binary images. Morphological operations are performed by probing an image with a structuring element. A structuring element is basically a small matrix of pixels with values of 1's forming a box or disc structure. The dimension of the matrix denotes the size of the structuring

117

element, the pattern of 1's denotes the shape of the structuring element, and one of its pixels is usually treated as the origin of the structuring element. A common practice is to have odd dimensional matrix as the structuring element where the center of the matrix is usually considered as the origin.

There are two basic morphological techniques in image processing named erosion and dilation. Other morphological operations like opening and closing are done using a combination of the erosion and dilation process. Both erosion and dilation follow a process similar to convolution, where a small structuring element is slid over the image in a row-wise manner so that the center pixel is positioned at all possible locations in the image. At each position, it is compared with the connected pixels, and based on how the pixels of the structuring element matches the pixels of the image, we can have three different operations:

- Fit: When all the pixels in the structuring element match with all the pixels of the image in the neighborhood, we can call it a fit.

- Hit: When at least one of the pixels in the structuring element matches with the corresponding pixel(s) in the image neighborhood, we can call it a hit.

- Miss: When none of the pixels in the structuring element has a match in the image neighborhood, we can call it a miss.

Erosion

To understand the process of erosion, consider the binary image block and structuring element shown in Figure 5-16. Here the dark pixels of the image have a value of "0", and the bright pixels have a value of "1". The structuring element of 1's is then used to traverse the image and find the pixel values where the element fits the neighborhood. The center pixel of the image block is maintained as "1" in the event of a fit, else they are changed to "0". The only place where the fit occurs is shown with a red bounding box, and the resulting output image is shown to the right. The erosion operation is denoted by the symbol ⊖.

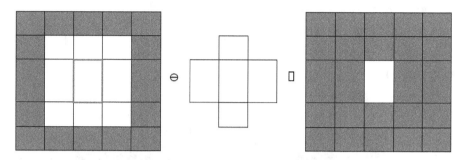

Figure 5-16. *Erosion of a binary image block using a structuring element*

It can be seen that the erosion with a small structuring element tends to shrink the structures in an image by stripping away a layer of pixels from the inner as well as outer boundaries of regions. The erosion process can be used to split or disassemble joint objects and to remove the extrusions from an object. This is illustrated from the following code, and the resulting image is given in Figure 5-17.

```
import cv2
import numpy as np
import matplotlib.pyplot as plt
# read image and convert it to binary image
img = cv2.imread('C:/Users/user/Pictures/erosion.jpg', 0)
(thresh, bwImage) = cv2.threshold(img, 127, 255, cv2.
THRESH_BINARY)
# define the structuring element
se = np.ones((3, 3), np.uint8)
# apply erosion
img_erosion = cv2.erode(bwImage, se, iterations=1)
```

119

```
# display the images
plt.subplot(121)
plt.imshow(bwImage,cmap='gray')
plt.title('Original image')
plt.subplot(122)
plt.imshow(img_erosion,cmap='gray')
plt.title('Eroded image')
plt.show()
```

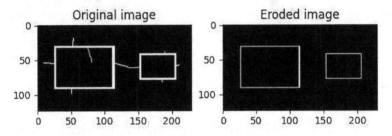

Figure 5-17. *Illustration of image erosion*

Dilation

Dilation, on the other hand, works by changing the pixel value of image covered by the center pixel of the structuring element to "1" if there is at least a single pixel value that is matched between the structuring element and the image neighborhood covered by it. In other words, we change the center pixel to "1" if the structuring element hits the image neighborhood. Let us consider the same image block and structuring element illustration as before. The places where the structuring element hits the image neighborhood are indicated by the red bounding box, and the resulting image is shown to the right in Figure 5-18. The dilation operation is denoted by the symbol $\oplus$.

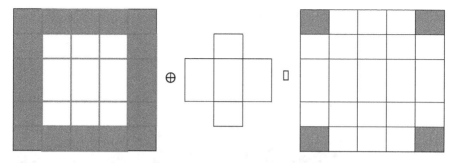

Figure 5-18. *Dilation of a binary image block using a structuring element*

It can be seen that the dilation with a small structuring element tends to expand the structures in an image by adding a layer of pixels from the inner as well as outer boundaries of regions. The dilation process can be used to repair any breaks or damages in the image and repair or correct intrusions in the image. This is illustrated from the following code, and the resulting image is given in Figure 5-19.

```
import cv2
import numpy as np
import matplotlib.pyplot as plt
# read image and convert it to binary image
img = cv2.imread('C:/Users/user/Pictures/chapter5_dilation.
jpg', 0)
(thresh, bwImage) = cv2.threshold(img, 127, 255, cv2.
THRESH_BINARY)
# define the structuring element
se = np.ones((5,5), np.uint8)
# apply dilation
img_erosion = cv2.dilate(bwImage, se, iterations=1)
# display the images
plt.subplot(121)
plt.imshow(bwImage,cmap='gray')
```

```
plt.title('Original image')
plt.subplot(122)
plt.imshow(img_erosion,cmap='gray')
plt.title('Dilated image')
plt.show()
```

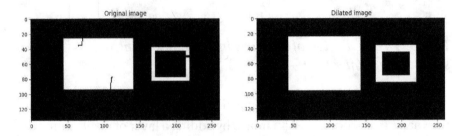

Figure 5-19.   *Illustration of image dilation*

Case Study: Morphological Filtering for Noise Removal

Morphological operations can be used for a wide range of applications including image segmentation, feature extraction, shape analysis, noise removal, etc. In this case study, we will see how a simple morphological operation can be used to remove small unwanted specks-like-noise scattered around a gear image. The following code illustrates the morphological closing operation on a gear image with varying kernel sizes. Initially, we read the gear image, convert it into a grayscale image, and then apply Gaussian blurring to smoothen the image. The *GaussianBlur()* function in the OpenCV library is used to achieve this. It can be observed that a Gaussian kernel size of (3,3) is used to blur the image. Then, we convert the blurred image into a black and white image using the Otsu's thresholding method which we will be discussing in the upcoming section. For simple understanding, the Otsu method is used to determine global intensity threshold for the blurred image; any pixel with intensity above the threshold will be converted to 255(white), and those with intensity below the threshold will be converted to 0 (black).

As seen in Figure 5-20, the gear segment as well as the noise segments around the gear image are converted to white color, and the background is converted to black color. Now we use the morphological "opening" operation which is nothing but an erosion operation followed by a closing operation. This will potentially remove the small irregularities around the gear segment, but since the noise segments are of varying sizes, we need to choose the size of kernel accordingly. Here, we use a rectangular kernel of various sizes filled with 1's which is used to demonstrate the effect of kernel size on the filtering operation. This is achieved using the *ones()* function in the numpy library, and the *uint8()* function in the same library is used to represent all the values in the kernel (all 1's) as 8-bit unsigned integers. Then, *morphologyEX()* function in the OpenCV library is used to perform the morphological operation. This function takes the black and white thresholded image as input, a second morphological operation parameter, which is *MORPH_OPEN* in our case, and the kernel as the third parameter. It can be seen from the figure that the kernel size (7,7) completely removed all the noise specks in the image. Another interesting aspect to note is that if we had used binary inverse thresholding, then white and black regions would be inversed, and the morphological closing operation would provide us the desired result in that case, *import cv2.*

```
import matplotlib.pyplot as plt
import numpy as np
# Load the image
img = cv2.imread('C:/Users/Lenovo/Pictures/New
Folder/20230917_113122.jpg', cv2.IMREAD_GRAYSCALE)
blurred=cv2.GaussianBlur(img,(3,3),0)
# Perform Otsu's thresholding
thresh = cv2.threshold(blurred, 0, 255, cv2.THRESH_BINARY+cv2.
THRESH_OTSU)[1]
```

```
# Perform morphological opening
kernel_1 = np.ones((3,3),np.uint8)
kernel_2 = np.ones((5,5),np.uint8)
kernel_3 = np.ones((7,7),np.uint8)
opening_1 = cv2.morphologyEx(thresh, cv2.MORPH_OPEN, kernel_1)
opening_2 = cv2.morphologyEx(thresh, cv2.MORPH_OPEN, kernel_2)
opening_3 = cv2.morphologyEx(thresh, cv2.MORPH_OPEN, kernel_3)
# Display images
plt.subplot(231)
plt.imshow(img,cmap='gray')
plt.title('Original Image')
plt.subplot(232)
plt.imshow(blurred,cmap='gray')
plt.title('Blurred Image')
plt.subplot(233)
plt.imshow(thresh, cmap='gray')
plt.title('Black and White Image')
plt.subplot(234)
plt.imshow(opening_1,cmap='gray')
plt.title('Morphological opening with 3x3 kernel')
plt.subplot(235)
plt.imshow(opening_2,cmap='gray')
plt.title('Morphological opening with 5x5 kernel')
plt.subplot(236)
plt.imshow(opening_3,cmap='gray')
plt.title('Morphological opening with 7x7 kernel')
plt.show()
```

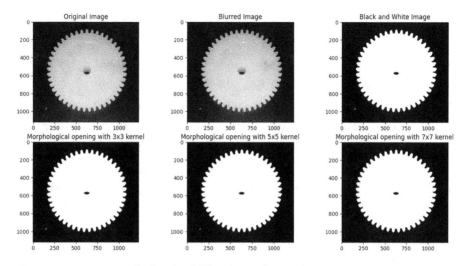

Figure 5-20. *Morphological filtering of gear image*

Thresholding Techniques with OpenCV

In image processing, thresholding is a simple method for segmenting images where the values of certain pixels are altered with respect to a certain threshold which in turn makes the image easier to analyze. Thresholding helps to highlight select regions of interest in an image while ignoring the rest of the image that we are not concerned with. There are a number of thresholding techniques of which we will discuss four common techniques in this section.

Binary Thresholding

This is the simplest form of thresholding where the pixel values of a grayscale image are compared to a threshold T. The pixels with value less than T are converted to black pixels with value "0", and those with value greater than T are converted to white pixels with value "1". In essence, the grayscale image is converted to a binary image. The application of binary threshold with three different values 63, 127, and 191 to our nut image is illustrated in the following code. Since 63 is closer to the black pixel value "0" and distant from the white pixel "255" in the grayscale image, a larger range of pixels is converted to white pixels in the resultant binary image which results in an image dominated by white intensity. The second threshold of 127 is in the midway between the black pixel "0" and the white pixel "255" that gives a better-balanced binary image. The third threshold of 191 is very close to the white pixel "255" resulting in a large range of pixels to be turned black in the binary image. The resulting images for these three thresholds are shown in Figure 5-21.

```
import cv2
import numpy as np
import matplotlib.pyplot as plt
# read image
img = cv2.imread('C:/Users/user/Pictures/Nut.jpg', 0)
# apply binary thresholding
(thresh1, bwImage1) = cv2.threshold(img, 63, 255, cv2.
THRESH_BINARY)
(thresh2, bwImage2) = cv2.threshold(img, 127, 255, cv2.
THRESH_BINARY)
(thresh3, bwImage3) = cv2.threshold(img, 191, 255, cv2.
THRESH_BINARY)
# display the images
plt.subplot(221)
plt.imshow(img,cmap='gray')
plt.title('original image')
plt.subplot(222)
plt.imshow(bwImage1,cmap='gray')
plt.title('Threshold value=63')
plt.subplot(223)
plt.imshow(bwImage2,cmap='gray')
```

```
plt.title('Threshold value=127')
plt.subplot(224)
plt.imshow(bwImage3,cmap='gray')
plt.title('Threshold value=255')
plt.show()
```

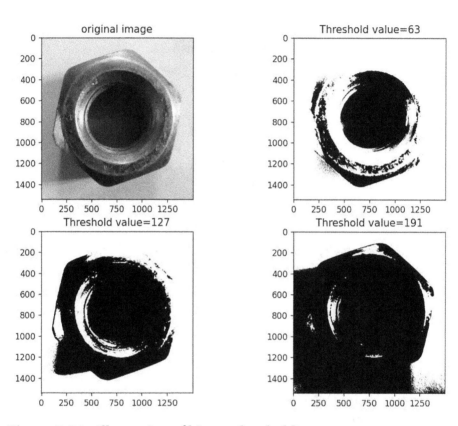

Figure 5-21. *Illustration of binary thresholding*

Binary Inverse Thresholding

This type of thresholding is the exact opposite of binary thresholding. Here, the pixels with values greater than the threshold T are converted to black pixels with value "0", and those with values lesser than the threshold T are converted to white pixels with value "1". The illustration of this technique with the same three thresholds as before is presented as follows, and the resulting images are shown in Figure 5-22.

```python
import cv2
import numpy as np
import matplotlib.pyplot as plt
# read image
img = cv2.imread('C:/Users/user/Pictures/Nut.jpg', 0)
# apply binary inverse thresholding
(thresh1, bwImage1) = cv2.threshold(img, 63, 255, cv2.THRESH_
BINARY_INV)
(thresh2, bwImage2) = cv2.threshold(img, 127, 255, cv2.THRESH_
BINARY_INV)
(thresh3, bwImage3) = cv2.threshold(img, 191, 255, cv2.THRESH_
BINARY_INV)
# display the images
plt.subplot(221)
plt.imshow(img,cmap='gray')
plt.title('original image')
plt.subplot(222)
plt.imshow(bwImage1,cmap='gray')
plt.title('Threshold value=63')
plt.subplot(223)
plt.imshow(bwImage2,cmap='gray')
plt.title('Threshold value=127')
plt.subplot(224)
```

```
plt.imshow(bwImage3,cmap='gray')
plt.title('Threshold value=255')
plt.show()
```

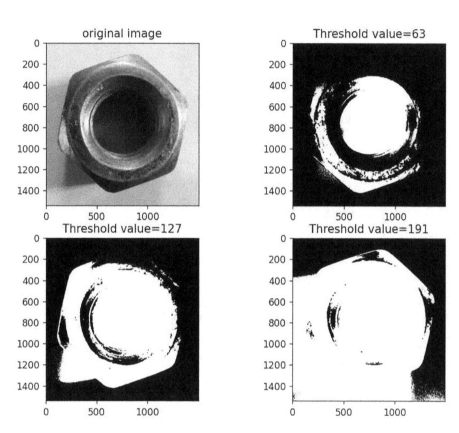

Figure 5-22. *Illustration of binary inverse thresholding*

Otsu's Thresholding

In both the thresholding methods that we have discussed, the threshold
for segmentation is selected manually. There are other methods where an
optimal threshold could be selected automatically by implementing a fixed
procedure. One common method for automated thresholding is Otsu's

method, named after Nobuyuki Otsu, the person behind the development of this algorithm. Otsu's thresholding is a simple method used to generate a threshold value that splits the images into two classes, the foreground and the background, by minimizing the intra-class variance. This method is well suited for bimodal images whose histogram shows two clear peaks, each representing different intensity range. So, if the intensity range of the foreground and background is clearly segregated from each other, then Otsu's threshold would produce a binary image with clear segmentation between the foreground and background. For our illustration, let us go with the same nut image. We will plot the histogram to check if there are two clear peaks. The result of binary thresholding with the middle value of 127 alongside the result of Otsu's thresholding shown in Figure 5-23 helps us to compare the two techniques.

```python
import cv2
import numpy as np
import matplotlib.pyplot as plt
# read image
img = cv2.imread('C:/Users/user/Pictures/Nut.jpg', 0)
# calculate histograk
hist = cv2.calcHist([img],[0],None,[256],[0,256])
# binary thresholding
(thresh1, bwImage1) = cv2.threshold(img, 127, 255, cv2.
THRESH_BINARY)
# Otsu thresholding
(otsu_thresh, bwImage2) = cv2.threshold(
    img, 0, 255, cv2.THRESH_BINARY + cv2.THRESH_OTSU,
)
# display the images
plt.subplot(221)
plt.imshow(img,cmap='gray')
plt.title('original image')
```

```
plt.subplot(222)
plt.plot(hist)
plt.title('Histogram of original image')
plt.subplot(223)
plt.imshow(bwImage1,cmap='gray')
plt.title('Binary thresholding with threshold value=127')
plt.subplot(224)
plt.imshow(bwImage2,cmap='gray')
plt.title(f'Otsu thresholding with threshold value =
%f'%otsu_thresh)
plt.show()
```

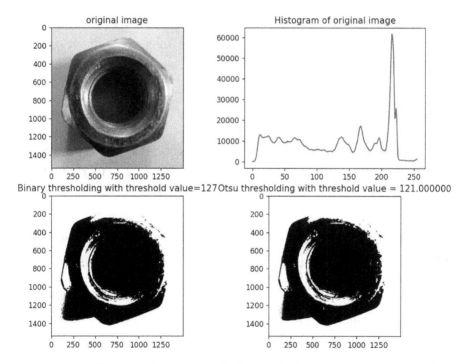

Figure 5-23. *Illustration of Otsu's thresholding*

131

We can see that the histogram of the nut image does not have two distinct peaks since there is no clear segregation between the foreground and background intensities. Around the top-right corner, the bright portions of the nut image are similar in intensity to the background at that area. Similarly, we can observe that the dark pixel intensities of the image to the left side are similar to the shadow created in the background. It can also be observed from the code segment for Otsu's thresholding that the initial value of the threshold is set to 0 and the Otsu method computes the optimal threshold to be 121 which is indicated in the title of the fourth image in the plot. From the histogram, it is evident that one cluster of pixels has a distribution with a clear peak, whereas the rest of the pixels are distributed widely with no clear peak. Otsu's method tries to find the optimal value between the two clusters and ends up with the value of 124. The readers can try to apply this method to an image with higher contrast between the foreground and background to see a much better result.

Adaptive Thresholding

In all the thresholding techniques discussed so far, a single threshold value is used for all the pixel values. Such a threshold is often termed as a global threshold. Alternatively, we can apply different threshold values for different parts of an image based on the local values of the pixels in each neighborhood. These threshold values are called local thresholds, and the techniques used to apply local thresholds are termed as adaptive thresholding techniques. These kinds of techniques are suited for images with uneven lighting conditions.

In adaptive thresholding, the threshold is calculated from either arithmetic mean or Gaussian mean of the pixel intensities in each region. All the pixel values contribute equally in the calculation of arithmetic mean value, whereas in Gaussian mean value, maximum weightage is given to the center pixel and the weights decrease as we move farther from the center pixel. The process of adaptive thresholding using arithmetic mean and Gaussian mean is illustrated here using the nut image, and the resulting images are shown in Figure 5-24.

```python
import cv2
import numpy as np
import matplotlib.pyplot as plt
# read image
img = cv2.imread('C:/Users/user/Pictures/Nut.jpg', 0)
# adaptive thresholding using arithmetic mean
bwImage1 = cv2.adaptiveThreshold(
    img,255,cv2.ADAPTIVE_THRESH_MEAN_C,cv2.THRESH_BINARY,11,4)
# adaptive thresholding using Gaussian mean
bwImage2 = cv2.adaptiveThreshold(    img,255,cv2.ADAPTIVE_
THRESH_GAUSSIAN_C,cv2.THRESH_BINARY,11,4)
# display the images
plt.subplot(131)
plt.imshow(img,cmap='gray')
plt.title('original image')
plt.subplot(132)
plt.imshow(bwImage1,cmap='gray')
plt.title('Adaptive thresholding with arithmetic mean')
plt.subplot(133)
plt.imshow(bwImage2,cmap='gray')
plt.title('Adaptive thresholding with Gaussian mean')
plt.show()
```

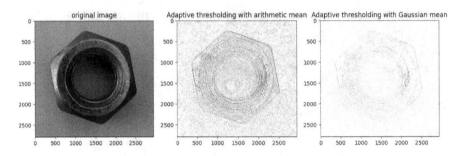

Figure 5-24. *Illustration of adaptive thresholding*

In the preceding code, the number 255 denotes the maximum value that is applied to pixel values exceeding the threshold. The number 11 indicates the size of the neighborhood area that is used to calculate the threshold for each pixel. The number 4 at the end is a constant value that is subtracted from the mean or Gaussian mean.

Binary Large Objects (Blob) Detection Using OpenCV

Blobs in an image can be considered as those regions with connected pixel in the image which share some common properties, such as the brightness or color, which are constant or approximately constant compared to the surrounding regions. These regions could indicate the presence of objects or parts of objects which could then be used for object detection or object tracking. In OpenCV, these blobs could be detected using a simple function SimpleBlobDetector(). The algorithm behind this function is composed of four steps:

- Thresholding: The first step is to convert the given image to several binary images thresholding it with different thresholds starting with a minimum specified threshold and then gradually increasing it by a specified constant step size till a maximum specified threshold is reached.

- Grouping: In each of the resulting images, the connected white pixels are grouped. These groups may be considered as blobs.

- Merging: The center for each of the detected binary blobs is computed, and those blobs that are separated by a distance less than a specified minimum distance are merged.

- Center and Radius Calculation: The centers and radii of the final merged blobs are then computed and returned.

The following code illustrates the blob detection on a standard "coins" image, which consists of a number of bright coins in a dark background. We use the predefined functions SimpleBlobDetector_create() and detector.detect() to detect the blobs in the image. Since these functions are suited for detecting dark blobs in bright background, we have to invert the grayscale image to make it as dark coins in bright background before using these functions. Finally, the OpenCV tool is used to display red circles around the detected blobs as shown in Figure 5-25.

```
import cv2
import numpy as np;
import matplotlib.pyplot as plt
# Read image
im=cv2.imread(
"C:/Users/user/Pictures/Coins.png",cv2.IMREAD_GRAYSCALE)
plt.imshow(im,cmap='gray')
plt.title('Original image')
plt.show()
```

```
inverted_img = cv2.bitwise_not(im)
# Set up the detector with default parameters.
detector = cv2.SimpleBlobDetector_create()
# Detect blobs.
keypoints = detector.detect(inverted_img)
print(len(keypoints))
# Draw detected blobs as red circles.
blobs = cv2.drawKeypoints(
im, keypoints, np.array([]), (0,0,255), cv2.DRAW_MATCHES_FLAGS_
DRAW_RICH_KEYPOINTS)
# Show keypoints
cv2.imshow("Detected Blobs", blobs)
cv2.waitKey(0)
```

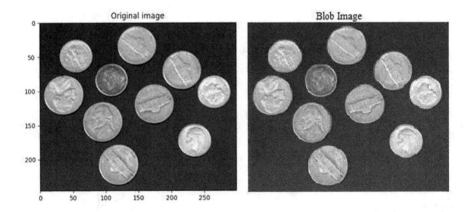

Figure 5-25. *Illustration of blob detection*

Contours Detection with OpenCV

A contour in an image is a closed curve joining all the continuous points along a boundary having the same intensity or color that represent the shape of objects in the image. Contours are widely used in applications such as shape analysis, object detection, object recognition, foreground/background segmentation, etc. OpenCV provides two simple functions findContours() and drawContours() to accomplish this task.

We will consider the most common "rice" image to illustrate this task. As the findContours() function has to be applied on a binary image, we need to apply thresholding to convert the input image to a binary image. In the illustration, a manual threshold of 130 is used, but it is always a good practice to go for automatic thresholding methods like OTSU or adaptive thresholding. In addition to the black and white image, the findContours() function accepts two more parameters. The first parameter cv2.RETR_TREE denotes the contour retrieval mode which retrieves all the contours in the image and creates a hierarchy list. Hierarchy is the representation of the relationships between the contours in an image. For example, if one contour is located inside another, the outer one is called parent and the inner one is called the child, thereby establishing a hierarchy between the two. The second parameter cv2.CHAIN_APPROX_SIMPLE denotes the method used to save the (x,y) coordinates of the boundary of a shape. The SIMPLE method removes redundant points thereby compressing the contour and saving memory. Once the contours are determined, the drawContours() function is used to draw the contours over a black canvas of the same size as the input image. This black canvas is simply created by defining a matrix of zeros with the same size as the input. The code for the contour detection process is illustrated as follows, and the corresponding outputs are shown in Figure 5-26.

```
import cv2
import numpy as np
import matplotlib.pyplot as plt
img = cv2.imread('C:/Users/user/Pictures/rice.jpeg')
img_grey = cv2.cvtColor(img,cv2.COLOR_BGR2GRAY)
#convert the grayscale image to binary image
thresh = 130
```

```
ret,thresh_img = cv2.threshold(img_grey, thresh, 255, cv2.
THRESH_BINARY)
#find contours
contours, hierarchy = cv2.findContours(thresh_img, cv2.RETR_
TREE, cv2.CHAIN_APPROX_SIMPLE)
#create an black canvas for contours
img_contours = np.zeros(img.shape)
# draw the contours on the black canvas
cv2.drawContours(img_contours, contours, -1, (0,255,0), 3)
#display all images
plt.subplot(221)
plt.imshow(img)
plt.title('original image')
plt.subplot(222)
plt.imshow(img_grey,cmap='gray')
plt.title('grayscale image')
plt.subplot(223)
plt.imshow(thresh_img,cmap='gray')
plt.title('original image')
plt.subplot(224)
plt.imshow(img_contours)
plt.title('contour image')
plt.show()
```

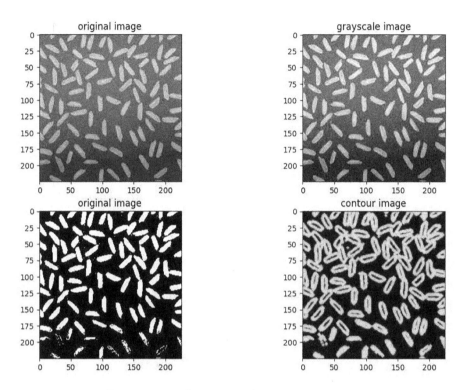

Figure 5-26. *Illustration of contour detection*

Summary

This brings us to the end of this chapter. We have elaborately discussed a wide variety of image processing techniques that are more relevant to industrial vision applications. Let us recall all the techniques that we discussed in the chapter:

- A brief introduction on image acquisition where we touched upon types of sensors, the importance of lighting, and image resolution

- Various image properties like resolution, aspect ratio, color depth, image size, and image file formats

- Common noise sources like Gaussian noise, salt and pepper noise, and speckle noise

- Common types of images like binary images, grayscale images, and color images

- Resizing of images with various interpolation techniques offered by both Pillow and OpenCV libraries

- Image transformation techniques like image negative, log transformation, power law transformation, and contrast stretching

- Commonly used filtering and edge detection techniques like mean filter, median filter, Sobel filter, and Canny filter

- Morphological operations like erosion, dilation, opening, and closing

- Thresholding techniques like binary thresholding, binary inverse thresholding, Otsu's thresholding, and adaptive thresholding

- Blob detection and contour detection

Having gone through such a comprehensive list of image processing techniques, we will discuss how to develop simple and easy-to-use user interfaces for the image processing techniques in the next chapter that will allow the users such as those in quality control team of an assembly line to carry out their tasks without the need to understand the coding behind the techniques.

CHAPTER 6

Graphical User Interface with OpenCV and tkinter

In this chapter, we will discuss the design of a basic graphical user interface (GUI) using a number of graphical components for an industrial vision system. There are multiple libraries available in Python for designing a GUI, and we will use the *tkinter* library in this chapter. We will start with the discussion of individual GUI components provided by tkinter along with a simple demonstration for each one of them and finally build a complete user interface for a simple vision system.

GUIs at a Glance

A GUI is a digital interface between the users and the underlying computer program behind an application that lets them interact with the program with the help of graphical elements such as icons, buttons, windows, sliders, menus, etc. A GUI makes life simple for common people without knowledge of technical details by providing a user-friendly way to interact with complex systems or software applications. Prior to GUIs, users interacted with computer programs using text commands in an interface

© K. Mohaideen Abdul Kadhar and G. Anand 2024
K. Mohaideen Abdul Kadhar and G. Anand, *Industrial Vision Systems with Raspberry Pi*,
Maker Innovations Series, https://doi.org/10.1007/979-8-8688-0097-9_6

called character user interface (CUI). Unlike CUI, the GUI provides visual elements to represent various functions and actions associated with the programs. Ranging from operating systems to browsers and multimedia applications, GUI have become the standard interface for interaction.

Following are the key components of a GUI:

- Windows: The primary component of GUI applications are windows that consist of various elements like buttons, menus, scrollbar, etc.

- Dialog Boxes: These are small windows to communicate information to the user and prompt response from them.

- Buttons and Icons: These are graphical elements that users click or tap to trigger some actions.

- Toolbars: Usually placed at the top of windows, they provide quick access, using buttons and icons, to commonly used functions in the application.

- Scrollbars: Usually provided at the side or bottom of a window to navigate across the entire window area when the contents of the window could not be fit within the visible area.

- Text Fields: Allows users to input and edit text.

- Checkboxes and Radio Buttons: These elements allow users to select options from a list. Checkboxes are meant for multiple selections, whereas radio buttons allow only a single selection.

When we talk about industrial vision system in manufacturing sector, the end users of the system include the likes of assembly line operators or technicians from quality control department. Industrial vision systems are comprised of cameras, sensors, and algorithms that work on the images and sensor data performing tasks such as object detection, measurement, defect identification, etc. The vision systems should be designed in a way that enables these personnel to use them with minimal training thereby making life easy for them. This can be achieved by providing a simple easy-to-use GUI for interaction thereby enhancing the efficiency and effectiveness of the process involved.

Tkinter

Tkinter is one of the most commonly used Python libraries for developing GUI. It is the standard Python interface to the Tk GUI toolkit where Tk is a cross-platform widget toolkit providing a library of GUI widgets. The name tkinter comes from the phrase "Tk interface," and it is an open source library released under Python license. tkinter comes bundled together with Python package, making it easily available for developers. The GUI code developed using tkinter can work on multiple platforms like Windows, MacOS, and Linux.

Tkinter offers a number of widgets that provide different ways for the users to interact with an application. Discussing all the widgets is beyond the scope of this book. We will only discuss some of the common widgets that are often used in vision systems as illustrated in Table 6-1. We will first learn to build simple GUIs with each of these widgets one by one. Later on, in the chapter, we will build a comprehensive GUI with multiple widgets for an industrial vision system.

Table 6-1. *Tkinter widgets*

Widget	Description
Label	Displays static text or images that users can just view but not interact with
Button	Enables users to initiate an action by clicking it
Entry	A single-line text field where users can type in strings involving text and numbers
Radiobutton	Let users choose one among several choices
Checkbutton	Allow users turn an action on or off
messagebox	Displays a message to the user which is non-editable multi-line text
Toplevel	Provides users with a separate window
filedialog	Used to get information from users like typing text or selecting files to open, inform them of some events, confirm an action, and more
Canvas	A widget intended for drawing pictures and placing graphics, text, and other widgets
Scale	A graphical slider that allows users to select values from a scale

Label

Let us start with a small program that creates a simple window with a label widget that displays a welcome message.

```
from tkinter import *
# create a window
root = Tk()
root.title("Sample Window")
# create a label
```

```
mylabel = Label(root, text="Hello World!")
# place the label in the window
mylabel.pack()
root.mainloop()
```

In the preceding code, the function Tk() creates the main window in which the required graphic widgets will be added. The *title()* function is used to provide a title to the window. All the widgets of the application window will be managed using the variable name created for the window which is *root* in our case. This is evident from the next line of code where we create a label widget using the *root* variable. We just provide the commonly used "Hello World!" string to be displayed in the Label widget so that we don't get a blank window. Now that the Label widget is created, the *pack()* function in tkinter is used to push it into the main window. The *mainloop()* window keeps the main window running in a loop so that it stays open as long as the user chooses to close the application. This GUI code can be executed in any Python IDE of our choice. For instance, the code can be typed in a new editor window in the IDLE IDE, as shown in Figure 6-1, and then it can be executed by clicking "Run Module" in the "RUN" menu at the top palette or by clicking the "f5" key in the keyboard. This will create the sample window as shown in the figure.

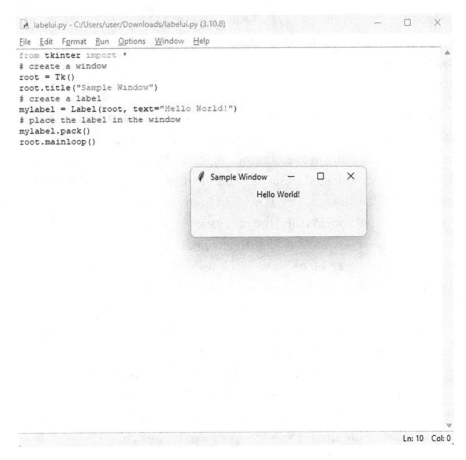

Figure 6-1. *GUI with a label widget in IDLE IDE*

We can use a grid system to place multiple widgets at desired locations using a row-and-column-based coordinate system. In the following code, we create two label widgets to be displayed at successive rows. To position the widgets, we use the *grid()* function instead of *pack()* function, and we provide the row index as 0 for the first label and 1 for the second label. To understand the column position, we also provide the column index as 0 for the first label and 1 for the second label. The positioning of the label widgets corresponding to the code can be witnessed from Figure 6-2.

```
from tkinter import *
# create a window
root = Tk()
root.title("Grid Window")
# create a label
mylabel1 = Label(root, text="Hello World!")
mylabel2 = Label(root, text="Let's play with GUI")
# place the labels in adjacent rows of a grid
mylabel1.grid(row=0,column=0)
mylabel2.grid(row=1,column=1)
root.mainloop()
```

Figure 6-2. *GUI with grids enable to display labels*

Button

Now that we know how to display labels, let us try to use a button widget to generate a label. A button widget needs two things: a text prompt on top of the button indicating its functionality and an action that needs to be carried out upon pressing the button. In our case, the action of generating a label can be created first with a user-defined function as illustrated in the following code. Once the action is defined, we can use the *Button()* function to create the button. Within the button function, the *text* option can be used to provide the text prompt, and the *command* option can be used to set the function call for the label generation function we created.

147

Recall that we need to use the *pack()* function to push the button into the main window. In addition, we can customize the button by providing the height and width of the button using the *padx* and *pady* options. We can also set the foreground color (color of the text over the button) and the background color (color of the button) using the *fg* and *bg* options. Readers can explore the other configuration options provided by the *Button* function from the official documentation. The window generated by the code is illustrated in Figure 6-3.

```python
from tkinter import *
root = Tk() # create a window
root.title("Button window")
# define button action
def click():
    mylabel = Label(root, text='Hello World!')
    mylabel.pack()
# create and pack a disabled button
mybutton = Button(root, text='Generate Label', command=click,
padx=10, pady=10, fg="white", bg="blue")
mybutton.pack()
root.mainloop()
```

Figure 6-3. *GUI with a button to generate label text*

Entry

In both of the previous examples, we programmed the text to be displayed in the label. In this section, we will use the entry widget to get the text from the user and use a button widget to push the text to the label widget. In the following code illustrated, we initially create the entry widget using the *Entry()* function. It can be seen that the function allows us to customize the widget by providing options like *width, borderwidth,* etc. The function provides an insert method with the syntax *insert(index, value),* where *index* is the position at which the value is inserted and *value* is the text to be inserted in the entry field. Note that we have provided a default string *"Enter text"* to be displayed as default. The index 0 enables us to replace this default string with the string that we type since we are inserting in the same position as the default string. Next, we create action function for the pushbutton wherein we create a label widget. Unlike the previous examples, here we use the *get()* function to get the text from the entry widget rather than giving our own text. And finally, we use the button function to initiate the action. The resulting window is shown in Figure 6-4.

```
from tkinter import *
# create a window
root = Tk()
root.title("Entry window")
# create an entry widget
entry = Entry(root, width=50, borderwidth=5)
entry.pack()
entry.insert(0,"Enter text")
# define button action
def click():
    mylabel = Label(root, text=entry.get())
    mylabel.pack()
# create and pack a disabled button
```

```
mybutton = Button(root, text='Generate Label', command=click,
fg="white", bg="blue")
mybutton.pack()
root.mainloop()
```

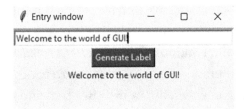

Figure 6-4. *Gui with entry widget to generate label text*

Radiobutton

In this section, we will use radio buttons to push integer values into the label widget. As illustrated in the following code, we first define a variable *r* using the *IntVar()* function to hold integer data which is then retrieved using the *get()* function while defining the action for the radiobutton widgets. Next, we define the action for radiobutton widgets with a user-defined function where we use the *config()* function to update the label widget. Following this, we create the radio buttons using the *Radiobutton()* function. This function takes in the following inputs: the text to be displayed for the radio button, the control variable to keep track of the user's choices, the value to be assigned to the control variable, and the action to be initiated upon clicking the radio button. Note that we use the Lambda function which gets the value assigned to the control variable r and provides it to the radio button action function we defined earlier. Finally, we create a label widget with empty text and push it to the window. When we click a radio button, the value assigned to the control variable corresponding to that button is displayed in the label widget as illustrated in Figure 6-5.

```
from tkinter import *
# create a window
root = Tk()
root.title("Radiobutton window")
r=IntVar() # define integer variable
# define action for radiobutton
def clicked(value):
    mylabel.config(text=value)
# define radio button
Radiobutton(root, text="Option 1", variable=r,
            value=1,command=lambda: clicked(r.get())).pack()
Radiobutton(root, text="Option 2", variable=r,
            value=2,command=lambda: clicked(r.get())).pack()
# define label
mylabel = Label(root, text="")
mylabel.pack()
root.mainloop()
```

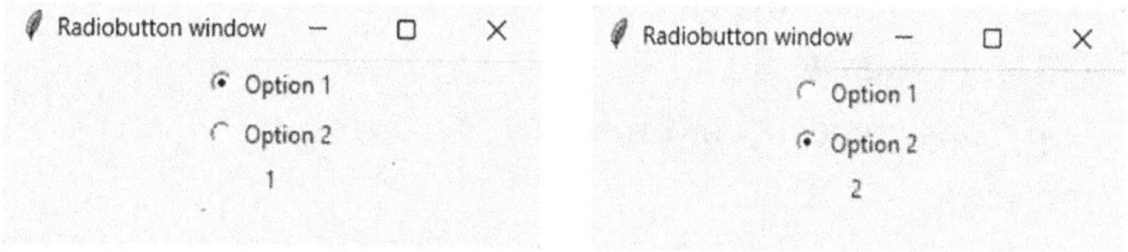

Figure 6-5. *GUI with radiobutton widgets to generate label text*

Checkbutton

Unlike the radio buttons that allow us to choose one among multiple options, checkbuttons allow us to select multiple options at once. In the code illustrated as follows, we use the *BooleanVar()* functions with the checkboxes where the value of the variables will automatically be updated to *True* when the corresponding buttons are selected and to *False* when the buttons are deselected. In the action function corresponding to the button widget, we generate a text string corresponding to the checkbutton selected and append it to a list. The reason for appending to a list is the fact that we can select multiple checkbuttons at a time, and the text string corresponding to all those buttons needs to be displayed. The generated text strings are then configured to the label widget. We also add a default text to be displayed in case none of the boxes are selected. The different scenarios corresponding to the selection of checkbuttons are illustrated in Figure 6-6.

```
from tkinter import *
# Create a window
root = Tk()
root.title("CheckButton Window")
# action statement for check buttons
def generate_label():
    options = []
    if option1_var.get():
        options.append("Option 1")
    if option2_var.get():
        options.append("Option 2")
    if options:
        mylabel.config(text="Selected options: " + ',
        '.join(options))
    else:
        mylabel.config(text="No options selected")
# Create variables to store the state of the check buttons
option1_var = BooleanVar()
option2_var = BooleanVar()
# Create check buttons
checkbutton1 = Checkbutton(root, text="Option 1",
variable=option1_var, command=generate_label).pack()
```

```
checkbutton2 = Checkbutton(root, text="Option 2",
variable=option2_var, command=generate_label).pack()
# Create a label to display selected options
mylabel = Label(root, text="No options selected")
mylabel.pack()
root.mainloop()
```

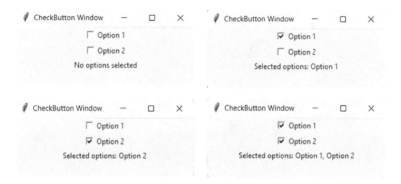

Figure 6-6. *GUI with checkbutton widgets to generate label text*

Messagebox

Oftentimes, we find the need to provide some warnings or convey some information regarding the application to the user. Message boxes provide a simple way of achieving this using a popup box that is triggered on the behest of an action initiated by the user. In the following simple code, we use a button action to trigger the messagebox widget. Figure 6-7 illustrates the result of the action.

```
from tkinter import *
from tkinter import messagebox
# create a window
root = Tk()
root.title('Window with popup')
```

```
# define action for button
def popup():
    messagebox.showinfo("Popup window","How are you?")
# create a button
Button(root, text="Popup", command=popup).pack()
mainloop()
```

Figure 6-7. *GUI with messagebox triggered by button action*

Toplevel

The toplevel widget can be used in an application when there is a need
for an extra window to represent some extra information to the user
or to provide a separate interface for a subset of the application. These
additional windows can be directly managed by using their own variable
name and do not need to be associated with a parent window. The simple
code given here illustrates the creation of an additional window with its
own label. The resulting windows are shown in Figure 6-8.

```
from tkinter import *
# create main window
root=Tk()
```

```
root.title('Main window')
# create additional window
top = Toplevel()
top.title('Sub window')
# create labels for both windows
mylabel1 = Label(root, text = 'This is the main window').pack()
mylabel2 = Label(top, text='This is the sub window').pack()
mainloop()
```

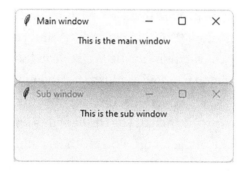

Figure 6-8. *GUI with two windows*

Fielddialog and Canvas

For ease of understanding, we just used simple labels to demonstrate the widgets that we discussed so far. In this section, we will see how to browse the files, select an image, and display it in our window which will be crucial for our vision system. We will use the *fielddialog* widget to browse for the image and *Canvas* widget to display the image. Images can also be displayed in the *Label* widget, but since it is a static widget, it does not allow for further interaction with the displayed image. Hence, we go for the *Canvas* widget where we can choose to draw over the image or make transformations like resizing, rotation, etc., to the image.

In the following code, we use a button widget to open the dialog widget for selecting an image and a *Canvas* widget for drawing the image. We will specify the width and height of the canvas according to the size of the image to be displayed. In our case, we use the same size as the image, that is, 512 x 512. Under the function defined for the button action, we use the *askopenfilename* function of the fielddialog widget to browse for image. The *askopenfilename* function takes three parameters as input in our code. The first one is the initial directory into which the fielddialog widget will open followed by a text to be displayed on the dialog window and then the filetypes to be shown in it. Note that we have provided two file types in the function: ".png" indicating PNG images and "*.*" indicating all other file types. These two types will therefore be available in the *file-type* drop-down menu in the dialog window as illustrated in Figure 6-9 (a). We can select an image available in the initial directory itself or navigate to other directories for selecting the image. The result of this *askopenfilename* would be the filename of the image along with its path.

To enable the file to be displayed in the canvas, we need to use the *PhotoImage* function in tkinter library to read the file. But the problem is that this *PhotoImage* function supports only GIF and PGM/PPM formats, whereas the commonly used image formats that we will be using are JPEG and PNG. A way around this problem is to use an alternative *PhotoImage* function provided by PIL library under the *ImageTk* class. We initially read the image using the *imread()* function of the OpenCV library. The reason for this is that, the image is read as a numpy array when using OpenCV, and this allows us to perform a number of numerical operations on the image as we discussed in Chapter 5. We then use the *fromarray()* function in the PIL library to convert the image into a PIL Image file format and then use the *PhotoImage* function in the same library to convert the image to image objects that could be displayed in the Canvas widget.

Next, we can use the *create_image* function to draw the image on the canvas. The first two numbers inside the function indicates the (x,y) coordinates used to position the image. We can vary the coordinates to

156

shift the position of the image either horizontally or vertically. The *anchor* value determines the position within the image that will be aligned with the coordinates. For instance, we have specified "nw" as the anchor which implies that the northwest anchor point of the image (top leftmost corner) will be placed at the coordinates (0, 0) on the canvas. After configuring the canvas, the image opened using the *PhotoImage* function is assigned to the *image* attribute of the Canvas widget. The resulting image displayed on the canvas widget is shown in Figure 6-9 (b). For all the GUI illustrations in this chapter, from this point onward, we use the image of a tipped saw blade.

```python
from tkinter import *
from tkinter import filedialog
from PIL import Image, ImageTk
import cv2
# create root window
root = Tk()
root.title('Window with dialogbox')
# define action for button widget
def click():
    filename = filedialog.askopenfilename(initialdir="C:/Users/
    user/Pictures", title="Browse", filetypes=(("png files",
    "*.png"),("all files","*.*")))
    o_img = cv2.cvtColor(cv2.imread(filename),
    cv2.COLOR_BGR2RGB)
    c_img = ImageTk.PhotoImage(Image.fromarray(o_img))
    canvas.create_image(20,20,anchor="nw",image=c_img)
    canvas.image=c_img
# create canvas widget
canvas = Canvas(root,width=500, height=500)
canvas.pack()
```

```
# create button widget
mybutton = Button(root, text='Browse', command = click)
mybutton.pack()
root.mainloop()
```

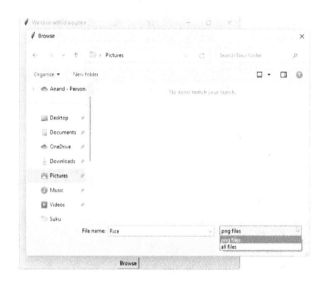

(a) Dialog window

(b) Canvas widget

Figure 6-9. *GUI for selecting and displaying image file*

Scale

Sliders are often used in vision-based GUIs to make real-time adjustment to certain parameters of an image. The scale widget allows us to create a slider in our GUI that covers a scale of values. In the following code, we click a button to browse and select an image and a slider to zoom-in or zoom-out of the image. Unlike our previous example, the canvas widget here will have to be updated by both the button action and the slider action. Therefore, we create separate functions for loading and displaying the image, which were previously implemented in the same function, so that the display function can be called for both the button action and the slider action.

Let's go over the functions one at a time. The *load()* function initiates the action for the button widget, same as the *click()* function in the previous case, where we browse and select an image using a dialog window. The difference here is that once we get the filename from the selected image and read the file using the *imread()* function, we call the *display()* function to push the image to the canvas widget. We have made a little tweak to this *display()* function as well. Since the display has to be updated with the corresponding zoomed image every time the slider is moved, we initially check if the canvas has an image displayed already and ensure that the image is removed before updating the new image.

Before displaying the image, we call the *update()* function to apply the zoom settings captured from the slider to the original image. In this function, we first get the zoom scale from the scale widget using the *get()* function and normalize the value. Next, we determine the new width and height by multiplying this normalized value with the width and height of the original image. Now that we have the new dimensions, we can use the *resize()* function to scale the original image accordingly. We need to provide the type of interpolation to be used for scaling the image, and in this example, we have used the linear interpolation. Finally, we use the

PhotoImage() function to convert the resized image to a format suitable for displaying, and then it is pushed to the canvas widget using the *create_image()* function inside the *display()* function.

The final function is the *zoom_image()* function which initiates the action for the scale widget. Within this function, we just call the two functions *update()* and *display()* functions to perform the zooming action and displaying the result in the canvas widget. Note that we have denoted the variables containing the original image, displayed image, and the zoomed image as global variables to enable smooth communication between the different functions. Following the functions, we have created all the widgets to be used in our application window. Note that the *Scale()* function is used to create the Scale widget, and the function takes as input the start and end scale of the zoom function, the orientation of the widget, a label to indicate the functionality of the widget and the function to initiate the zooming action. The *set()* function is used to set the initial position of the scale widget at a value of 100. Note that this value is normalized to 1 within the *update()* function which indicates the original image size as multiplying the width and height of the original image with 1 leading to the same image.

One other important thing to note here is that we initialize all the global parameters we described earlier as Nonetype. This will lead to an AttributeError in the *update()* function while running the code because the scale widget will automatically initiate action, and since the original image is initiated as Nonetype, we will not be able to obtain the height or width inside the *update()* function. To avoid getting this error, we create an exception to replace the error statement with a blank response. The GUI window displaying the tipped saw blade image at three different scales is illustrated in Figure 6-10.

```
from tkinter import *
from tkinter  import filedialog
from PIL import Image, ImageTk
```

```
import cv2
# action for Button widget
def load():
    filename = filedialog.askopenfilename(filetypes=[("Image
    files", "*.png *.jpg *")])
    if filename:
        global displayed_img, img_cv, img
        img_cv=cv2.cvtColor(cv2.imread(filename), cv2.COLOR_
        BGR2RGB)
        display()
# function to update the canvas widget
def display():
    global displayed_img, img_cv, img
    if displayed_img:
        canvas.delete(displayed_img)
    displayed_img = None

    if img_cv is not None:
        update()
        displayed_img = canvas.create_image(0, 0, image=img,
        anchor=NW)
        canvas.image = img
# resize the image to the new dimensions
def update():
    try:
        global displayed_img, img_cv, img
        zoom_level= zoom_scale.get() / 100.0
        h,w,c=img_cv.shape
        width = int(w * zoom_level)
        height = int(h * zoom_level)
        resized_img=cv2.resize(img_cv,(width,height),interpolat
        ion= cv2.INTER_LINEAR)
```

161

```
        img = ImageTk.PhotoImage(Image.fromarray(resized_img))
    except AttributeError:
        print("")
# action for Scale widget
def zoom_image(value):
    update()
    display()
# create the root window
root = Tk()
root.title("Image Zoom App")
# create a canvas to display the image
canvas = Canvas(root, width=512, height=512)
canvas.pack()
# create a button to load the image
load_button = Button(root, text="Load Image", command=load)
load_button.pack()
# create a scale widget to zoom the image
zoom_scale = Scale(root, from_=10, to=200, orient="horizontal",
label="Zoom", command=zoom_image)
zoom_scale.set(100)  # Initial zoom level (100%)
zoom_scale.pack()
# intialize the global variables
img_cv = None
displayed_img = None
img = None
root.mainloop()
```

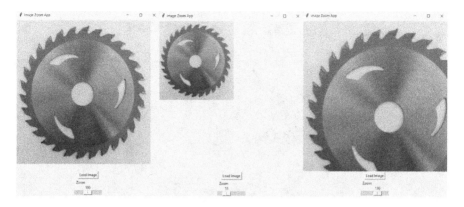

Figure 6-10. *GUI with scale widget to zoom image*

GUI for Industrial Vision System

Now that we have gone over the components that are commonly used in a GUI application individually, let us bring together multiple graphical components to build a comprehensive vision system that can be used for identifying defective products in an assembly line. We use the grid arrangement to place the different components of the GUI shown in Figure 6-11. The GUI window is divided into grids with five rows and two columns.

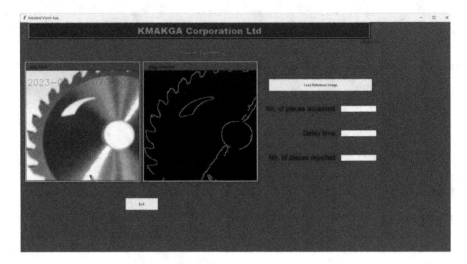

Figure 6-11. *GUI for identifying defective products in assembly line*

The first row consists of a *label* widget displaying the name of the organization for which the GUI is developed. Here, a bogus corporation name comprised of the initials of the authors is used for the purpose of illustration. This widget is extended to cover both columns by specifying the value for *columnspan* and *sticky* option in the *grid()* function. The *sticky* option *"ew"* indicates that the label must stretch from the left (west) to the right (east) side of its cavity defined using the *columnspan* option. Also the *borderwidth* and *relief* options are used in the *Label()* function to create a visual boundary effect to the *label* widget.

In the second row, the version of the GUI is displayed toward the end of the row in the second column. The positioning of the widget at the rightmost corner of the second column is achieved by setting the *sticky* option in the *grid()* function as *"e"*. We have simply provided a bogus version number 1.0 for the purpose of illustration. The title of the application is positioned at the center of the third row using the *columnspan* and *sticky* option similar to the first label. Again, we have simply provided the title "Vision System" for the purpose of illustration.

In the fourth row, we have used two *frame* widgets which we have not discussed so far in this chapter. The *frame* widget is simply used to group multiple widgets together. In the first frame, two *canvas* widgets are grouped together. The first canvas is used to display live video feed from the USB camera. We have already discussed how to capture the video and read the frames in Chapter 2. The only thing we have done here is to display the time stamp over the video using the *datetime.now()* from the *datetime* library to get the current time and the *putText()* function in the OpenCV library to push the time into the frames of the video. Timestamps could be handy for managers in assembly line as saving the timestamp of detection for each product could help them perform some analysis later. The second canvas is used to perform edge detection over the frames of the video and display the edge detected video. The Canny edge detector discussed in Chapter 5 is used here.

The second frame consists of a button widget and a set of labels and entry widgets grouped together. The button widget is used to browse and select a reference image which can then be used to compare with the product image captured in the assembly line with the help of image processing algorithms to identify defective products. The first and third entry widgets are used to display the number of accepted and rejected pieces in the assembly line. These widgets get updated each time a product is detected by our vision system. The second entry widget is used to provide a delay time which is set according to the time delay between the arrivals of two successive products in the assembly line. Finally, an exit button is provided in the fifth row which is used to close the root window. The action for the button is defined using the *close_window()* function as illustrated in the code. Ample comments are provided to explain each and every part of the code illustrated as follows. As this chapter is mainly focused on GUI design, the illustration is focused mainly on building the GUI and does not include the background process involved in identifying the defective product by comparing the captured product image with the reference image. This will be discussed in the subsequent chapters.

```python
from tkinter import *
from tkinter import filedialog
import cv2
from PIL import Image, ImageTk
import datetime

# Create the main application window
root = Tk()
root.title("Industrial Vision App")
root.geometry("1600x1000")
root.configure(bg="blue")

# Function to close the window
def close_window():
    root.destroy()

# Create labels
company_label = Label(root, text="KMAKGA Corporation Ltd",
                      borderwidth=5, relief="ridge",
                      font=("Arial Black", 24),fg="red",
                      bg="dark blue")
company_label.grid(row=0,column=0,columnspan=4,padx=30,pady=0,
sticky="ew")
version_label = Label(root, text="Version 1.0",bg="blue")
version_label.grid(row=1,column=2,padx=0,pady=0,sticky="e")
vision_label = Label(root, text="Vision System",
font=("Helvetica", 16,"bold"), fg="red", bg="blue")
vision_label.grid(row=2,column=0,columnspan=3,padx=0,pady=10,
sticky="ew")

# Create a frame to hold the canvases
frame = Frame(root,width=800,height=800,relief="ridge",
borderwidth=1,bg="blue")
```

```
frame.grid(row=3,column=0,padx=10,pady=0)

# Create canvases
video_canvas1 = Canvas(frame, borderwidth=2, width=400,
height=400, bg="blue")
video_canvas1.grid(row=3,column=0,padx=5,pady=5)
video_canvas2 = Canvas(frame, borderwidth=2, width=400,
height=400, bg="blue")
video_canvas2.grid(row=3,column=1,padx=5,pady=5)
video_canvas1.create_text(80, 10, text="Video Feed",
font=("Helvetica", 10), anchor="ne")
video_canvas2.create_text(110, 10, text="Edge detection",
font=("Helvetica", 10), anchor="ne")

# Load image to the reference image canvas
def click():
    global img
    filename = filedialog.askopenfilename(
        initialdir="C:/Users/user/Pictures/",
        title = "Select a file", filetypes = (("png files",
        "*.png"), ("all files","*.*")))
    img = ImageTk.PhotoImage(Image.open(filename))

# Create a frame to hold the configuration options
entry_frame = Frame(root, width = 200, height = 600, bg="blue")
mybutton=Button(entry_frame,width=20,height=2,borderwidth=2,
relief="ridge",text='Load Reference Image',command = click)
mybutton.grid(row=0,column=0,columnspan=2,
padx=20,pady=20,sticky="nsew")
labels = ["No. of pieces accepted:", "Delay time:", "No. of
pieces rejected:"]
entries = [Entry(entry_frame, borderwidth=2, relief="ridge")
for _ in range(3)]
```

```
for i, label_text in enumerate(labels):
label = Label(entry_frame, text=label_text, font=("Helvetica",
18), fg="black", bg="blue")
    label.grid(row=i+1, column=0, padx=5, pady=25, sticky="e")
    entry = entries[i]
    entry.grid(row=i+1, column=1, padx=5, pady=25, sticky="w")
entry_frame.grid(row=3, column=2, padx=5, pady=5)

# create a close button
close_button = Button(root,width=15,height=2,borderwidth=2,
relief="ridge",text="Exit", command=close_window)
close_button.grid(row=4,column=0,columnspan=2,padx=0,pady=50,
sticky="n")

# Function to update the video canvas with webcam feed
def update_video_canvas():
    ret, frame = cap.read()
    if ret:
        # Convert frame to grayscale
        gray_frame = cv2.cvtColor(frame, cv2.COLOR_BGR2GRAY)
        # Edge detection using Canny
        edges = cv2.Canny(gray_frame, 100, 200)
        # Convert to a format suitable for Tkinter
        edges_rgb = cv2.cvtColor(edges, cv2.COLOR_GRAY2RGB)
        edge_photo = ImageTk.PhotoImage(image=Image.
        fromarray(edges_rgb))
        # Display edge detection in the second canvas
        video_canvas2.create_image(0, 30, image=edge_photo,
        anchor=NW)
        video_canvas2.photo = edge_photo
        # Push the timestamp into the frame
        font = cv2.FONT_HERSHEY_SIMPLEX
```

```
        dt = str(datetime.datetime.now())
        frame_rgb = cv2.cvtColor(frame, cv2.COLOR_BGR2RGB)
        frame_rgb = cv2.putText(frame_rgb, dt,
        (10,50),font,1,(255,0,0))
        # Display original video in the first canvas
        orig_photo = ImageTk.PhotoImage(image=Image.
        fromarray(frame_rgb))
        video_canvas1.create_image(0, 30, image=orig_photo,
        anchor=NW)
        video_canvas1.photo = orig_photo
        video_canvas1.after(10, update_video_canvas)

# Open the webcam
cap = cv2.VideoCapture(0)

# Call the update_video_canvas function to start displaying the
video feed
update_video_canvas()

# Start the tkinter main loop
root.mainloop()

# Release the webcam and close OpenCV when the window is closed
cap.release()
cv2.destroyAllWindows()
```

Summary

We have now made a solid foundation for the design of GUI for vision systems by discussing the following topics in this chapter along with a sample demonstration for each topic:

- A basic understanding of the *tkinter* library and the various widgets provided by it

- Demonstration of a sample GUI to understand the working of the different widgets in *tkinter* library

- A comprehensive GUI design by putting multiple widgets we learned earlier together for creating a simple vision system

Now that we have a solid understanding of GUI design, we will shift our focus to extracting meaningful information with the help of various features in the next chapter.

Feature Detection and Matching

We explored how to combine OpenCV and Tkinter to make graphical user interfaces (GUIs) for image processing applications in the last chapter. Let us now explore how we can extract useful features from a given image. Feature detection allows us to identify distinguishing points or patterns in an image that serves as the basis of applications like object recognition, image segmentation, pattern matching, etc. In this chapter, we will start with a basic understanding of what image features are. Then we move on to discuss different methods for detecting what we call keypoints in an image. We will then discuss a special algorithm that will allow us to detect corner points in an image. Finally, we will see how to detect the shapes of objects in an image.

Image Features

Image features are the unique components or patterns in an image that provides information about the visual characteristics of the image. These features help to break down the visual information of an image and are a crucial aspect of computer vision systems as the features learned from the image help to perform tasks like object recognition, image segmentation, and classification. The features can be categorized into two types: global

© K. Mohaideen Abdul Kadhar and G. Anand 2024
K. Mohaideen Abdul Kadhar and G. Anand, *Industrial Vision Systems with Raspberry Pi*,
Maker Innovations Series, https://doi.org/10.1007/979-8-8688-0097-9_7

and local features. The global features represent the overall characteristics of the whole image, whereas the local features represent information about specific regions or objects in the image.

For instance, the color histogram of a digital image gives a representation of the color distribution in the image, and global statistics such as skewness and kurtosis help to describe the pixel intensity distribution of the image. These features are represented by a single vector which provides a holistic understanding of the given image. On the other hand, features like points, edges, corners, etc., are unique to particular patches in the image and are distinct from their immediate neighborhood.

The extraction of these local features requires two steps: detecting points or regions of interest that are invariant to scale, illumination and rotation, and converting the detected features into a numerical representation. These points of interest are also called keypoints, whereas the numerical features that provide a description of these keypoints are called descriptors.

In this chapter, we will be discussing some of the common techniques that are used widely to extract these features from the images.

SIFT Features

In computer vision, scale-invariant feature transform (SIFT) is an algorithm for keypoint detection and description that can be employed to extract unique local features from an image. As the name of the algorithm implies, the extracted features are robust to the changes in the image caused by the changes in its scale or illumination levels as well as rotation of the image. Numerous applications such as object detection, image matching, and image stitching make extensive use of the SIFT features. For instance, in an object detection task, the keypoints of an object in an image can be extracted to provide a description of the object which can then be used to detect that object in other images.

The extraction of SIFT features is comprised mainly of four steps:

1. Scale-Space Peak Selection: First, we create a scale-space representation of the image, which is made up of a series of blurred images at various scales. Next, we find the local maxima in the scale space using the difference of Gaussians (DoG) approach, and these are recognized as potential keypoints.

2. Keypoint Localization: SIFT uses a Taylor series expansion to refine the keypoint locations to sub-pixel precision. If a keypoint's contrast or edge response falls below a predetermined level, it is eliminated.

3. Orientation Assignment: Each of these refined keypoints is then assigned an orientation based on their local image gradients. This is accomplished by creating a histogram of gradients corresponding to each keypoint and assigning the orientation of the peak in the histogram as the orientation of that keypoint.

4. Keypoint Descriptor: The last stage is the creation of a descriptor for each keypoint which is a vector that represents the local appearance of the image around that point. For each keypoint, the surrounding neighborhood is divided into 16 sub-blocks, and a histogram of gradient directions is computed for each sub-block which are then concatenated to form the keypoint descriptor.

The following code illustrates the extraction of keypoints from a gear image using SIFT features. The SIFT_create() function in the OpenCV library is used to create a SIFT object, and the detectAndCompute method in the object can be used to detect the keypoints in the image and their descriptors. Finally, the drawKeypoints() function in the OpenCV library can be used to mark the keypoints over the original image. Figure 7-1 shows the descriptors marked in red color over the gear image, and it can be observed that they are mostly distributed over the edges of the gear teeth that form the important features of the gear. In the production line, the alignment of the gear teeth need to be verified before they are integrated into the actual products, and these descriptors could serve the purpose as they are invariant to scale and rotation.

```python
# Load the image
img = cv2.imread('C:/Users/user/Pictures/gear.jpg',0)
# Create a SIFT detector
sift = cv2.SIFT_create()
# Detect keypoints and descriptors
keypoints, descriptors = sift.detectAndCompute(img, None)
# Mark the keypoint on the image using circles
img_k=cv2.drawKeypoints(img ,
                keypoints ,
                img ,
                (255, 0, 0) ,
                flags=cv2.DRAW_MATCHES_FLAGS_DEFAULT)
# Display original image and image with keypoints
plt.subplot(121)
plt.imshow(img, cmap='gray')
plt.title('Original image')
plt.subplot(122)
plt.imshow(img_k)
plt.title('image-with-keypoints')
plt.show()
```

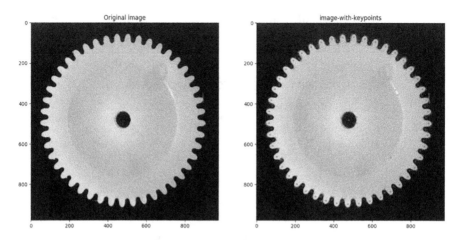

Figure 7-1. *Illustration of keypoints extraction using SIFT features*

SURF Features

SURF, which stands for Speeded-Up Robust Features (SURF), is a sort of accelerated version of SIFT features and can detect keypoints that are invariant to scale, illumination, and rotation. The steps involved in keypoint detection and description using SURF features comprises of four steps:

1. Scale-Space Extrema Detection: In order to identify features at various sizes, SURF operates on an image at many scales. It locates local extrema in the scale space using a method similar to the difference of Gaussians (DoG) used in SIFT. To find areas of interest, the image is convolved using Gaussian filters at various scales, followed by the subtraction of successive blurred images.

175

2. Keypoint Localization: After the identification of potential keypoints, SURF performs keypoint localization by fitting a 3x3 Hessian matrix at the location of each candidate keypoint to determine scale and rejection points with low contrast or poorly defined edges.

3. Orientation Assignment: Next, SURF assigns an orientation to each keypoint to make them rotation invariant. In order to create a 2D vector that represents the dominant orientation, the Haar wavelet responses in the x and y directions are computed surrounding the keypoint. The orientation is then determined based on the angle of this vector.

4. Descriptor Calculation: Following the detection of scale and keypoint orientation, SURF computes a descriptor for the keypoint's neighborhood which is a vector of values characterizing the intensity distribution around the keypoint.

Since SURF is patented, and OpenCV excludes patented algorithms by default. In order to access SURF, we can explicitly enable the non-free modules during OpenCV compilation or installation. This will activate the *xfeatures* library which consists of the SURF and other patented algorithms, but it is our responsibility to ensure that necessary license or legal permission has been obtained to use them especially for commercial uses. The following code extracts the key points corresponding to SURF features from the gear image. Once we read the gear image, the xfeatures2d.SURF_create method is used to create a SURF object with a Hessian threshold of 10000. The sensitivity of the feature detector is controlled by the Hessian threshold where a higher value detects fewer but stronger key points. The *detectAndCompute* method of the SURF object can then be used to detect the key points and compute the descriptors in the grayscale image 'img'.

To draw the colored key points on the image, we convert the grayscale image '*img*' to a BGR image '*img1_color*'. Next, we iterate over the key points and draw circles using the *circle()* method with the coordinates of the key points as the center and radius equal to 1/4th the size of the key points. Finally, we display the gear image with the key points alongside the original image as shown in Figure 7-2. It can be seen that the circles indicating the key points are capturing all the distinctive features of the gear including the edges as well as the center of the gear.

```python
import cv2
import numpy as np
import matplotlib.pyplot as plt
# Load the gear image
img = cv2.imread('Gear.jpg', cv2.IMREAD_GRAYSCALE)
# Create a SURF object
surf = cv2.xfeatures2d.SURF_create(10000)
# Detect key points and compute descriptors
keypoints, descriptors = surf.detectAndCompute(img, None)
# Convert grayscale image to BGR for colored keypoints
img1_color = cv2.cvtColor(img, cv2.COLOR_GRAY2BGR)
# Draw keypoints with increased thickness
for kp in keypoints:
    x, y = int(kp.pt[0]), int(kp.pt[1])
    radius = int(kp.size / 4)
    # Use thickness of 2 for the circle
    img1=cv2.circle(img1_color, (x, y), radius, (255, 0, 0),
    thickness=2)
# Display the image
plt.subplot(121)
```

```
plt.imshow(img, cmap='gray')
plt.title('Original Image')
plt.subplot(122)
plt.imshow(img1)
plt.title('Image with keypoints')
plt.show()
```

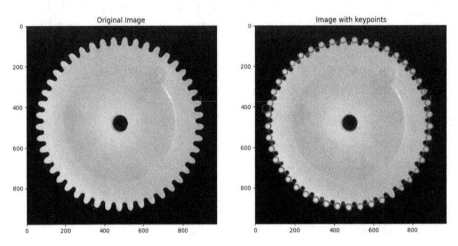

Figure 7-2. *Illustration of Keypoints extraction using SURF features*

FAST Features

FAST stands for Features from Accelerated Segment Test. This corner detector algorithm published in 2006 is computationally efficient and hence is faster than other algorithms thereby justifying its acronym. Therefore, this detector is well suited for real-time video processing applications that require high-speed computations with limited resources.

The steps involved in determining the interest points using FAST features are as follows:

1. Select a pixel, say p, that is to be identified as an interest point or not, and let I_p be the intensity of that pixel.

178

2. Select a threshold value for the intensity, say T.

3. Consider a circle of 16 pixels with our selected pixel p at the center of the circle.

4. The selected pixel, with intensity I_p, is considered as an interest point if there are n contiguous pixels in the circle that have intensity values of order T greater than ($> I_p + T$) or less than ($< I_p - T$) that of the chosen pixel. The originally proposed and commonly used value of n is 12.

5. A high speed test can then be used for faster detection of the interest points with the help of step 4. This test can be done in two parts:

   a. First, the intensity of the pixels 1, 5, 9, and 13 of the circle are tested for the threshold criterion in step 5. If the selected pixel p is an interest point, then the intensities of at least three of these pixels would all be either greater than I_p+T or less than I_p-T.

   b. The threshold criterion is then carried out for all the n pixels for those candidates that pass the initial four-pixel test.

The following code illustrates the extraction of keypoints from the gear image using FAST features. The FastFeatureDetector_create() function in OpenCV library can be used to create a FAST object, and the detect() method can be used to get the keypoints. Here, we use the circle() function to draw the keypoints as well as the 16 pixels on the circle surrounding the keypoint. As all these little circles are closely packed together, they appear like circular patches on the image, and we can see from Figure 7-3 that most of these patches are distributed across the edges of the gear.

```python
import cv2
import matplotlib.pyplot as plt
# Read the image
image = cv2.imread('C:/Users/user/Pictures/gear.jpg', 0)
# display the original image
plt.subplot(121)
plt.imshow(image,cmap='gray')
plt.title('Original image')
# Define the FAST detector
fast = cv2.FastFeatureDetector_create()
# Find the interest points
keypoints = fast.detect(image, None)
# Draw the interest points and the 16 pixels on the circle
for keypoint in keypoints:
    circle = cv2.circle(image, (int(keypoint.pt[0]),
    int( keypoint.pt[1])), 3, (255,0 , 0), 2)
    for i in range(-7, 8):
        for j in range(-7, 8):
            if (i**2 + j**2) <= 49:
                cv2.circle(image, (int(keypoint.pt[0]) + i,
                int(keypoint.pt[1]) + j), 1,
                (255, 0, 0), 1)
# Display the image with keypoints
plt.subplot(122)
plt.imshow(image,cmap='gray')
plt.title('Image with keypoints')
plt.show()
```

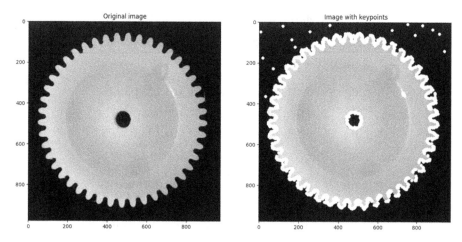

Figure 7-3. *Illustration of keypoints extraction using FAST features*

BRIEF Features

While using feature descriptors for applications like object recognition, there is a need for faster and memory-efficient matching which in turn would require short descriptors. One way to achieve this is to reduce the descriptors by applying a dimensionality reduction algorithm (like LDA or PCA) to the original descriptors and then converting the descriptor vector into binary strings with fewer bits. But this would still require us to first compute the full descriptors before applying dimensionality reduction. The BRIEF descriptors overcome this by computing binary strings directly from image patches surrounding the keypoints instead of computing the descriptors.

BRIEF, which stands for Binary Robust Independent Elementary Features, is a feature descriptor that works in tandem with keypoint detection algorithms like SURF, FAST, or HARIS. As mentioned above, BRIEF uses binary strings as efficient keypoint descriptors, making it ideal for real-time applications. The following are the steps involved in determining the BRIEF features.

1. Use keypoint detection algorithms like SURF, SIFT, or Harris corners to detect the distinctive keypoint locations in the given image.

2. For each detected keypoint, a local square patch of pixels in the neighborhood around that pixel is extracted. The height and width of the patch will determine the scale of the BRIEF descriptor.

3. Since the BRIEF features deal with the intensities at pixel level, it is very noise sensitive. Therefore, the selected patches are smoothed with the help of Gaussian kernels before further processing.

4. For each patch, select a set of n random location pairs of pixels (x,y) where n is the length of the binary feature vector. The pixel intensities are compared for each pair of pixels to get the corresponding binary values. For instance, if the intensity of pixel x is less than that of pixel y, then the corresponding binary value is 1, whereas the value will be 0 if the intensity of x is greater than that of y. Here the location pairs are randomly selected from a Gaussian distribution.

Following these steps results in a binary descriptor for each of the keypoints in the image. The following code illustrates the extraction of descriptors from the gear image. It can be seen that the keypoints from the image are detected using FAST features as discussed earlier. Then the create() method from the BriefDescriptorExtractor object can be used to extract the binary descriptors from the detected keypoints. From the output shown following the code, we can see that the extracted descriptors variable is a numpy array. The descriptor for a single keypoint is printed, and it can be seen that the descriptor is a vector of integers. To get the binary descriptors, we convert each integer in the vector into 8-bit binary representation using the binary_repr() function in the numpy library.

```
import cv2
import numpy as np
# Load the input gear image
img = cv2.imread('C:/Users/user/Pictures/gear.jpg', 0)
# Initialize a FAST detector and detect keypoints
f = cv2.FastFeatureDetector.create()
kp= f.detect(img)
# Initialize an extractor and extract BRIEF descriptors for the
keypoints
b = cv2.xfeatures2d.BriefDescriptorExtractor.create()
keypoints,descriptors = b.compute(img, kp)
# Print the characteristics of the descriptors
print("The data type of the descriptors variable
is:",type(descriptors))
print("\nDescriptor size:", len(descriptors))
#Print the first descriptor
print("\nThe first descriptor is:")
print(descriptors[0])
# Print the descriptor as binary
print("\nThe first descriptor in binary:")
print(' '.join([np.binary_repr(num,8) for num in
descriptors[0]]))
```

Output:
The data type of the descriptors variable is: <class 'numpy.
ndarray'>

Descriptor size: 8802

The first descriptor is:
[8   7   12 124   43   50 228   72   16 131   26 152 184
236   0   10   70 248
  82 150 44   8 200 44 205 216 164 123 184   76   4 245]

The first descriptor in binary:
00001000 00000111 00001100 01111100 00101011 00110010 11100100
01001000 00010000 10000011 00011010 10011000 10111000 11101100
00000000 00001010 01000110 11111000 01010010 10010110 00101100
00001000 11001000 00101100 11001101 11011000 10100100 01111011
10111000 01001100 00000100 11110101

ORB Features

ORB was developed as an efficient alternative to SIFT and SURF features
in terms of computation as well as matching performance. Another key
aspect is the fact that both SIFT and SURF features were patented at the
time of development of ORB features thereby making it a free alternative to
these features. Currently, the patent for SIFT features has expired making it
freely available, whereas the SURF features are still patented requiring the
purchase of license if the features are to be used for commercial purposes.

ORB stands for Oriented FAST and Rotated BRIEF. As the name
implies, it is a combination of the FAST keypoints and BRIEF descriptors
with certain modifications to overcome their shortcomings. The following
are the steps involved in computing ORB features:

1. Detect FAST Keypoints: ORB begins by detecting
    the keypoints in a given image using the FAST
    algorithm. Here, ORB also uses a multi-scale
    pyramid approach to apply FAST at different scales
    enabling the algorithm to capture features of
    varying sizes.

2. Assign Orientation: The next step is to assign an
    orientation to each keypoint to make the features
    rotationally invariant. ORB does this for a keypoint
    by computing the intensity weighted centroid of

a patch with the keypoint at its center and then determining the direction of the vector from the keypoint to the centroid.

3. Calculate BRIEF Descriptors: Finally, ORB computes the BRIEF descriptors for each of the detected keypoints and rotates the descriptors based on the orientation assigned to each keypoint to ensure rotation invariance.

The following code illustrates the extraction of ORB features from the gear image. We use the ORB_create() function in the OpenCV library to create an ORB object and then use the detectAndCompute() method to detect the keypoints as well as descriptors. We then use the drawKeypoints() function in the OpenCV library to plot the image along with the detected keypoints as shown in Figure 7-4. Though ORB is computationally more efficient than SIFT and SURF, it can be seen from the figure that it is not as accurate as those features since it fails to capture some of the teeth in the gear image.

```python
import cv2
import numpy as np
import matplotlib.pyplot as plt
# Read the input image
img = cv2.imread('C:/Users/user/Pictures/gear.jpg',0)
# Display the original image
plt.subplot(121)
plt.imshow(img,cmap='gray')
plt.title('Original Image')
#  Detect and compute the keypoints and descriptors
orb = cv2.ORB_create()  # Create an ORB object
kp, des = orb.detectAndCompute(img, None)
```

```
# Draw the keypoints on the image
img2 = cv2.drawKeypoints(img, kp, img, color=(255, 0, 0),
flags=cv2.DRAW_MATCHES_FLAGS_DEFAULT)
# Display the keypoint image
plt.subplot(122)
plt.imshow(img2,cmap='gray')
plt.title('Keypoint Image')
plt.show()
```

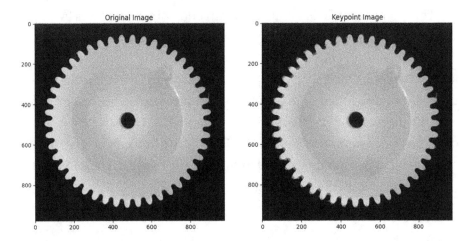

Figure 7-4. *Illustration of keypoints extraction using FAST features*

Corner Detection

The terms keypoints, corners, and features are used interchangeably in
literature, but there is a subtle distinction between a corner and a keypoint.
A corner can be considered as the intersection of two edges or boundaries
thereby making it an important feature for vision tasks such as object
recognition and tracking. In the context of image processing, corners can
be considered as those points in an image where the image will undergo

significant intensity change in multiple directions. On the other hand, a keypoint can represent various features in an image including a corner, isolated points of intensity maximum or minimum, and line endings.

Assume that we are moving a small rectangular window over an image. When the window is over a very flat region, then there will not be any large changes in intensity. If the window is placed over an edge, the intensity change will occur only in a single direction in which the window is moving. If the same window is placed over a corner, there will be large intensity changes in all directions. One of the most commonly used methods for corner detection is the Harris corner detector which measures the variation in intensity within a window as it moves in different directions across the image and detects the presence of a corner when there is a significant change in intensity in multiple directions. The following are the steps involved in Harris corner detection:

1. Gradient Computation: The first step is to calculate the image gradients by taking partial derivatives in the horizontal and vertical directions.

2. Structure Tensor: A structure tensor, which is a 2 x 2 matrix computed from the image derivatives, is then created.

3. Corner Response Function: A corner response function is then calculated using the structure tensor which scores the presence of a corner inside the patch. High value of this function indicates the presence of a corner.

4. Nonmaximum Suppression: The nonmaximum suppression, which is a post-processing technique for removing duplicates, is applied to retain only the most significant corners.

The following code illustrates the extraction of corner points from a grid image that was specifically created for this purpose. The cornerHarris() function in the OpenCV library is used to detect the corner points in the image. The function takes the grayscale image as the input along with other parameters. The number 2 is the block size of the neighborhood that is considered for corner detection which implies a 2x2 neighborhood. The selection of block size often involves a tradeoff as a large size may miss small corners despite providing smooth results, whereas a smaller size may be more sensitive to noise despite detecting small corners. Since we have a manually created image that is free of noise, a smaller size of 2 will suffice.

The number 3 is the size of the Sobel kernel that is used to compute the image derivatives as mentioned in the first step earlier. Therefore, we are using 3 x 3 kernels to compute the horizontal and vertical gradients. The last number 0.04 is a free parameter of the Harris corner detector which is used to adjust the sensitivity of the detector. Following the detector function, the dilate() function is applied to the result of the detector, and then a threshold is applied to suppress the spurious corners produced by image noise. It can be seen from Figure 7-5 that all the 9 corner points in the grid image are detected accurately.

```
import numpy as np
import cv2 as cv
import matplotlib.pyplot as plt
# Read the grid image
img = cv.imread('C:/Users/user/Pictures/grid.jpg')
# Display the original image
plt.subplot(121)
plt.imshow(img)
plt.title('Grid image')
gray = cv.cvtColor(img,cv.COLOR_BGR2GRAY) # Convert the image
                                          to grayscale
```

```
# Apply Harris corner detector
dst = cv.cornerHarris(gray,2,3,0.04)
dst = cv.dilate(dst,None)
# Apply threshold to get the optimal corner points
img[dst>0.01*dst.max()]=[255,0,0]
# Display the grid image with corner points
plt.subplot(122)
plt.imshow(img)
plt.title('Grid Image with Corner points')
plt.show()
```

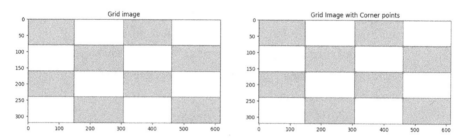

Figure 7-5. _Illustration of corner detection using Harris detector_

Line and Shape Detection in Images

Detecting lines and other shapes form a crucial aspect of detecting objects in images with respect to various computer vision applications. Hough transform is one of the popular techniques used for this purpose. Proposed by Paul Hough in 1962, the Hough transform was originally used for detecting lines but was later modified to detect other shapes like circles and ellipses. The algorithm has since been widely used in the areas of pattern recognition and computer vision.

Traditional techniques like edge detection and thresholding tend to be ineffective in detecting shapes especially if the shapes are incomplete or distorted. Hough transform overcomes this difficulty by transforming the image space into a different parameter space. First let us consider the case of detecting lines in images where the parameter space is composed of two parameters: slope of the line and its y-intercept. The following are the steps involved in detecting lines using Hough transform:

1. Detect Edges: The first step normally involves detecting edges in the image using standard techniques like the Canny edge detector.

2. Accumulator Array: For each edge point, multiple lines may pass through it leading to multiple slopes (m) and intercept (b). The accumulator array is a collection of these parameters. In other words, each cell in the accumulator array might represent a particular m and b. Since vertical lines will have infinite slope, these parameters will be converted to polar form using the expression $r = x\cos\theta + y\sin\theta$ where (x,y) denotes the point for which we are computing the parameters, r is the perpendicular distance from the origin to the line, and θ is the angle between the x-axis and the line.

3. Voting: With respect to each edge point in the image, the corresponding cells in the accumulator array are incremented, the process being termed as voting. The idea behind this procedure is that if multiple edge points lie on the same line, then their votes will accumulate at the corresponding entries in the accumulator array.

4. Thresholding: The peaks in the accumulator array after the voting process represent potential lines in the image. An additional step of thresholding is applied to select significant peaks thereby avoiding noise.

5. Backprojection: The selected peaks in the accumulator array are then transformed back to the original space to obtain the parameters of the detected lines.

The following code illustrates the detection of lines from the same grid image that we used in our last section with the help of Hough transform. It can be seen that we are using a Canny edge detector with two thresholds to detect the edge points in the image. Then, we pass these points to the HoughLines() function in the OpenCV library to detect the lines in the image to which some of the edge points are associated with. The number 1 given to the function is the resolution of the parameter r in pixels which implies that we are using a resolution of 1 pixel. Similarly, the value $\pi/180$ given to the function is the resolution of parameter θ in radians which implies that we are using a resolution of 1 degree as it is equivalent to $\pi/180$ in radians. Then, we are providing a threshold of 100 which is the minimum number of votes required to be considered as a line. The parameter minLineLength of 100 implies that line segments shorter than that are rejected. Similarly, the parameter maxLineGap of 10 is the maximum allowed gap between points on the same line to link them. The resulting image is shown in Figure 7-6 which shows that every line in the image is detected accurately using the Hough transform.

```
import cv2
import numpy as np
import matplotlib.pyplot as plt
# Load the nut image
image = cv2.imread('C:/Users/user/Pictures/grid.jpg')
# Display the original image
image = cv2.cvtColor(image, cv2.COLOR_BGR2RGB)
plt.subplot(121)
plt.imshow(image)
plt.title('Orignal image')
```

```
# Convert image to grayscale
gray = cv2.cvtColor(image, cv2.COLOR_BGR2GRAY)
# Apply Canny edge detection
edges = cv2.Canny(gray, 50, 150)
# Apply Hough transform
lines = cv2.HoughLinesP(edges, 1, np.pi / 180, 100,
                        minLineLength=100, maxLineGap=10)
# Draw the detected lines on the image
for line in lines:
    x1, y1, x2, y2 = line[0]
    cv2.line(image, (x1, y1), (x2, y2), (0, 0, 255), 2)
# Display the image
plt.subplot(122)
plt.imshow(image)
plt.title('Image with detected lines')
plt.show()
```

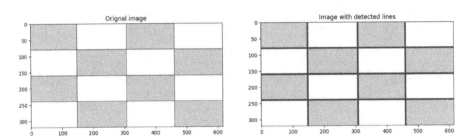

Figure 7-6. *Illustration of line detection with Hough transform*

Another variant of the Hough transform called the Hough circle transform works in a similar fashion, except that it detects circles instead of straight lines. This transform works by transforming the image space into a parameter space with three parameters x, y, r instead of two (slope and intercept in case of lines), where x, y denotes the coordinates of the center of the circle and r denotes the radius of the circle. The following code illustrates the detection of circles in a gear image using Hough circle transform. The parameters that we provide as input to the HoughCircles() function in the OpenCV library are as follows:

gray: The grayscale version of the input image.

method: Detection method; two methods are available: HOUGH_GRADIENT and HOUGH_GRADIENT_ALT.

dp: Inverse ratio of the accumulator resolution to the image resolution; dp = 1 implies that accumulator has the same resolution as the input image.

minDist: Minimum distance between the centers of detected circles; we are selecting a size of 20.

param1: Represents the higher threshold of the two passed to a Canny edge detector that is internally used by the Hough circle transform; we are selecting a value of 120.

param2: Accumulator threshold for the circle centers; the smaller the value, the more the false circles detected; we are selecting a value of 50.

minRadius: Minimum circle radius; we are selecting a value of 5.

maxRadius: Maximum circle radius; we are selecting a value of 100.

Finally, the circles are drawn over the image with the help of circle() function in the OpenCV library where we provide the original image, the coordinates (x, y, r) for the circles, the desired color by specifying (R, G, B) values, and then the desired thickness. The HoughCircles() function provides the coordinates (x, y ,r) as floating-point values. There, we convert them to integers while providing them to the circle() function. Figure 7-7 shows that the circle at the center of the gear image is detected perfectly. This in turn can be applied in the manufacturing assembly line to verify the bore of gears without human intervention.

```python
import cv2
import matplotlib.pyplot as plt
# Read the gear image
image = cv2.imread('C:/Users/user/Pictures/Gear.jpg')
# plot the original image
plt.subplot(121)
plt.imshow(image)
plt.title('Gear image')
# Convert the image to grayscale
gray = cv2.cvtColor(image, cv2.COLOR_BGR2GRAY)
# Detect circles
circles = cv2.HoughCircles(gray, cv2.HOUGH_GRADIENT, dp=1,
minDist=20, param1=120, param2=50, minRadius=5, maxRadius=100)
# Draw the detected circles
for (x, y, r) in circles[0]:
    cv2.circle(image, (int(x), int(y)), int(r), (255, 0, 0), 10)

# Display the image with detected circles
plt.subplot(122)
plt.imshow(image)
plt.title('Gear image with detected circles')
plt.show()
```

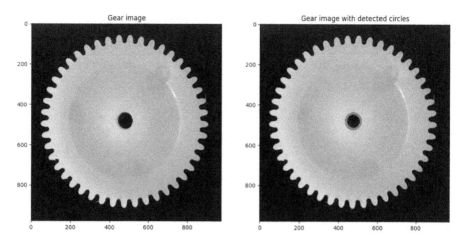

Figure 7-7. *Illustration of circle detection with Hough transform*

To detect other shapes in an image, contours are commonly used in computer vision and image processing. Simply put, a contour is a curve that joins all the continuous points with the same color or intensity along the boundary of objects in an image. So, the contours are an ideal choice for identifying and analyzing shapes in an image. The following code illustrates the detection of the shapes in the gear image. We begin by converting the image to grayscale and then applying a threshold to get the binary image. Here we are using OTSU thresholding to get the binary image. Next, we feed the binary image as input to the findContours() function in the OpenCV library. This function takes two other parameters: the mode of contour retrieval algorithm and the contour approximation algorithm. For the retrieval algorithm, we are using RETR_TREE which retrieves all the contours in the image and reconstructs a full hierarchy of nested contours. For the approximation algorithm, we are using CHAIN_APPROX_SIMPLE which compresses the horizontal, vertical, and diagonal segments leaving only their endpoints. We then use the drawContours() function to draw the boundary over the image. This function takes the image and the detected contours as input along with other parameters like the contour index which should be -1 to draw all the contours, the desired

(R, G, B) colors, and the thickness of the boundary. From Figure 7-8, we can see that three levels of contours are detected: the overall boundary of the frame, the boundary of the outer gear teeth, and the boundary of the inner circle in the gear.

```
import cv2
import matplotlib.pyplot as plt
# Load the gear image
img = cv2.imread('C:/Users/user/Pictures/gear.jpg')
# Display the original image
plt.subplot(121)
plt.imshow(img)
plt.title('Original gear image')
# Convert the image to grayscale
gray = cv2.cvtColor(img, cv2.COLOR_BGR2GRAY)
# Apply thresholding to binarize the image
thresh = cv2.threshold(gray, 0, 255, cv2.THRESH_BINARY_INV |
cv2.THRESH_OTSU)[1]
# Find contours in the image
contours = cv2.findContours(thresh, cv2.RETR_TREE, cv2.CHAIN_
APPROX_SIMPLE)[0]
# Draw contours on the image
for contour in contours:
    cv2.drawContours(img, [contour], -1, (255, 0, 0), 10)
# Show the image with contours
plt.subplot(122)
plt.imshow(img)
plt.title('Gear image with contours')
plt.show()
```

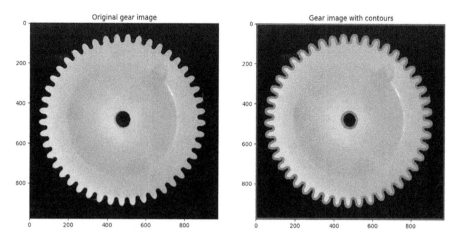

Figure 7-8. *Illustration of shape detection with contours*

Summary

In this chapter, we have navigated through a diverse array of techniques used for deriving features of interest from a given image which is essential for interpreting images in computer vision. Following are the key concepts that we discussed in this chapter:

- Keypoint detectors such as SIFT, SURF, FAST, BRIEF, and ORB for identifying distinctive points in an image

- Harris detector for effectively detecting corner points in an image that are usually found at the conjunction of two edges or boundaries

- Hough transform for detecting lines and circles in a given image precisely

- Contours to detect other random shapes or boundaries of objects in an image

In the next chapter, we will discuss another set of crucial techniques for detecting and extracting objects in an image called the segmentation techniques.

CHAPTER 8

Image Segmentation

An important aspect of vision systems is to differentiate between objects in a scene. The first step toward this goal is to segregate the various objects in a given image. This is accomplished by a process called segmentation wherein all pixels corresponding to various regions (objects) are grouped together thereby segregating the given image into its constituent objects. In the field of computer vision, image segmentation is an essential and fundamental process that forms the basis for many applications, including autonomous vehicles, medical imaging, object recognition, and more. Building on the knowledge gained in earlier chapters, this chapter explores the complex field of segmentation with a focus on advanced approaches and procedures.

We looked at thresholding methods as a foundation for image segmentation in Chapter 5 that utilized intensity thresholds to help discern between various regions in a given image. Although thresholding works well in some situations, it might not be enough for complicated images with a lot of noise, varying illumination, or complex structures. This chapter will broaden our comprehension of segmentation techniques and explore more sophisticated approaches in addition to thresholding.

Image Segmentation Using Thresholding

Thresholding, a simple and powerful technique for image segmentation, involves setting a pixel value to one of two levels based on whether it is greater than or less than a predefined threshold. Pixels with attribute

© K. Mohaideen Abdul Kadhar and G. Anand 2024
K. Mohaideen Abdul Kadhar and G. Anand, *Industrial Vision Systems with Raspberry Pi*,
Maker Innovations Series, https://doi.org/10.1007/979-8-8688-0097-9_8

values above or below a threshold are divided into two groups by the threshold value, which often represents distinct objects or backgrounds. Thresholding techniques can be broadly classified into global and local methods. We have already discussed some of these techniques in Chapter 5. In this section, we will recall how to segment a given image using a global threshold technique as well as a local threshold technique.

For the global thresholding technique, we will take the Otsu thresholding technique that we discussed earlier in Chapter 5. The following code illustrates the segmentation of a given image using Otsu's thresholding. Let us take the image of a U-bolt for this demonstration. The first step is to read the image and convert it into a grayscale image. Then we will apply a Gaussian filter using the *GaussianBlur()* function with a filter size of 7 x 7 which will help to get rid of any high-frequency noises present in the image. The *threshold()* function is then used to apply thresholding to the filtered image. The attribute *THRESH_OTSU* is used to determine the optimal threshold for the image starting with the initial value of 0 provided in the function, and then the attribute *THRESH_BINARY* is then used to apply binary thresholding on the image using the determined threshold. It can be seen that the U-bolt object is clearly segmented from the background as shown in Figure 8-1. It can also be observed that the shadow caused by the lighting is also segmented as part of the object which reiterates the importance of uniform lighting requirements. The determined optimal threshold value is displayed in the title of the segmented image in the figure and is equal to 146.

```
import cv2
import numpy as np
import matplotlib.pyplot as plt
# Load the image in grayscale
image = cv2.imread('C:/Users/User/Pictures/New folder/U-Bolt.
jpg', cv2.IMREAD_GRAYSCALE)
blurred = cv2.GaussianBlur(image, (7, 7), 0)
```

```
# Apply OTSU's thresholding
(T, thresh) = cv2.threshold(blurred, 0, 255,
            cv2.THRESH_BINARY | cv2.THRESH_OTSU)
# Display the original and binary images
plt.subplot(121)
plt.imshow(image, cmap='gray')
plt.title('Original Image')
plt.subplot(122)
plt.imshow(thresh, cmap='gray')
plt.title('Segmented Image(Otsu Thresholding) with threshold =
'+str(T))
plt.show()
```

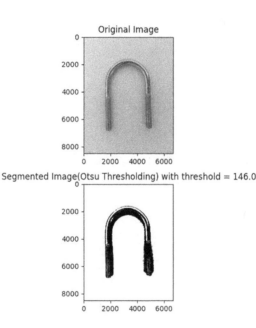

Figure 8-1. *Segmentation using Otsu's thresholding*

The Otsu method is a global thresholding method, where a single threshold value (146 in our example) will be applied all over the image. As different threshold values may work well for different regions of the

201

image, let us apply adaptive thresholding to the same image. This method considers multiple small regions in the given image and computes a threshold using the set of pixels in those regions. The following code illustrates the process of applying adaptive thresholding to the same U-bolt image. The *adaptiveThreshold()* function in the OpenCV library is used to accomplish this task. The *ADAPTIVE_THRESHOLD_GAUSSIAN_C* attribute indicates that the threshold value will be a Gaussian-weighted sum of the neighborhood values in the selected region minus a constant "c", the value of which is specified as 3 in the function. The number 17 in the function indicates that the thresholding is applied across 17 x 17 regions in the given image. The segmented image illustrated in Figure 8-2 shows that segmentation attained is much better than the Otsu thresholding method that was greatly affected by the shadows in the image.

```
import cv2
import numpy as np
import matplotlib.pyplot as plt
# Load the image in grayscale
image = cv2.imread('C:/Users/User/Pictures/New folder/U-Bolt.
jpg', cv2.IMREAD_GRAYSCALE)
blurred = cv2.GaussianBlur(image, (7,7), 0)
# Apply OTSU's thresholding
thresh = cv2.adaptiveThreshold(blurred, 255,
        cv2.ADAPTIVE_THRESH_GAUSSIAN_C,cv2.THRESH_
        BINARY, 17, 3)
# Display the original and binary images
plt.subplot(121)
plt.imshow(image, cmap='gray')
plt.title('Original Image')
plt.subplot(122)
```

```
plt.imshow(thresh, cmap='gray')
plt.title('Segmented Image(Adaptive Thresholding)')
plt.show()
```

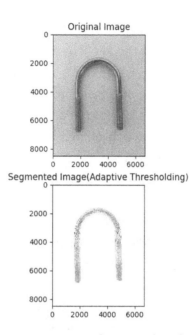

Figure 8-2. *Segmentation using adaptive thresholding*

Image Segmentation Using Contour Detection

Another prevalent method of segmenting objects from a given image is using contour detection which relies on identifying and creating boundaries of objects in the image. The continuous boundaries or curves that connect points with the same color or intensity are called contours. When trying to extract relevant information from images, like object borders, shapes, and structures, this method is quite helpful. More complex analysis and comprehension of visual data are made possible by the ability to recognize contours, which allow one to isolate and characterize specific regions in an image.

The following code illustrates the segmentation of a gear image using contour detection. We start with the same steps as discussed in the case of thresholding. We convert our image into grayscale, apply Gaussian filter to remove high-frequency noise, and then extract a threshold using Otsu's technique. We then provide 0.5 times the Otsu threshold as the lower threshold and the actual Otsu threshold as the higher threshold to a Canny edge detector which detects the edges from the filtered image. We then perform dilation operation on the edge image to enhance and connect the edges in the image. This is done in two steps. The *getStructuringElement()* function in the OpenCV library is used to define a rectangular structuring element of size 3x3 for performing the morphological operation. Following this, the *dilate()* function is used to apply the structuring element to the edge image. We then provide the dilated image as input to the *findContours()* function to determine the contours. This function takes two other attributes in addition to the dilated image as inputs: the attribute *RETR_EXTERNAL* denotes the contours retrieval mode which retrieves only the outer contours, and the parameter *CHAIN_APPROX_SIMPLE* denotes the contour approximation mode which compresses horizontal, vertical, and diagonal segments and leaves only their endpoints. Finally, the *drawContours()* function is used to draw the detected contours over a copy of the original image created using the *image.copy()* function. The segmented image in Figure 8-3 clearly shows the contour enclosing the object in the image.

```
import cv2
import numpy as np
import matplotlib.pyplot as plt
# Load the image
image = cv2.imread('C:/Users/User/Pictures/New
folder/20230917_113209.jpg')
gray = cv2.cvtColor(image, cv2.COLOR_BGR2GRAY)
blurred = cv2.GaussianBlur(gray, (3, 3), 0)
```

```python
# Apply OTSU thresholding
T, thresh = cv2.threshold(blurred, 0, 255, cv2.THRESH_BINARY +
cv2.THRESH_OTSU)
edges = cv2.Canny(blurred, 0.5*T, T)
# define a (3, 3) structuring element
kernel = cv2.getStructuringElement(cv2.MORPH_RECT, (3, 3))
# apply dilation operation to the edged image
dilate = cv2.dilate(edges, kernel, iterations=2)
# find the contours in the edged image
contours, _ = cv2.findContours(dilate, cv2.RETR_EXTERNAL, cv2.
CHAIN_APPROX_SIMPLE)
image_copy = image.copy()
# draw the contours on a copy of the original image
cv2.drawContours(image_copy, contours, -1, (255, 0, 0), 10)
plt.subplot(121)
plt.imshow(image)
plt.title('Original Image')
plt.subplot(122)
plt.imshow(image_copy)
plt.title('Image segmented using contour detection')
plt.show()
```

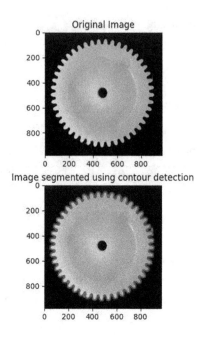

Figure 8-3. *Segmentation using contour detection*

Image Segmentation Using Watershed Algorithm

Watershed algorithm is one of the prominent methods for segmenting objects in a given image. The way water flows on a topological region serves as the inspiration for this technique. The goal of the algorithm is to divide an image into meaningful regions, much like the way the valleys in a terrain map might collect rainwater. To put things into perspective, think of the image as a landscape in which elevation is represented by the pixel intensities. Darker regions in the image resemble valleys and depressions, whereas the brighter regions resemble peaks and hills. The "catchment basins" in this terrain, where water would naturally gather and be separated by ridges, are what the watershed algorithm seeks to locate. The following are the steps involved in the watershed algorithm:

1. Preprocessing: To increase segmentation accuracy, the image is usually converted to grayscale and undergoes preprocessing (such as noise reduction).

2. Marker Identification: Sure background and sure foreground regions are designated as key areas. These serve as the water flow simulation's initial points.

3. Distance Transform: The "elevation" from each pixel to the closest sure foreground point is determined by applying a distance transform.

4. Simulated Flooding: Imagine that at the designated foreground locations, water is beginning to fill. With respect to the topography information (based on variations in pixel intensity), it "floods" the image gradually.

5. Watershed Lines: "Watershed lines" are drawn to divide areas where water from different basins begins to mix. The boundaries between various objects in the image are represented by these lines.

6. Segmentation Map: The output is a segmented image in which each pixel is labeled according to the catchment basin it is located in.

The following code illustrates the segmentation of gear image using the watershed algorithm. Similar to what we have done so far, we read the image, convert it to grayscale, and then create a binary image by using Otsu thresholding technique. Next, the background region is identified by dilating the binary image using the *cv2.morphologyEx()* function in the OpenCV library. We provide the attribute *MORPH_DILATE* to this function along with a 3x3 kernel of ones. The dilation usually adds pixels to the object boundaries in an image thereby enabling the clear identification of background. We then move on to find the foreground image by finding the distances of each pixel to the nearest background pixel by using the *distanceTransform()* function. This function takes the dilated image as input along with two other attributes: the distance type attribute *DIST_L2* denotes the simple Euclidean distance, and the number 5 indicates the size of the distance transform mask indicating that we are applying a 5x5 mask.

A threshold is applied to the output image of distance transform to separate the background and foreground pixels. The connected components of the thresholded image are then labeled using the *connectedComponents()* function following which watershed algorithm is applied to these labels using the *watershed()*. These labels are then passed as markers to the watershed algorithm which uses these markers to detect the exact boundaries between the foreground and background using watershed lines as explained earlier. Finally, before applying a color to the boundary lines, we increase the thickness of the lines by applying dilation with a 5x5 kernel. We use the dilated mask labels to mark the boundaries in the original image with red color by providing the color attributes [255,0,0] which indicates the corresponding values red, green, and blue components. The segmented image is illustrated in Figure 8-4.

```
import cv2
import numpy as np
import matplotlib.pyplot as plt
# Load the image
img = cv2.imread('C:/Users/User/Pictures/New
folder/20230917_113209.jpg')
imgRGB = cv2.cvtColor(img, cv2.COLOR_BGR2RGB)
# Convert the image to grayscale
gray = cv2.cvtColor(img, cv2.COLOR_BGR2GRAY)
# Apply thresholding to create a binary image
```

```python
ret, thresh = cv2.threshold(gray, 0, 255, cv2.THRESH_BINARY_INV
+ cv2.THRESH_OTSU)
# Find the background region
kernel = np.ones((3, 3), np.uint8)
imgD = cv2.morphologyEx(thresh, cv2.MORPH_DILATE, kernel)
# Find the foreground region
disT = cv2.distanceTransform(imgD, cv2.DIST_L2, 5)
_,disThres = cv2.threshold(disT, 5, 255, cv2.THRESH_BINARY)
# Label connected components
disThres = np.uint8(disThres)
_,labels = cv2.connectedComponents(disThres)
# Apply watershed
labels = np.int32(labels)
labels = cv2.watershed(img, labels)
# Increase thickness of line by dilating the segmented mask
dilate_kernel = np.ones((5, 5), np.uint8)
segmented_mask = np.zeros_like(gray)
segmented_mask[labels == -1] = 255
dilated_mask = cv2.dilate(segmented_mask, dilate_kernel)
# Apply the dilated mask to the original image
img[dilated_mask == 255] = [255, 0, 0]
plt.subplot(121)
plt.imshow(gray,cmap='gray')
plt.title('Original Image')
plt.subplot(122)
plt.imshow(img)
plt.title('Image segmented with watershed algorithm')
plt.show()
```

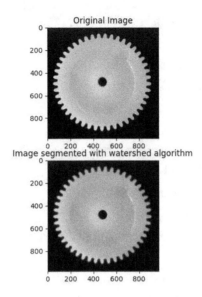

Figure 8-4. *Segmentation using watershed algorithm*

Image Segmentation Using Clustering

K-means clustering is a widely used algorithm for image segmentation due to its effectiveness and simplicity. K-means clustering, an unsupervised machine learning technique, is used to partition a dataset into a set of K unique, non-overlapping groups or clusters. The ultimate goal is to assign each data point to one of the K clusters in such a way that the points in a cluster are nearest to the centroid of that cluster compared to their distance from the centroids of the other clusters. Let us try to understand the logic behind K-means algorithm before going forward with the segmentation process. The following are the steps involved in K-means clustering algorithm:

1. Initialization: This step involves the initialization of two parameters:

    a. The number of clusters (K) that you want the data to be divided into

    b. Random centroids for the K clusters representing the center of the cluster

2. Assignment: In this step, all the data points are assigned to one of the clusters selected based on their distance from the cluster centroids using a distance measure such as Euclidean distance, Manhattan distance, cosine similarity, etc. Each data point is assigned to the cluster whose centroid is the closest.

3. Update: Once all the data points are allotted to a specific cluster, the cluster centroids are recomputed by taking the mean of all the data points assigned to them. The resulting new centroids are then considered as the updated cluster centers.

4. Iteration: Repeat the assignment and update step until convergence which occurs when there is no significant change in the assignment of data points to clusters.

There are much more technical details associated with the K-means algorithm which are beyond the scope of the book. So we will move forward to discuss how this algorithm can help us in segmenting the objects in an image. In our context of image segmentation, the data points correspond to the pixels in an image, and the K-means algorithm is used to group similar pixels together. The following code illustrates the segmentation of the gear image using K-means clustering algorithm. Before applying the algorithm, we need to reshape the image to a format suitable for clustering. Our gear image is an RGB image with a 2D matrix of pixels for each of the R, G, and B planes. So, we begin by reshaping the 2D matrix for each plane into a 1D matrix using the *reshape()* function. Then we provide the number of clusters (K) to the algorithm. Since our image has only a single gear object and we need to segment the object from the background, we give a K value of 2, one each for the object and the background.

Next, we create an instance of *KMeans* by providing the number of clusters defined earlier using the *n_cluster* attribute. Then we can fit the model to the reshaped image using the *fit()* function. This function will result in two variables *labels* and *cluster_centers* where the *labels* indicate the label of each pixel which can be either 0 or 1 as we have only two clusters and the *cluster-centers* indicate the centroids of the final clusters. Finally, we can assign each pixel to its centroid and display the image. It can be seen from the image in the Figure 8-5 that the entire object is converted to a single color, whereas the background is in another color (black in this case), indicating the clear segmentation of the object.

```
from sklearn.cluster import KMeans
import numpy as np
import matplotlib.pyplot as plt
import cv2
# Load the image
img = cv2.imread('C:/Users/User/Pictures/New
folder/20230917_113209.jpg')
img = cv2.cvtColor(img, cv2.COLOR_BGR2RGB)
# Reshape the image to a 2D array of pixels
pix = img.reshape((-1, 3))
k = 2 # Number of clusters (K)
# Apply K-means clustering
```

```
kmeans = KMeans(n_clusters=k)
kmeans.fit(pix)
# Get the labels and centroids
labels = kmeans.labels_
centroids = kmeans.cluster_centers_
# Assign each pixel to its corresponding cluster centroid
seg_image = centroids[labels].reshape(img.shape)
# Display the original and segmented image
plt.subplot(121)
plt.imshow(img)
plt.title('Original Image')
plt.subplot(122)
plt.imshow(seg_image.astype(np.uint8))
plt.title('Image segmented using Kmeans clustering')
plt.show()
```

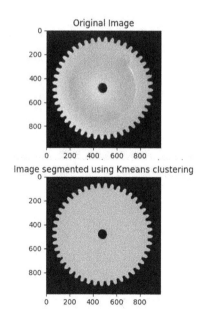

Figure 8-5. *Segmentation using K-means clustering*

Summary

Segmenting objects from an image could help us further in applications like object detection and tracking, medical imaging, face recognition, etc. In this chapter, we have explored different techniques to segment an object in a given image as listed here:

- Segmentation of a U-bolt in an image using global and local thresholding techniques

- Segmentation of a gear in an image using techniques like contour detection, watershed algorithm, and K-means algorithm

In the next chapter, we will discuss another crucial component of computer vision which is the extraction of text from images using optical character recognition.

CHAPTER 9

Optical Character Recognition

Optical character recognition, shortly called OCR, is a technology used to detect text characters from scanned text documents or digital images captured by a camera and convert them into an editable data. To put it in different terms, the OCR technology extracts machine-encoded text from the text characters recognized within scanned documents or images. OCR technology began to emerge in the early twentieth century. The primary purpose of early OCR systems was to identify printed text in documents that were typewritten or typeset. Later on, techniques like pattern matching and template matching were employed to create commercial character recognition systems. With the rise in popularity of machine learning methods as well as the development of advanced computing capabilities, these techniques gained prominence in implementing highly accurate OCR systems. Deep learning methods have improved OCR performance tremendously in the recent years, making it possible to recognize intricate handwritten text.

OCR has been widely adopted in multiple vision system applications like verifying information printed on packaging labels, reading and logging number plates of vehicles, automatic inventory management using serial numbers printed on products, extracting data from invoices, bills, or inspection reports for further analysis, etc. By incorporating OCR techniques for performing these operations, accuracy can be

K. Mohaideen Abdul Kadhar and G. Anand, *Industrial Vision Systems with Raspberry Pi*, Maker Innovations Series, https://doi.org/10.1007/979-8-8688-0097-9_9

greatly improved as it removes the possibilities for human error, and the productivity can be greatly improved as it minimizes the time spent in these tasks. As with every technology, there are some limitations with OCR systems as well. For instance, the quality of the OCR output is highly dependent on the quality of the input images. Therefore, poor-quality inputs can degrade the performance of the system. Also, OCR systems are still facing a lot of challenges with respect to handwritten text recognition owing to the variety of handwriting styles.

Despite the challenges, OCR has become an integral part of industrial automation across the world, especially in handling of diverse document formats. In this chapter, we will start with the fundamentals of OCR application exploring the various stages of the OCR pipeline. Then we will explore some of the leading OCR libraries and APIs that are readily available to be used for real-time applications.

Stages of OCR Pipeline

Although modern-day OCR systems are built on top of deep learning frameworks, we will start with the discussion of traditional OCR systems that will provide us better insights into the various stages in the OCR pipeline and how they transform the given image to recognize the characters in the image. Developing traditional OCR systems involved various stages, each serving a specific purpose, in order to achieve an efficient character recognition system. In each of these stages, the image will undergo various transformations ultimately leading to the recognition of the characters in the image. In this section we will discuss these stages one by one and try to build a deep understanding of the processes behind every OCR system.

Image Preprocessing

This stage involves preparing the input image for character recognition by improving its quality and transforming it to a form suitable for further processing. The key techniques involved in this stage are discussed as follows.

Noise Reduction:

As discussed in Chapter 5, images captured in real time are often susceptible to noise which reduces the quality of the image making it difficult for further processing. Therefore, these noises need to be treated first to enhance the image quality by smoothing them out using suitable filters like Gaussian blurring or median filtering. Recall from our earlier discussions that the suitable kernel size has to be selected while applying these filters to get better results.

i. Contrast Enhancement

A lot of photos, industrial images, and scanned documents have low contrast, which makes the text and background appear washed out or blended together. Because of this, OCR algorithms have trouble telling them apart, which might result in mistakes. We can simplify the process of distinguishing individual characters from the background by increasing the contrast. By making the segmentation process simpler, each character may be isolated by the OCR software to ensure accurate recognition. Popular techniques like contrast stretching, histogram equalization, adaptive histogram equalization, etc., can be used to enhance the contrast of the image. We can guarantee that our OCR system receives the cleanest and most readable input by using the appropriate contrast enhancement technique

ii.   Binarization

As we are interested only in recognizing the characters present in the given image, the color information becomes irrelevant, and hence, it would be better to convert the image into black and white. This would serve two purposes: reducing the computational complexity as the 3-plane RGB image is converted to a single plane binary image with just two values (0 for black and 1 for white) and clearly distinguishing the text from the background. Recall from our earlier discussions that binarizing a color image will involve two steps: convert the image into a grayscale image, and then apply thresholding (global or local) to convert it into a black and white image.

iii. Skew Correction

Skew correction is the process of correcting slanted or tilted text in an image so that it can be recognized accurately by making it horizontal. Common causes of skew in an image are imperfect scanning or photography of objects (or documents) with the text, camera angles during capture, or the physical distortion of the objects. Skew correction is very crucial because slanted text can significantly hinder the performance of OCR systems as character segmentation becomes more challenging. Such misaligned characters could lead to incorrect character recognition and degrade the accuracy of the system. Prominent techniques like Hough transform can be used to determine the skew of the text, and then rotation transformation can be applied to correct the skew to make the text horizontal.

Character Segmentation

Once the image is prepared for further processing, the next stage in the pipeline is to segment the individual characters in the image. We will discuss some of the prominent techniques for character segmentation in this section.

i. Connected Component Analysis

A commonly used method for character segmentation in OCR is connected component analysis (CCA). It entails locating and isolating clusters of related pixels that are probably going to depict distinct characters in an image. The following are the steps involved in this analysis:

a. Labeling: In the binary image, a unique label is assigned to every black pixel. Initial segments are produced by this labeling process, each of which represents a potential character.

b. Neighborhood Analysis: As it moves across the image, the algorithm compares the labels of nearby pixels. Two neighboring pixels are regarded as belonging to the same connected component if they share the same label. If their labels differ, it suggests that there might be a potential boundary between characters.

c. Label Propagation: Labels are upgraded iterative to combine connected components. The component is united when two nearby pixels with different labels are recognized as belonging to the same character and one label is changed to the other.

    d. Component Extraction: Following label propagation, every connected component in the image is assigned a unique label that corresponds to a different character or symbol. After that, these components are taken out as distinct images so that the OCR pipeline may process them further.

One important aspect of connected component analysis is that it is fairly robust to variations in font size and orientation. Though this technique is simple and effective, it will struggle with touching or overlapping characters. This technique is an ideal choice for industrial applications which usually involve recognizing bar codes, labels, or serial numbers where the text is well defined and controlled.

ii.   Projection-Based Methods

The key idea behind this technique is to project the pixel intensities in the binary image onto a single axis, horizontal or vertical, to create a projection profile which will reveal the patterns in the text arrangement. Segmenting lines of text and word segmentation inside lines are accomplished using the horizontal profile, which entails adding pixel values along each row of the image, whereas segmenting characters within words is accomplished using vertical profile, which entails adding pixel values along each column of the image. The valleys or dips in the projection profile can be used to identify the boundaries between characters. Projection-based methods are computationally efficient and work well for text with clear spacing and consistent font sizes. Similar to the connected component analysis, this technique can also struggle with overlapping characters. This technique is usually used in conjunction with other techniques like the connected component analysis for improved accuracy.

Feature Extraction

Once we have segmented the characters, the next step would be to represent the characters in a suitable way for recognition algorithms. We will discuss some of the prominent feature extraction techniques here:

i. Statistical Features

Statistical feature extraction plays a crucial role in optical character recognition (OCR) by converting raw pixel data into numerical representations that reflect the fundamental properties of characters. The statistical qualities of the pixel intensity in a character's image are utilized by statistical features. The pixel intensities within each character region are used to generate statistical features such as mean intensity, variance, skewness, kurtosis, histogram properties, texture features, co-occurrence matrix features, run-length features, and moment-based features. Each character's visual attributes, such as shape, texture, intensity distribution, and spatial relationships, can be compactly and informatively represented by the retrieved statistical features. Additionally, feature selection techniques can be used to identify the most discriminative features.

ii.   Shape Descriptors

A significant class of features known as shape descriptors capture the geometric characteristics and contours of characters, which are essential for differentiating between them. The input image containing text needs to be preprocessed and segmented to separate individual characters before shape descriptors can be used. Any of the segmentation techniques that we discuss in the previous chapter can be utilized for this purpose. The contours or boundaries can then be extracted from the segmented characters to represent their shapes. Contours are represented as a series of coordinates denoting each character's boundary. To capture the geometric properties of characters, shape descriptors are generated using the retrieved contours. Some of the common shape descriptors include bounding box, Fourier descriptors, region-based shape descriptors (such as moments), etc.

Character Recognition

The characters in a given image can be recognized and extracted with the help of the features derived from the image. One of the earlier techniques that was commonly used in tradition OCR systems was template matching. Some traditional machine learning techniques were also commonly used for recognizing characters. We will discuss both these techniques briefly to understand the underlying principle.

i. Template Matching

Traditional OCR systems used a basic technique called "template matching" to recognize characters in images. This technique compares predefined character patterns or templates with corresponding regions of the input image. Templates are first created to depict each character's visual appearance at different scales and orientations. The input image to the OCR system is then preprocessed to improve readability. The image is methodically scanned during the matching process, and similarity metrics between the templates and the image regions are calculated. In regions where the character templates closely reflect the image content, high match values are generated. Regions showing a substantial degree of similarity are flagged as possible character matches. In order to identify each character region in the image, the template with highest match value is associated with them. Despite being a simple and straightforward technique, template matching cannot handle variations in scale, rotation, or different font styles.

ii. Machine Learning

Machine learning techniques can learn patterns and relationships between features extracted from the characters and leverage the knowledge to effectively recognize the text within images. Supervised learning algorithms, such as k-nearest neighbors (kNN), support vector machines (SVM), artificial neural networks (ANNs), etc., are commonly used wherein a large dataset of character images along with the corresponding labels are used for training. Feature extraction techniques, like the ones we discussed in the previous section, can be applied to extract meaningful information from the characters in the image. These features can then be fed into the machine learning model during the training phase, and the model will learn to associate the features with the appropriate character labels. To achieve optimal performance, the model's parameters are iteratively changed to minimize the classification error on the training dataset. The trained model can then be used to classify unseen character images that are previously not available in the training dataset. Though traditional machine learning-based OCR systems are not as flexible and adaptable as modern deep learning-based approaches, they can still be effective when abundant labeled training data is available and there is a requirement for simple technique with minimized complexity.

In the coming section, we will discuss a traditional machine learning-based OCR system where we will use kNN to extract handwritten digits from the given image. This will give the readers a hands-on experience in creating a machine learning model trained on a large dataset. In the subsequent sections, we will discuss some of the state-of-the-art deep learning-based APIs and libraries that can be leveraged to perform text extraction even from complex images.

Handwritten Digit Extraction Using kNN

A crucial component of optical character recognition (OCR) technology, which extracts the digits from an image, is the handwritten digit recognition. To learn the features and patterns of each handwritten digit, machine learning algorithms can be trained on a large dataset of images of handwritten digits. The trained model can then be used to recognize digits in new images. In this section, we will use the MNIST (Modified National Institute of Standards and Technology database) dataset, which is a sizeable collection of handwritten digits frequently used to train different image processing systems. The dataset is comprised of 70,000 grayscale images of handwritten digits (0–9). Each image is of size 28 x 28 and has a corresponding label representing the digit it depicts. The images are categorized into 60,000 training images and 10,000 test images. The training images and the associate labels will be provided to the model so that the model can learn to determine the labels from the images. The test images on the other hand can be used to test the learned model and determine the accuracy of the model by comparing the predicted labels and actual labels. Through its *mnist* module, the *keras* Python library offers easy access to this dataset, making it perfect for both novice and seasoned practitioners.

We will use k-nearest neighbors (kNN) algorithm, a simple and effective supervised learning algorithm commonly used for classification and regression tasks, to train the model for classifying the handwritten digits. In the kNN classification process, every data point in the dataset is associated with a class label, and the model will be trained to determine the labels corresponding to the data points. When a new data point without a label needs to be classified, the algorithm uses a predefined distance metric to determine how far it is from every other data point in the training set. The k closest neighbors of the unlabeled point are then determined. A majority vote among the new data point's k closest neighbors determines the class designation for that point. The kNN classification algorithm relies on the idea that data points that share comparable features are probably members of the same class. This approach is easy to use and understand, which makes it appropriate for a variety of classification problems.

The following code illustrates the implementation of handwritten digit recognition using kNN. Let's discuss the code one step at a time:

1. We start by importing the libraries required for the implementation of the digit recognition system.

2. The *load_data()* function from the *keras* MNIST dataset loads the training and testing data for handwritten digit recognition. Here, *x_train* and *x_test* represent the training and testing images, and *x_test* an *y_test* represent the training and testing labels, respectively. The *x_train* and *x_test* will be of size (60000,28,28) and (10000,28,28), whereas the *y_train* and *y-test* will be of size (60000) and (10000), respectively.

3. We plot the first four images in the *x_train* array to visualize samples of the handwritten digits. We use the labels from *y_train* array denoting the corresponding digits as the plot title as shown in Figure 9-1.

4. Next, the images of size 28 x 28 are reshaped to a 1D array of size 784 (which is the product 28*28) using the *reshape()* function. The size of the training and testing dataset will now be (60000,784) and (10000,784), respectively.

5. We then use the *StandardScaler()* function from the *sklearn* library to scale the image data to have zero mean and unit variance. The corresponding scaled training and test image data are stored in the variables *x_train_scaled* and *x_test_scaled*, respectively.

6. We proceed to define kNN model with five neighbors which implies that for every image data the five nearest neighbors will be compared and a majority voting among their class values will be used to determine the labels. The *KNeighborsClassifier()* function from *sklearn* library is used to define the model.

7. The *fit()* method is then used to train the model. The scaled training image data *x_train_scaled* and the corresponding label data *y_train* are provided to this method.

8. The *predict()* function is used to predict the labels for the scaled test image data *x_test_scaled*. The predicted labels are stored in the variable *y_pred*.

9. The *accuracy_score()* method from the *sklearn* library can then take the actual labels *y_test* and the predicted labels *y_pred* and provide the accuracy of the prediction which is the percentage of images correctly identified by the model. The model predicts the handwritten digits with an accuracy of 94.43%.

10.   Finally, we take a sample image data from the *x_test_scaled* variable and then use the *predict()* function to get the predicted label for the image. We then display the corresponding original image from the *x_test* variable using *matplotlib* library and then use *text()* function to display the label in the same figure as shown in Figures 9-1 and 9-2.

```
from sklearn.neighbors import KneighborsClassifier
from sklearn.preprocessing import StandardScaler
from sklearn.metrics import accuracy_score
from tensorflow.keras.datasets import mnist
import matplotlib.pyplot as plt
# Load mnist data
(x_train, y_train), (x_test, y_test) = mnist.load_data()
print(x_train.shape)
print(y_train.shape)
# Display the first four images in the training dataset
for i in range(4):
    plt.subplot(2,2,i+1)
    plt.imshow(x_train[i],cmap='gray')
    plt.title('Label: {}'.format(y_train[i]))
plt.show()
# Reshape data to 1D arrays
x_train = x_train.reshape(len(x_train), 28 * 28)
x_test = x_test.reshape(len(x_test), 28 * 28)
print(x_train.shape)
# Scale data
scaler = StandardScaler()
x_train_scaled = scaler.fit_transform(x_train)
x_test_scaled = scaler.transform(x_test)
# Define KNN model
```

```
knn = KneighborsClassifier(n_neighbors=5)
# Train the model and make predictions
knn.fit(x_train_scaled, y_train)
y_pred = knn.predict(x_test_scaled)
# Evaluate performance
accuracy = accuracy_score(y_test, y_pred)
print("Accuracy: {}%".format(accuracy*100))
# Sample prediction
new_image = x_test_scaled[0].reshape(1, 28 * 28)
prediction = knn.predict(new_image)
plt.imshow(x_test[0].reshape(28,28),cmap='gray')
plt.title('Test Image')
plt.text(10, 3, 'Label: {}'.format(prediction[0]), fontsize=12,
bbox=dict(facecolor='white', alpha=0.9))
plt.show()
```

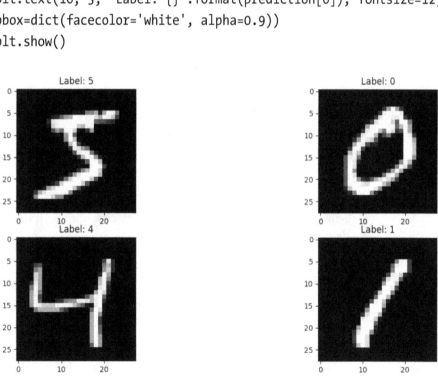

Figure 9-1. *Sample images from the MNIST dataset*

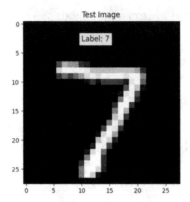

Figure 9-2. *Test image with the label detected by the kNN model*

Cloud APIs for OCR

An API, or application programming interface, is a collection of rules and tools that facilitate communication between various software programs. APIs can be used for a number of things, including developing apps that make use of the features of other software components, integrating third-party functionality, and accessing web services. APIs are essential in the context of cloud computing because they enable programmatic interaction between developers and cloud resources and services.

Cloud APIs offer developers scalable and practical ways to extract text from documents or images utilizing cloud-based services. Rather than having to create and maintain OCR capability from scratch, these APIs usually provide developers with an easy-to-use, standardized interface via which they may include OCR capabilities into their applications. Users can submit files to the cloud service, which uses advanced OCR algorithms to process the material. Along with other metadata like bounding boxes, confidence scores, etc., the extracted text is given back to the user. Cloud OCR APIs use deep learning techniques and robust computational resources to achieve high efficiency and accuracy in text extraction activities. In this section, we will discuss two most prominent computer vision APIs, provided by the world's leading cloud service providers Google˙ and Microsoft˙. These APIs have the capability to detect multiple languages from more complex images.

OCR with Google® Cloud Vision API

Google˙ offers a range of cloud computing services under the Google˙ Cloud Platform (GCP) suite. With the help of its extensive array of platform and infrastructure services, customers may build, deploy, and scale applications and services on Google˙ cloud's infrastructure. The key components and services offered by CGP can be categorized as compute services, storage and databases, networking, big data and machine learning, identity and security, developer tools, Internet of Things (IoT), and management tools. Developers can integrate their applications with different Google˙ Cloud services by using the extensive set of APIs provided by Google˙ Cloud Platform.

One of the key APIs offered by GCP is the Google˙ Cloud Vision API which provides powerful pre-trained machine learning models that allows developers to perform various image analysis tasks like classification, object detection, OCR, and more. OCR is supported by two annotation features: TEXT_DETECTION that detects and extracts text from any type of image and DOCUMENT_TEXT_DETECTION that is optimized for dense text and documents. Google˙ Cloud offers these OCR solutions via access to pre-trained ML models that can be deployed through an API. Before we get into the discussion of how this API can be used, the readers are hereby informed that a Google˙ Cloud subscription that is configured with a billing account would be required to use the API. Also, a new project will need to be created in the Google˙ Cloud Console to start configuring the API, and this project needs to be linked to the billing account. These aspects are beyond the scope of this book, and we will restrict out discussion to the configuration and usage of the API in this session.

Implementing OCR using Google˙ Cloud Vision API will require two separate procedures. The first one is to configure the Vision API and create an access key to utilize the API, and the second step is to download the Google˙ Cloud Vision library for python to implement the text detection algorithm. Let us start with the steps involved in enabling and configuring the Vision API using the Google˙ Cloud Console.[1]

1. Go to the menu bar in the Google˙ Cloud Console window, click *APIs & Services*, and select *Library* in the resulting submenu as shown in Figure 9-3. Note that a project has already been created (project name displayed at the top of the page), and all these configurations are done within the ambit of the project.

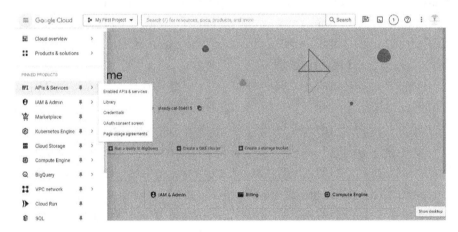

Figure 9-3. *Selection of API Library from Google˙ Cloud Console Menu*

---

[1] https://console.cloud.google.com/

2. In the resulting *Library* page, search for "vision API,"
    and then click *Cloud Vision API* from the search
    results. This will open the *Cloud Vision API* page as
    shown in Figure 9-4. Click *Enable* to enable the API
    for the Cloud account.

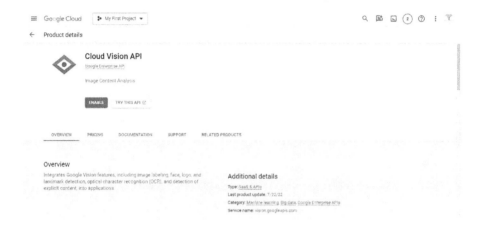

Figure 9-4. *Cloud Vision API Home Page*

3. Once enabled, we will be directed to the *API/
    Service Details* page for the API. In this page, go to
    Credentials and click *Create Credentials*. This will
    generate a menu as shown in Figure 9-5. In the
    menu, click *Service account*.

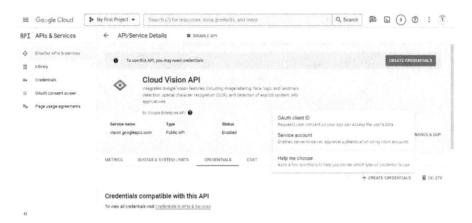

Figure 9-5. *Credentials menu in API/Service Details page of Cloud Vision API*

4. In the resulting setup page for service account, provide the *Service account name, Service account ID*, and *Service account description* as illustrated in Figure 9-6. Here we have given the ocr-example for our account. Then, click *Create and Continue* to move on to the access control settings for the service account.

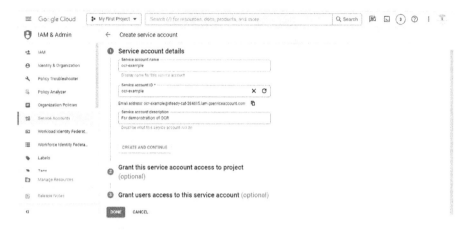

Figure 9-6. *Setting up Service account details*

5. In the *Service account access* settings, click *Add another role*, navigate to the *Basic* submenu, and select *Owner* as illustrated in Figure 9-7. Click *Done* to create the service account.

Figure 9-7. *Setting up Service account access to project*

6. Once the service account is created, we will be
    directed back to the *API/Service Details* page where
    the *ocr-example* account we have created will be
    listed under *Service Accounts* section as illustrated
    in Figure 9-8. Click the account to be redirected to
    its configuration page.

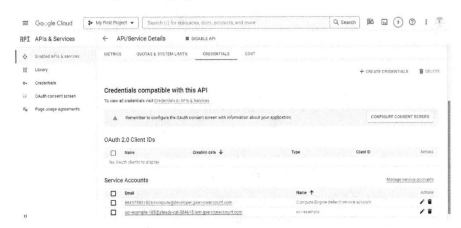

Figure 9-8. *Service account listed in the API/Service Details page*

7. In the *ocr-example* configuration page, navigate to
    the *Keys* section and click *Add Key*. This will result
    in a pop-up window with two options as illustrated
    in Figure 9-9. Click the *JSON* option to download the
    key in JSON format. This key will be used to access
    the Vision API services via our Python code.

Figure 9-9. *Downloading the key required for availing Vision API services*

After configuring the Google® Cloud console, the next step is to install the required python libraries to access the Vision API. The following are the essential libraries to utilize the services of the Vision API services via our python code:

i. google-auth-oauthlib: The purpose of this function is to authenticate our user credentials by integrating with OAuth 2.0 which is a standard authorization protocol.

ii. google-cloud-vision: This library will allow us to integrate vision detection features into various applications including OCR.

These libraries can be installed using the pip function that we discussed in previous chapters. For instance, the cloud vision library can be installed using the command *pip install google-cloud-vision* in the command prompt or terminal. Once the cloud configurations are complete and the required libraries are installed, we can proceed with the development of code for text detection. In this illustration, we will use the saw blade image shown in Figure 9-10. Our goal is to detect the text provided over the label of the saw blade.

Figure 9-10. *Tipped saw blade image*

The following code illustrates the process involved in extracting the text from the saw blade image. We begin, as always, by importing the required libraries for the code. The function *service_account.Credentials. from_service_account_file* creates a *Credentials* object from the service account JSON key file that we created earlier. The path to the file is given as input to the *filename* parameter. The parameter *scopes* define the permissions granted to the service account, and the Cloud Vision API URL provided as input to this parameter provides access to the service account to utilize the API services. The *ImageAnnotatorClient* class creates a client object using the credentials created in the previous step.

We then load the input saw image as a raw binary file using the *io.open* function so that it can be submitted to the Google˙ Cloud Vision API. Next, we create an image object from the binary file using the *vision.Image* function and then make a request to the Cloud Vision API to detect the text in the image by using the *client.text_detection* function. The resulting text annotations will be stored in the *response* object which can then be extracted by looping over the results and saving the text description in each iteration to a variable name *ocr*. Finally, we can print this *ocr* variable to display the entire text extracted from the label as illustrated in the following code. It can be seen that the Google˙ Cloud Vision API produces fairly good results. You may observe some minor mistakes in the text which can be attributed to the quality of the image.

```python
from google.oauth2 import service_account
from google.cloud import vision
import cv2
import io
import matplotlib.pyplot as plt
# create the client interface
credentials = service_account.Credentials.from_service_
account_file(
        filename="C:/Users/User/Downloads/storied-
        fuze-356305-48525d5682b6.json",
        scopes=["https://www.googleapis.com/auth/cloud-
        platform"])
client = vision.ImageAnnotatorClient(credentials=credentials)
# load the input image
filename = "C:/Users/Lenovo/Downloads/Gear_new.png"
with io.open(filename, "rb") as f:
```

```
      byteImage = f.read()
# create an image object make request to Vision API
image = vision.Image(content=byteImage)
response = client.text_detection(image=image)
# loop over the results
ocr=''
for text in response.text_annotations[1::]:
      ocr+= text.description+' '
print("Detected Text: \n", ocr)
```

Detected Text:
 110mm 4³1 , 3 " 20 to 16 mm N.MAX 14000RPM POWFRIEE PPT FOWER HOOLD POWERTEX 30T POWER TOOLS QUALITY BLIM GUT TDKWA10430 Tungsten Carbide Tipped Saw Blade SKU NO.182100 Unplug saw before mounting blade . Do not operate without saw blade querd . Always wear eye protection.Pailure to head all warnings could resultin serious bodily injury .

OCR with Azure Compute Vision API

Just like Google, Microsoft° offers an all-inclusive cloud computing platform referred to as Azure that offers a wide variety of services for developing, implementing, and managing applications and services via data centers managed by Microsoft°. Without having to invest in and maintaining physical infrastructure, Azure's Infrastructure as a Service (IaaS), Platform as a Service (PaaS), and Software as a Service (SaaS) capabilities allow businesses to take advantage of scalable computing resources, storage, networking, and other functionalities.

In this section we will discuss how to leverage Azure's computer vision API service to perform text extraction from the same saw blade image. Similar to our previous discussion with respect to Google cloud, we need to create and configure the Vision API services in the Azure portal[2]. Before that, users must create an Azure subscription and then assign a Resource group to that subscription. Since these processes are out of scope of this book, we will begin with the creation of computer vision API as illustrated in the following steps.

1.   The home page of the Azure portal shows the subscription created before and the associated resource group as illustrated in Figure 9-11. Now, click the *Computer Vision* icon at the top of the page.

Figure 9-11. *Azure portal home page*

2. In the *Computer* Vision page, click *Create* icon at the top to create a new Computer Vision service. This opens a configuration page as illustrated in Figure 9-12. In this page, select the *Resource Group* and the *Region* from their respective drop-down menu, and then provide a name for the Vision service.[2]

Select the pricing tier from the drop-down menu. The free tier that allows 20 calls per minute has been selected for our demonstration. Finally, scroll down to tick the acknowledgment checkbox, and then click *Review+create*. This will take us to a new page displaying all the details that we have selected. Click *Create* at the bottom of the page and Azure will start deploying the Vision service.

Figure 9-12. *Computer Vision service configuration page*

---

[2] https://portal.azure.com/

3. Once the deployment is complete, we will see the message as illustrated in Figure 9-13. Click *Go to resource* to open the page for the deployed Vision service.

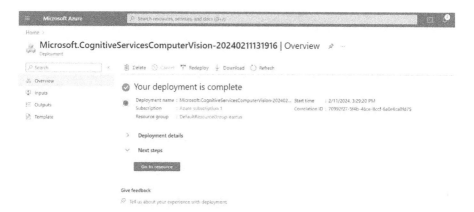

Figure 9-13. *Deployment completion message after creation of Computer Vision service*

4. In the deployed Vision Service page illustrated in Figure 9-14, click *Keys and Endpoints* in the menu available to the left side of the page.

Figure 9-14. *Home page of deployed Computer Vision service*

5. In the resulting page shown in Figure 9-15, copy any one of the two keys and the endpoint to a notepad so that it can be used in our Python code.

Figure 9-15. *Keys and Endpoint for the Computer Vision service*

Once the above configurations are completed in the Azure portal, the next step is to install the necessary libraries for Python. The following two libraries need to be installed in order to access the Azure Vision services via Python code:

i. msrest: This package offered by Microsoft® acts as a common framework for communicating with different Microsoft® REST APIs.

ii. azure-cognitiveservices-vision-computervision: This library is a software development kit (SDK) provided by Microsoft® Azure for interacting with the Computer Vision service with Azure Cognitive Services.

The following code illustrates the process of extracting the text from the saw blade image using computer vision API. As always, we start by importing all the necessary libraries for implementing the OCR system. We then get the endpoint URL and the API key that we saved to the notepad earlier, and then create a client using these credentials. Once the client is set up, we go to read the input image data from a file-like object in memory using the function io.*BytesIO*. The *read_in_stream()* method of the Azure Computer Vision client object takes the image data as a binary stream, performs an asynchronous analysis operation, and then returns a response object which contains the location of the operation in the Azure service. The *Operation-Location* parameter (an URL) is then extracted from the response header and can be used to track the status of the operation and retrieve its results. Then, we use the *split()* function to extract the operation ID from the Operation-Location URL string.

The *get_read_result()* method of the Azure Computer Vision client is used to retrieve the results of the asynchronous image analysis. The *result.status* provides us the status of the operation. Initially the status is in *not started or running* mode, and we use this block of code in a *while* loop to wait until the status turns to *succeeded*. The *sleep()* method in the *time* library is used to pause the execution of the *while* loop for 10 seconds so that the status is checked every 10 seconds. The code breaks out of the loop once the status is changed to *succeeded*. Then we iterate overt the *analyze_result.read_results* property of the *'ComputerVisionResult'* object. Each item in the *read_results* list consists of text content corresponding to the lines of text in the image. Next, we iterate over the *result.lines* property to read the text contents of each line in the image which are then appended to the *text* variable which we created as an empty string before the *for* loop. Once all the lines are extracted, the *text* variable can be printed the result of which is shown following the code. It can be seen that, similar to the Google Cloud Vision output, there are few mistakes in reading the text owing to the poor quality of the image.

```
import io
from msrest.authentication import CognitiveServicesCredentials
from azure.cognitiveservices.vision.computervision import
ComputerVisionClient
from azure.cognitiveservices.vision.computervision.models
import OperationStatusCodes
from msrest.authentication import CognitiveServicesCredentials
import requests
import time
API_KEY = 'fea22b23dbf848b3b7562f583948c41a'
ENDPOINT = 'https://ocr-example.cognitiveservices.azure.com/'
client = ComputerVisionClient(ENDPOINT,CognitiveServicesCredent
ials(API_KEY))
# load the input image
filename = "C:/Users/Lenovo/Downloads/20240202_082924.png"
with io.open(filename, "rb") as f:
      image = io.BytesIO(f.read())
# perform analysis operation and get the operation id
```

```python
response = client.read_in_stream(image, raw=True)
operationLocation = response.headers['Operation-Location']
operation_id = operationLocation.split('/')[-1]
# wait for operaion status to change to 'succeeded'
while True:
    # get the result
    results = client.get_read_result(operation_id)
    # check if the status is not "not started" or "running",
    # if so, stop the polling operation
    if results.status.lower() not in ["notstarted",
    "running"]:
        break
    # pause execution for 10 seconds before making another
    request to the API
    time.sleep(10)
# iterat over the results to read the text line by line
text = ''
for result in results.analyze_result.read_results:
    for line in result.lines:
        text+=line.text+' '
print("Text description: " text)
```

Text description:
POWERTEE PPT SLIM GUT FOWER FOOLS POWERTEX 30T QUALITY POWER
TOOLS 110mm 4318' 3 " 20 to 16 mm N.MAX 14000RPM TOKWA10430
Tungsten Carbide Tipped Saw Blade SKU NO.182100 Unplug saw
before mounting blade. Do not operate without saw blade querd.
Always wear eye protection. Pallure to head all warnings could
result In serious bodily Injury.

OCR with Python Libraries

Optical character recognition (OCR) packages for Python give programmers powerful tools for text extraction from various sources like scanned documents, images, and other visual media. These libraries enable automatic text extraction and analysis by accurately recognizing and interpreting characters within images using machine learning methods, such as deep learning models. Python OCR packages are crucial for activities like document digitalization, data extraction, and automated text recognition in domains like document management, natural language processing, and computer vision because of their versatility in handling different text formats, fonts, and languages. In this section, we will see a couple of popular OCR libraries

EasyOCR

EasyOCR is a user-friendly and versatile optical character recognition (OCR) package for the Python programming language. The library offers pre-trained text detection and identification models with support for several languages, and an emphasis on speed and efficiency in word recognition from images. EasyOCR consists of three primary parts: feature extraction, sequence labeling, and decoding. Feature extraction uses deep learning models like ResNet and VGG to extract meaningful features from the input image. The next phase, sequence labeling, makes use of Long Short-Term Memory (LSTM) networks to interpret the sequential context of the retrieved features. Lastly, the Connectionist Temporal Classification (CTC) method is used in the decoding phase to decode and transcribe the labeled sequences into the actual recognized text. As a detailed explanation of these techniques is beyond the scope of the book, readers are encouraged to explore them on their own.

The EasyOCR library can be installed using the command *pip install easyocr* in the Windows command prompt. Once the library is installed, the code illustrated as follows can be utilized for extracting the text from a given image. In this illustration, we are using a partial image of the top view of Raspberry Pi board. Once we read the image, we use *imshow()* method from *opencv* library to display the original image. Next, we create a *reader* object of the *Reader* class provided in the *easyocr* module. The argument *en* passed to the *Reader* class specifies that the OCR should be performed for English language, and the argument *gpu=False* indicates that the OCR should be performed on the CPU and not the GPU. The system will take some time to create this *reader* object. The *gpu* argument can be set to *True* if we have a CUDA-capable GPU, and this would speed up the process.

The *readtext* method in the *reader* object can then be used to extract the text from the given image. The output of this method will be a list of pairs where each pair consists of the bounding box coordinates for each text detected in the image and the corresponding text extracted. We then use a *for* loop to iterate over the detected pairs. In each iteration, we create a rectangle around the detected text with the help of the bounding box coordinates using the *cv2.rectangle()* function and then display the extracted text about the bounding box using the *cv2.putText()* function. The original as well as the text detected imags are illustrated in Figure 9-16. It can be noticed that this library does a fairly decent job of extracting the text from the image.

```
import easyocr
import cv2
img = cv2.imread('C:/Users/Lenovo/Documents/Piboard1.jpg')
cv2.imshow("Original Image",img)
cv2.waitKey(0)
# create a reader object and extract text from the image
reader = easyocr.Reader(['en'],gpu=False)
```

```
results = reader.readtext(img,paragraph=True)
# Create bounding box and display extracted text over the image
for (bbox, text) in results:
    (tl, tr, br, bl) = bbox
    tl = (int(tl[0]), int(tl[1]))
    tr = (int(tr[0]), int(tr[1]))
    br = (int(br[0]), int(br[1]))
    bl = (int(bl[0]), int(bl[1]))
    cv2.rectangle(img, tl, br, (0, 0, 255), 2)
    cv2.putText(img, text, (tl[0], tl[1]-5),
        cv2.FONT_HERSHEY_PLAIN, 1, (0, 0, 255), 2)
cv2.imshow("Text Deteccted Image", img)
cv2.waitKey(0)
```

Figure 9-16. *Illustration of text extraction using easyOCR*

Keras-OCR

Based on TensorFlow and Keras, keras-ocr is an open source Python framework that provides an extensive toolkit for text extraction from images. It is based on the combination of two major deep learning techniques. The CRAFT model, which is based on convolutional neural networks (CNN), can effectively identify text regions in the image and is capable of handling intricate layouts and overlapping characters. The character recognition is then achieved by a convolutional recurrent neural network (CRNN) which takes the pre-detected text section and then converts them into character sequences. We will be discussing about CNN in Chapter 10, whereas the readers can explore CRNN on their own accord.

The keras-ocr library allows us to perform text extraction with just a few lines of code. The library is a flexible tool for a wide range of OCR applications because it supports multiple languages and text styles. We can either use pre-trained models directly for out text extraction, or we can train the end-to-end OCR pipeline on custom dataset to meet our specific requirements. In this illustration, we will use the pre-trained model pipeline to extract the text from our Raspberry Pi board image.

The following code illustrates the process of text extraction from the given image. We use *the keras_ocr.pipeline.Pipeline()* method to initialize a *Pipeline* object, which is a pre-configured model pipeline with a pre-trained model. This object can then be used to extract the text from a given image in a simple and effective way. The *keras_ocr.tools.read()* reads the input image and converts it into a format that can be passed to the *Pipeline* object. Next, the *recognize()* method can be called on the *Pipeline* object to extract the text from the image. The extracted details will consist of the bounding box coordinates for each text region detected and the corresponding text. We can then iterate over these predictions and use the *keras_ocr.tools.drawAnnotations()* method to draw text annotations onto the given image. These annotations are illustrated in Figure 9-17. It can be seen that the predictions are not as accurate as easyocr, but still keras-ocr can come in handy when we need to train the model for a unique set of images.

```python
import keras_ocr
import cv2
import matplotlib.pyplot as plt
img = cv2.imread('C://Users/user/Documents/Piboard1.jpg')
pipeline = keras_ocr.pipeline.Pipeline()
predictions = pipeline.recognize([img])
fig, (ax1, ax2) = plt.subplots(2, 1, figsize=(10, 20))
ax1.imshow(img)
ax1.set_title("Original Image")
keras_ocr.tools.drawAnnotations(image=img,
                                predictions=predictions[0],
                                ax=ax2)
ax2.set_title("Annotated Image")
```

Figure 9-17. *Illustration of text extraction using keras-ocr*

Summary

Optical character recognition is an important component of industrial vision system that can be used to automatically check text engraved on or stickers pasted or printed on the surface of manufactured equipment and components. Also, it can be used to automate text entries into systems that were otherwise done manually in various scenarios. In this chapter, we discussed about the following aspects with respect to OCR systems:

- The steps and processes involved in developing a traditional OCR system from scratch

- Illustration of handwritten digit recognition from images using the traditional kNN approach

- Discussion of the computer vision API features in Google Cloud Platform (GCP) and Azure along with the illustration of text extraction using the API services

- Discussion and illustration of text extraction using prominent Python OCR libraries like easyOCR and keras-ocr.

Though we have touched upon simple machine learning algorithms like k-means clustering and k-nearest neighbors algorithm so far, we will dig deeper into other prominent machine learning and deep learning algorithms in the next chapter.

CHAPTER 10

Machine Learning Techniques for Vision Application

In traditional programming, we will manually write the code based on a well-defined algorithm that takes the input data and provides the desired output data. Machine learning (ML), on the other hand, learns the algorithm from the data without being explicitly programmed. The data can be of any format, but in the domain of computer vision, it primarily refers to images. ML algorithms for vision systems analyze the image data and learn to identify patterns relevant to the task at hand. Over time, the algorithm gains experience and improve its ability to perform the task. The term task here can refer to a wide range of computer vision applications like image classification, object tracking, image segmentation, OCR, etc. This ultimately leads to intelligent systems that are able to learn and adapt by enabling machines to make data-driven predictions and automate complicated decisions. The groundwork for using machine learning with image data in your Raspberry Pi-based vision system will be laid out in this part. As with all the traditional image processing system that we have discussed so far, ML-based image processing systems will also require certain preprocessing steps that can enable the system to learn faster. We

K. Mohaideen Abdul Kadhar and G. Anand, *Industrial Vision Systems with Raspberry Pi*,
Maker Innovations Series, https://doi.org/10.1007/979-8-8688-0097-9_10

will start by discussing these techniques briefly and then begin to explore some of the traditional ML models for image data. We will then delve into deep learning techniques that are better suited to handle image data than the traditional ML techniques.

Image Preprocessing

Just like the way we prepare the ingredients for cooking in accordance with the dish that we are going to make, we will preprocess images to convert them to a suitable format before feeding them to the machine learning models for computer vision tasks. This plays a crucial part in enhancing the performance of the learning model in a number of ways:

- Standardization: We cannot always expect to get images with the same properties from the real world. The images may be of different sizes and formats and may be captured in varying lighting conditions. Therefore, preprocessing is essential to convert the images to a consistent format so that the model could effectively focus on the actual content rather than these technical flaws.

- Model Performance Improvement: Feeding consistent images to the machine learning models can help them to converge faster resulting in higher accuracy during training. Relatively large disparities in image formats will make it difficult for models to learn reliable patterns.

- Training Time Reduction: Implementing ML model-based systems in resource-constrained platforms like Raspberry Pi board can be quite challenging. By reducing the size of images without loss of information during preprocessing, the model can process them with less computational power thereby leading to faster training times.

Even though we are already familiar with a number of preprocessing techniques, we will have a brief discussion of some of the most commonly used techniques for ML-based vision systems.

1. Image Resizing: To ensure that every image conforms to the model's input requirements, images are scaled to a specified width and height. As a result, the data is formatted consistently for the model to evaluate.

2. Normalization: Another common practice in ML based vision systems is to normalize the pixel values of the input images to a smaller range. The pixel values of real-world images are normally in the range of 0 to 255. Normalization helps to scale down these values to a smaller range of 0 to 1, or -1 to 1. The smaller values of pixels in turn enable the model to converge faster during training thereby improving the overall performance.

3. Noise Reduction: Real-world images are often corrupted by noise from various sources, either while capturing or in transit, as we discussed earlier in Chapter 5. Noise reduction techniques play a crucial part in removing unwanted artifacts created by these noise sources thereby leading to cleaner images which in turn improves the feature extraction for the model.

4. Image Augmentation: The machine learning model must be trained with as much images as possible in order to build a vision system that is robust to variations in real-world images. One of the early challenges in developing a ML-based vision system from scratch is the lack of sufficient images to train the model. Augmentation is a powerful technique that can help us to expand our minimal dataset by generating new images from them with random variations such as zooming, cropping, rotation, flip, or brightness/contrast variations. Incorporating augmentation in our system can help the model to generalize well to unforeseen changes in real-world images.

These preprocessing methods help us to get our image data ready for the best possible performance from our machine learning model. This lays the groundwork for our Raspberry Pi-based vision system to analyze images accurately and train the model effectively.

Machine Learning Algorithms

Without being specifically programmed to do so, computers can learn from data and make predictions or decisions thanks to machine learning algorithms. The goal of machine learning, a branch of artificial intelligence (AI), is to create algorithms that can continuously learn from data and perform better over time. The ML algorithms are distributed over four broad categories:

1. Supervised Learning

    - These classes of algorithms are provided with input data along with the corresponding output labels, hence the name supervised learning.

    - The algorithm then learns a mapping function from this labeled data to map the input data features to the target outcomes.

    - The two most common types of supervised learning are regression and classification.

    - Common examples of supervised learning techniques include linear regression, logistic regression, decision trees, random forest, support vector machines (SVM), and neural networks.

2. Unsupervised Learning

    - As the name suggests, this type of learning deals with unlabeled data, that is, the output labels corresponding to the input data are not available.

    - In this case, the algorithm will try to find patterns and structures in the data without any labels for guidance.

    - Some of the common types of unsupervised learning are clustering, dimensionality reduction, and association rule learning.

    - Common examples of unsupervised learning techniques include k-means clustering, hierarchical clustering, and principal component analysis (PCA).

3.   Semi-supervised Learning:

- Semi-supervise learning is a class of machine learning that combines both supervised and unsupervised learning by making use of both labeled and unlabeled data for training

- This method is preferred when we have a small set of labeled data and a large amount of unlabeled data

4.   Reinforcement Learning:

- This is a class of machine learning that learns by trial and error.

- It involves training an agent to interact with an environment for making decisions.

- The agent receives feedback for its decisions in the form of rewards or penalties.

- With the goal of maximizing cumulative rewards, the algorithm over time learns to make the right decisions.

Not all the traditional ML techniques are suited for image processing tasks. Recall that we have already covered how to use k-means clustering algorithm for image segmentation in Chapter 8. Apart from segmentation, traditional machine learning algorithms like SVM and decision trees played a significant role in image classification tasks. But, with the rapid development of computing capabilities and advanced hardware technologies, deep learning algorithms have become the frontrunner in dealing with image processing tasks.

Artificial Neural Networks (ANN)

Neural networks, a class of machine learning algorithms that mimic the human brain, form the heart of deep learning algorithms. Theses algorithms became immensely popular due to their ability to learn complex patterns from the data. They are composed of multiple layers, each comprising a number of nodes that perform specific computations. All the nodes in these layers are interconnected in a complex fashion similar to that of the neurons in our brain. Therefore, these nodes are often referred to as artificial neurons, and the classes of algorithms that use this structure to learn from the given input are termed as artificial neural networks (ANNs). The layers can be classified into three categories: the input layer followed by one or more hidden layers and then the output layer. Each of these layers has a vertical stack of nodes, and the nodes in each layer are connected to the nodes in the subsequent layer. If each node in every layer is connected to every other node in the subsequent layer as illustrated in Figure 10-1, we call it as a fully connected network.

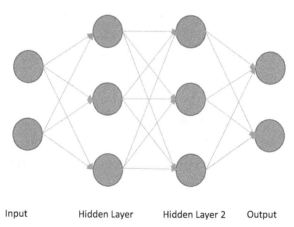

Input   Hidden Layer   Hidden Layer 2   Output

Figure 10-1. *Fully connected neural network*

The input layer is the actual data that is passed to the network. In case of images, each node in the input layer corresponds to a pixel value in the image. Suppose that a digital image to be processed by the neural network is of size 30 x 30 pixels, the image will be reshaped to a single vector consisting of 30x30 = 900 pixels, and hence, the input layer will consist of 900 nodes each holding a pixel value.

These values are then passed on to the hidden layers which learn and extract higher-level features from the input data. These layers are called hidden because the computations they perform are not directly observable. The neurons in the hidden layer compute a weighted sum of the inputs they receive from the previous layers or directly from the input layer (in the case of first hidden layer) and then pass the results through an activation function. A single node in a hidden layer is illustrated in Figure 10-2. The value of Z is the weighted sum of the inputs given by $Z = w_1x_1 + w_2x_2 + \dots + w_nx_n$ where $(x_1, x_2, \dots x_n)$ are the inputs to the node received from the previous hidden layer or the input layer and $(w_1, w_2, \dots w_n)$ are the model weights which the model learns iteratively. In addition to the input nodes, neural networks will have an additional bias node which is a constant value added to the above result. This bias is used to offset the result of each node and helps in shifting the activation function toward the positive or negative side. The function f(.) is the activation function which introduces nonlinearities into the network thereby allowing it to learn complex mapping between inputs and outputs. Some of the common activation functions include rectified linear unit (ReLu), Sigmoid, Softmax, and tanh. Readers are encouraged to explore the math behind these functions and their respective applications.

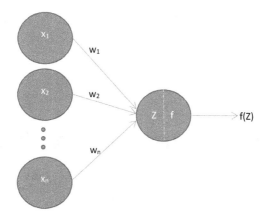

Figure 10-2. *Functionality of a single node (neuron)*

By acting as feature extractors, hidden layers produce higher level representation of the input data through a process called forward propagation. Each hidden layer extracts features pertinent to the current task via forward propagation. Multiple hidden layers in deep neural networks allow them to learn hierarchical representations of images, in which simple features like edges and textures are captured by lower layers and abstract features like shapes and objects are captured by higher layers.

In the training phase, the network uses optimization algorithms like gradient descent and backpropagation to modify the weights and biases of neurons in hidden layers. Effective weight updates across the network are made possible by the computation of the gradients of the loss function with respect to the network parameters during backpropagation. Hidden layers determine how errors are backpropagated through the network.

The output layer is the final layer of the neural network that produces the network's outputs. In case of regression task, that involves prediction of continuous values, the output layer will consist of a single node with a linear activation function. The single neuron will output the predicted value, and the loss function will be a measure of the difference between the predicted values and actual values. For classification task, the output layer will consist of multiple neurons, corresponding to the number of classes. In the output layer of multi-class classification, activation functions such as softmax are frequently utilized to generate probability distributions across the classes.

Convolutional Neural Networks (CNN)

CNNs are a class of deep neural networks with its architecture specifically tailored to handle grid-like data such as images, and hence, it is more common in the field of computer vision. When we pass an image into a traditional neural network, it will treat each pixel independently and don't understand the spatial relationships between neighboring pixels. What makes CNN so special compared to traditional ANN is its ability to leverage this spatial structure in the image data through a set of computing layers upfront called convolution layers and pooling layers, as shown in Figure 10-3, which we will be discussing in this section.

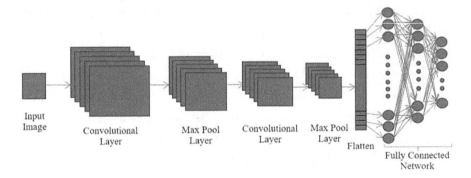

Figure 10-3. *Convolutional neural network*

Convolutional layers are the fundamental units of CNN. These layers apply a set of learnable filters, which are often called kernels, to the input image data. This filtering is applied by a process called convolution which involves sliding the kernel across the image, computing a sum of products of the filter coefficients and the image pixels covered by the kernel, and replacing the center pixel in the region covered by the kernel with the result. This operation is the same as the filtering operation we discussed earlier in Chapter 5. Figure 10-4 illustrates the convolution of a random grid data with a random kernel.

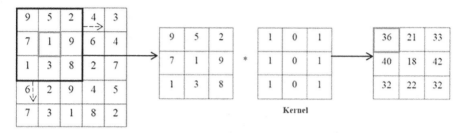

***Figure 10-4.** Convolution process*

In this illustration, a kernel of size 3x3 is moved over a grid-data to compute the convolution at different neighborhoods and then replace the center pixel in the neighborhood with the corresponding result. Let us consider the first 3x3 grid of data as shown in the figure. Element-wise multiplication of this grid data and the kernel is carried out, and the sum of the results $(9x1 + 5x0 + 2x1 + 7x1 + 1x0 + 9x1 + 1x1 + 3x0 + 8x1 = 36)$ is then replaced at the center pixel shown in red. This process, also called as dot product, is repeated by moving the kernel column-wise. In our example, the kernel will take two more steps to the right producing the values 21 and 33. Once it reaches the end of the column, the kernel will then shifted down to the beginning of the next row and then shifted column-wise to produce the values 40, 18, and 42. The same process will again be repeated by shifting the kernel by another row. In its entirety, the convolution process would produce 9 values converting the original matrix of size 5x5 to a 3x3 matrix.

This iterative process of sliding the kernel over the entire image and performing convolution transforms the input image to convolved features or feature maps that represent certain features in the image. Multiple filters make up a convolutional layer, and each filter therefore is in charge of identifying a certain pattern or feature from the input image. Similar to the fully connected layers, activation function can be applied element-wise to the output of the convolutional layers as well. These functions introduce nonlinearities to each element of the feature maps thereby enabling the neural network to learn more complex patterns. CNNs can automatically extract pertinent features from the data by learning appropriate filter weights during training and then passes these interpreted feature information to subsequent deep layers.

The convolution layer in CNN is usually followed by another critical component called pooling layer which helps to reduce the spatial dimension of the feature map data produced by the convolution layer thereby improving the network's computational efficiency. There are two commonly used pooling techniques named max pooling and average pooling as illustrated in Figure 10-5. The max pooling in this illustration is done with a grid size of 2 x 2 where each grid of data is converted to a single number which is the maximum of the 4 numbers in the grid as shown in the dark box. Similarly, each grid of size 2 x 2 is replaced by the average of the 4 numbers in the grid in case of average pooling. As the 4x4 matrix is composed of 4 grids, it is converted to a matrix of size 2 x 2 after the pooling operation.

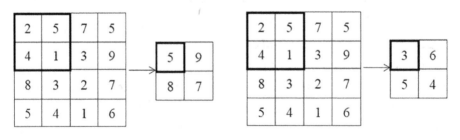

(a) Max Pooling   (b) Average Pooling

Figure 10-5. *Max-pooling process*

The number of convolution layers as well as the number of kernels to be used in each layer and the number of the max pooling layers depend upon a variety of factors like the complexity of the task involved, the nature and size of the input data, and the amount of computational resources available. Building a CNN from scratch will often involve a process of trial and error guided by domain knowledge as there is no one-size-fits-all solution to the number of convolutional and max pooling layers.

The output of the final layer in this sequence is flattened to create a single vector and then fed as input to a fully connected network. High-level reasoning is carried out by the fully connected network on the features that the convolutional layers have extracted. The fully connected layers can identify global dependencies in the data by discovering intricate patterns and relationships among features. This allows the network to make predictions or decisions that are pertinent to the current task. The fully connected layers essentially map the learned features to the output space that is appropriate for the given task, thereby functioning as a classifier or regressor.

Handwritten Digit Recognition with CNN

In the previous chapter, we developed a system to recognize handwritten digits using an unsupervised learning algorithm called k-means clustering. In this section, we will develop a CNN-based system to recognize handwritten digits with much better accuracy. We will begin by importing all the necessary libraries and methods. Here, we use the TensorFlow Keras library to import all the components required to build the model as illustrated here. Each of the model layers like 2D convolution, 2D max pooling, and dense layer is imported along with the *Flatten* function from *keras.layers*. The MNIST handwritten digits dataset is also imported from *keras.datasets*. The *Sequential* function is imported from *keras.models* to pack all the layers into a sequential model. The *to_categorical* function from *keras.utils* can be used to perform one hot encoding of the output labels.

```
import cv2
import numpy as np
from keras.datasets import mnist
from keras.layers import Dense, Flatten
from keras.layers import Conv2D, MaxPooling2D
from keras.models import Sequential
from keras.utils import to_categorical
from matplotlib import pyplot as plt
```

The dataset is initialized using the *load_data()* and separated into training with 60,000 images and testing set with 10,000 images. As we have already visualized some sample images in the previous chapter, we will skip that part and proceed with reshaping the dataset to a format suited for the model. Recall that the images in MNIST dataset are black and white images of size 28 x 28 with pixel values of either 0 or 255. We add another dimension of shape 1 using the *reshape()* function which signifies that the image is grayscale thereby changing the size of images to 28 x 28 x 1. We then normalize the image by dividing the pixels by 255.0 so that they are rescaled to the range [0, 1]. We then use the *to_categorical()* function to perform one-hot encoding of both the train and test labels. These operations are illustrated as follows:

```
# load dataset
(trainX, trainy), (testX, testy) = mnist.load_data()
# reshape dataset to have a single channel
trainX = trainX.reshape((trainX.shape[0], 28, 28, 1))
testX = testX.reshape((testX.shape[0], 28, 28, 1))
# normalize to range 0-1
trainX = trainX / 255.0
testX = testX / 255.0
# one hot encoding
trainY = to_categorical(trainy)
testY = to_categorical(testy)
```

As the data preparation is now complete, we now move on to the model development. The code illustrated as follows defines a convolutional neural network (CNN) model using the Keras Sequential API. A 2D convolution layer with 32 filters and kernel size of (3, 3) is created using the *Conv2D* function. The ReLu activation function is provided to introduce nonlinearities in this layer. As this is the first layer in the network that receives the input, the input shape (28, 28, 1) is provided as a parameter as well. A max-pooling layer with kernel size 2 x 2 is created as the second layer using the *MaxPooling2D*. The *Flatten()* function is then used to convert the output of the max pooling. We then define a fully connected network with a hidden layer consisting of 100 nodes and an output layer with 10 nodes corresponding to the 10 digits using the *Dense()* function. The *compile()* function is used to configure the learning process by specifying parameters like the optimizer, loss function, and evaluation metrics. Here we are using the most common "Adam" optimizer. For the loss function, we are using the "categorical_crossentropy" which is predominantly used for multi-class classification problems like our handwritten digit recognition problem. We provide "accuracy" as the metric for evaluating our model performance. The model is trained with the training dataset using the *fit()*. We provide a batch size of 32 which implies that 32 samples will be used in each training batch, and the model weights are updated after each batch. The number of epoch indicates the number of times the model will iterate over the entire training dataset during training. In our case, we select the number of epochs as 10. Additionally, we provide the test data and labels as validation data for the model. The *summary()* function is used to print the model summary which shows the details of each layer as shown in Figure 10-6.

```
# define cnn model
model = Sequential()
model.add(Conv2D(32, (3, 3), activation='relu', input_
shape=(28, 28, 1)))
```

```
model.add(MaxPooling2D((2, 2)))
model.add(Flatten())
model.add(Dense(100, activation='relu' ))
model.add(Dense(10, activation='softmax'))
# compile model
model.compile(optimizer='adam', loss='categorical_
crossentropy', metrics=['accuracy'])
print(model.summary())
history = model.fit(trainX, trainY, batch_size=32, epochs=10,
validation_split=0.2)
```

```
Model: "sequential"
```

Layer (type)	Output Shape	Param #
conv2d (Conv2D)	(None, 26, 26, 32)	320
max_pooling2d (MaxPooling2D)	(None, 13, 13, 32)	0
flatten (Flatten)	(None, 5408)	0
dense (Dense)	(None, 100)	540,900
dense_1 (Dense)	(None, 10)	1,010

```
Total params: 542,230 (2.07 MB)
Trainable params: 542,230 (2.07 MB)
Non-trainable params: 0 (0.00 B)
```

Figure 10-6. *CNN model summary*

The learned metrics are stored in the variable "history." To visualize how the model learning improves with each epoch, we plot the training accuracy and loss with respect to epochs as shown in Figure 10-7 using the following code. It can be seen that the accuracy increases with each epoch, whereas the loss decreases with each epoch indicating that the model is learning incrementally. The CNN model achieves more than 99% accuracy compared to the accuracy of 94.43% obtained in the kNN based recognition system that we discussed in Chapter 9.

```
plt.subplot(121)
plt.plot(history.history['accuracy'])
plt.title('Model accuracy')
plt.xlabel('Epoch')
plt.ylabel('Accuracy')
plt.subplot(122)
plt.plot(history.history['loss'])
plt.title('Model loss')
plt.xlabel('Epoch')
plt.ylabel('Loss')
plt.show()
```

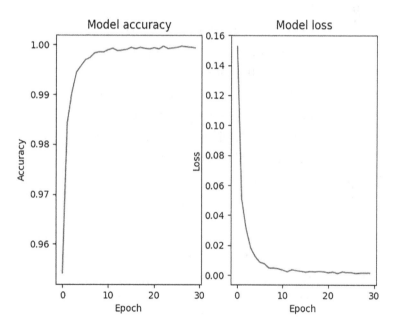

Figure 10-7. *Model training accuracy and loss vs epochs*

Now that we have trained the model and visualized it's learning performance on the training dataset, the next step is to evaluate the model's performance on the test dataset. We use the *evaluate()* method to do this which takes the test data as well as the corresponding labels as

271

input and provided the test accuracy as well as loss as the output. We can use a print statement to view this accuracy, and we get a value of 0.9853 which is equivalent to 98.53%. Therefore the model performance on the unseen test data, which it has not encountered during the training phases, is also close to the training performance indicating that the model adapts well to new data. To test the model prediction, we take the first image in the test data set using the index *testX[0]*, reshape it to the size (1,28,28,1) suitable for the model, and then use the *predict()* function to generate the prediction for the image. This function will generate an array of probabilities where each element represents the probability that the image corresponding to a particular digit class (0-9). The *argmax()* function can then be used on the prediction output to determine the index of the largest probability among the array, and this index corresponds to the output class of the digit. For example, in our case, the first image in the test dataset corresponds to digit 7, and the value in index 7 of the prediction array will be maximum (equal to 1) indicating that the detected number is 7. Readers can verify this by printing the prediction array. Finally, we can display the test image with predicted digit as its title as illustrated in Figure 10-8. The model can be saved as a *'h5'* model using the *save()* method from the tensorflow library. This will save the model architecture, learned weights, and optimizer configuration into a single file.

```
# Evaluate the model
test_loss, test_acc = model.evaluate(testX, testY)
print('Test accuracy:', test_acc)
# Predict the first digit from the test set
first_image = testX[0]  # Get first image from test set
prediction=model.predict(first_image.reshape(1,28,28, 1))
predicted_class = np.argmax(prediction[0])
plt.imshow(first_image.reshape(28, 28), cmap='gray')
plt.title('Predicted Digit: ' + str(predicted_class))
plt.show()
model.save('my_model.h5')
```

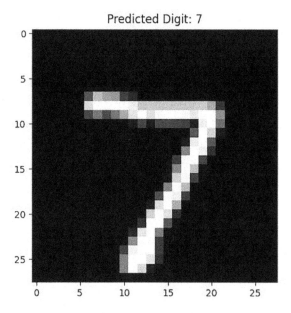

Figure 10-8. *Prediction of sample image from test dataset*

Digit Recognition from Test Scripts Using CNN

In this section, we will apply the trained model that we saved in the previous section to recognize handwritten digits from the front page of a student's test script where the section-wise marks are entered by a teacher. This use case will give an idea of how well the model trained on a standard dataset applies to other real-world documents. The handwritten digits for the MNIST dataset are actually taken from American Census Bureau employees and American high school students. Further, these images are preprocessed into 28 x 28 grayscale images to ensure uniformity and consistency. The same cannot be expected of the real-world images.

Before developing the code for the use case, let us first understand the challenges involved in dealing with images of real-world documents with handwritten digits. The foremost issue with real documents is the variability with respect to a number of factors like writing style, stroke thickness, slant, etc. The MNIST dataset with clean, standardized digit images will definitely not be able to capture this variability. MNIST may not generalize well to images with noise or distortion caused by various factors like imperfect writing conditions, scanning errors, etc. Addressing these issues require sophisticated models trained on large and diverse datasets representative of these variations and complexities.

Setting aside all the challenges for now, let us see how well our trained model detects the handwritten digits at different locations in the front page of an answer script. We start by importing the necessary library and loading the trained model using the *load_model()* method. Next we load the image followed by the coordinates for each of the boxes in the format [x,y,w,h], where x, y indicates the coordinates of the top-left corner of the boxes and w, h indicates the width and height of the boxes. To visualize how these coordinates correspond to the boxes of interest, we create a mask image with same size as the original image where the pixel values corresponding to the boxes are 255 and all the other pixel values of zero. The original image as well as the mask image is illustrated in Figure 10-9.

```
import cv2
import numpy as np
import matplotlib.pyplot as plt
from keras.models import load_model
# Load the model
model = load_model('my_model.h5')
# load the image and mask coordinates
img = cv2.imread('Scripts\script_new.jpeg')
mask_coordinates = [[221,227,382,283], [223,287,384,343],
[224,343,382,400], [224,398,382,455],
```

```
                [224,458,382,515],  [224,515,382,570],
                [222,570,382,626],  [224,627,384,683],
                [224,684,382,746],  [224,748,382,807],
                [224,803,382,862],  [224,862,382,921],
                [790,226,952,285],  [952,229,1113,285],
                [1117,229,1278,285],  [788,343,952,401],
                [951,341,1114,399],  [1113,342,1279,399],
                [789,400,952,454],  [952,400,1115,454],
                [1115,400,1279,456],  [788,514,952,570],
                [954,512,1113,568],  [1116,512,1278,567],
                [788,570,952,628],  [953,568,1117,626],
                [1113,569,1281,626],  [788,683,952,746],
                [955,683,1113,748],  [1114,685,1281,746],
                [789,748,952,803],  [953,749,1116,804],
                [1114,750,1279,807],  [789,861,951,919],
                [952,863,1114,921],  [1115,862,1278,919]]
# Create mask image
new_array = np.zeros_like(img)
for i in mask_coordinates:
    new_array[i[1]:i[3],i[0]:i[2]] = 1
image_rgb = cv2.cvtColor(img, cv2.COLOR_BGR2RGB) # Convert
                                                BGR to RGB

plt.figure()
plt.subplot(211)
plt.imshow(image_rgb)
plt.title('Original Image')
plt.subplot(212)
plt.imshow(255*new_array)
plt.title('Mask Image')
plt.show()
```

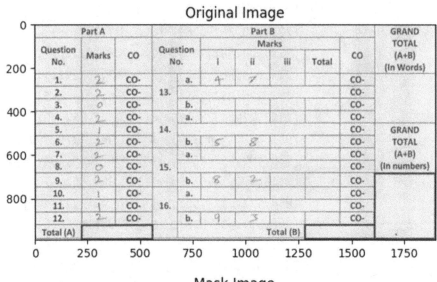

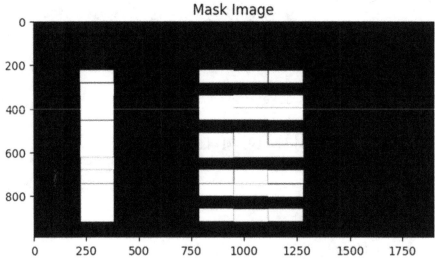

Figure 10-9. *Answer script image and mask image*

From the image, it can be seen that there are two sections in the answer script. The first section under "Part A" is composed of 12 questions, and the second section under "Part B" is composed of 4 questions (with subsections), with corresponding marks entered for both sections. Now, we have to extract the regions specified by the mask coordinates from the original image, preprocess them to make them compatible to the model, and then predict the digits in the image regions using the trained model.

The following code illustrates these operations. First, we start by initializing two figures *fig1* and *fig2* with subplots using *matplotlib* library to display the original and preprocessed images of the digits. To obtain these images, we iterate through the list of mask coordinates and extract specific regions of the script image. From Figure 10-9, we can also note that a number of boxes in the "Part B" section are empty. To drop these empty boxes from further execution, we use a conditional statement to allow only those boxes where the variance of pixel values, determined using *var()* method in the *numpy* library, is greater than 200. If the region contains a digit, the image is displayed in a corresponding subplot in the second figure *fig1* and then preprocessed by converting it to grayscale, applying a binary threshold, and resizing it to 28x28 pixels to match the input size of the trained machine learning model. The preprocessed image is displayed in a corresponding subplot in the second figure *fig2* and then normalized to a range of 0-1, reshaped to a 4D tensor (batch size, height, width, channels) and passed to the *model.predict()* method to obtain the digit prediction. The predicted digit is appended to the out list and the loop continues to the next digit. Finally, the extracted and preprocessed images of the digits are displayed using plt.show() method as shown in Figures 10-10 and 10-11, respectively.

```
out=[]
fig1, ax1 = plt.subplots(4, 5)
fig2, ax2 = plt.subplots(4, 5)
ax1_flat = ax1.flatten()
ax2_flat = ax2.flatten()
m=0
for i in mask_coordinates:
    img_i = image_rgb[i[1]+5:i[3]-5,i[0]+5:i[2]-5]
```

```
    if np.var(img_i)>200:
        ax1_flat[m].plt(img_i)
        # preprocess the image
        gray = cv2.cvtColor(img_1[:,50:100], cv2.COLOR_
        RGB2GRAY)
        ret, thresh = cv2.threshold(gray, 190, 255, cv2.THRESH_
        BINARY_INV)
        resized = cv2.resize(thresh, (28, 28))
        ax2_flat[m].plt(resized, cmap='gray')
        # Normalize the image
        normalized_image = resized / 255.0
        # Reshape the image to be compatible with the model
        reshaped_image = normalized_image.reshape(1, 28, 28, 1)
        # Predict the digit using the model
        prediction = model.predict(reshaped_image)
        # Get the index of the highest confidence digit
        predicted_digit_index = np.argmax(prediction)
        out.append(predicted_digit_index)
        m+=1
fig1.suptitle('Digit images extracted from their boxes')
fig2.suptitle('Preprocessed digit images')
plt.show()
```

Digit images extracted from their boxes

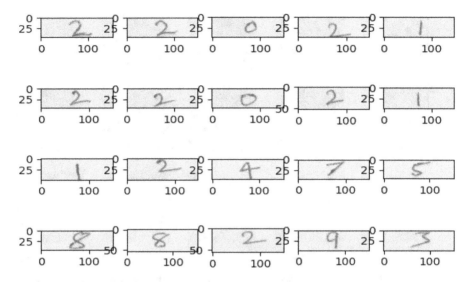

Figure 10-10. *Digit images extracted with mask coordinates*

Preprocessed digit images

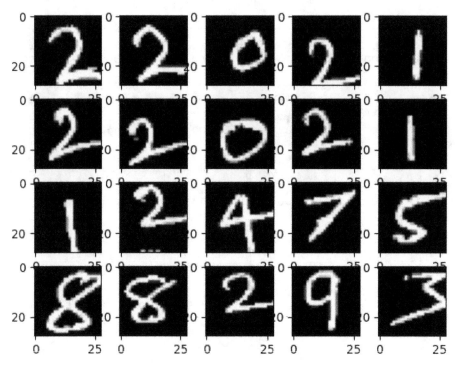

Figure 10-11. *Digit images after preprocessing*

All the predicted digits are now available in the list "*out.*" Rather than directly printing out the list, we use the following code to iteratively print the digits by associating them with their corresponding question number as illustrated in the following. This will help us to easily verify our results with the original image. It can be seen that the marks for questions 4, 5, 11, and the second part of questions 13 and 16 are incorrectly detected by the model. So, the model trained on MNIST dataset is still able to successfully predict 15 out of 20 digits from the images extracted from an external document that it was not previously trained on. As mentioned at the start of this section, this performance can be improved further by training more complex models than this simple CNN model on even larger and diverse datasets.

```
# Print the predictions along with question numbers
print('The predicted digits are:')
print('Part A:')
for i in range(12):
    print('{}. {}'.format(i+1,out[i]))
n = 13
print('Part B:')
for i in range(12,19,2):
    print('{}. ({}, {})'.format(n,out[i],out[i+1]))
    n+=1
```

Output of the code is:

```
The predicted digits are:
Part A:
1. 2
2. 2
3. 0
4. 7
5. 7
6. 2
7. 2
8. 0
9. 2
10. 1
11. 9
12. 2
Part B:
13. (4, 2)
14. (5, 8)
15. (8, 2)
16. (9, 5)
```

We can enhance this application by including alphabets. For example, readers can try developing a text extraction system by using the Extended MNIST (EMNIST) dataset that includes uppercase and lowercase letters along with digits. Further, this application can be extended to industrial applications, wherever manual data entries are still being processed, to digitize the data. Apart from text extraction, other techniques like image classification, object detection, object tracking, etc., find wide applications in industries.

For instance, a number of highly advanced open sources CNN-based models like YOLO (You Only Look Once), SSD (Single-Shot MultiBox Detector), Faster R-CNN, Mask R-CNN, etc., have been developed over the years that are highly effective in real-time object detection. Different pre-trained versions of these models are available that are trained on large datasets with multiple classes of images like COCO (80 classes), CIFAR-100 (100 classes), ImageNet (1000 classes), etc. These pre-trained models can be readily applied to real-world images and videos with reasonably good accuracy. On the other hand, these models can also be custom trained with images corresponding to our own applications making them more flexible and adaptable. Readers are encouraged to explore these models in order to truly appreciate the overwhelming research and developments happening in this domain.

Additionally, we can use the APIs for advanced pre-trained models offered by leading cloud service providers. For instance, we have already discussed the OCR application using the Vision API services offered by Google Cloud Platform (GCP) and Microsoft Azure. In addition to this, their Vision API services offer other applications such as image classification, face detection, object detection, etc., that can be leveraged for our applications. But readers need to be mindful of the fact that these services are offered in a restricted manner for free tier, whereas they are charged based on usage with respect to other pricing models.

Summary

In this chapter, we have explored the fundamental machine learning techniques used widely in image processing techniques. The chapter is organized as follows:

- The basic preprocessing steps involved in developing machine learning applications

- The basic categories of traditional machine learning techniques

- The detailed process behind artificial neural networks (ANN) techniques that mimic the behavior of the human brain

- The detailed process behind convolutional neural networks (CNN) and the additional capabilities that enable them to learn patterns from images

- Handwritten digit extraction from MNIST dataset images using CNN

- Application of the learned model for handwritten digits to real-time student answer script to extract the marks for section-wise questions

With this solid understanding of machine learning fundamentals, we will move on to develop industrial vision applications in the next chapter based on all the knowledge we have acquired so far in this book.

Industrial Vision System Applications

We have covered a lot of ground with respect to vision systems, starting from basic image processing techniques to more complex algorithms that can be used to develop advanced systems capable of performing crucial tasks. By using such complicated vision systems for industrial applications, a number of tasks ranging from quality control to safety monitoring can be performed in real time which can help to avoid human errors. We will take our learnings from all the chapters and develop vision systems for four different industrial applications in this chapter (Case Studies 11.1 through 11.4). We will further make the systems more user friendly by incorporating them into easily understandable user interfaces.

Interfacing Cameras with a Raspberry Pi

Interfacing cameras with a Raspberry Pi can be a common and useful task for various applications, such as computer vision, surveillance, or image processing. Here is a general guide to help you get started:

© K. Mohaideen Abdul Kadhar and G. Anand 2024
K. Mohaideen Abdul Kadhar and G. Anand, *Industrial Vision Systems with Raspberry Pi*,
Maker Innovations Series, https://doi.org/10.1007/979-8-8688-0097-9_11

1. Choose a Camera Module: Raspberry Pi supports
    various camera modules. The official one is the
    Raspberry Pi Camera Module, which comes in
    different versions (V1, V2, HQ). Choose the one that
    fits your requirements.

2. Connect the Camera Module: Connect the camera
    module to the Raspberry Pi's camera port. Make
    sure to power off the Raspberry Pi before connecting
    or disconnecting the camera module.

3. Enable the Camera Interface: Use raspi-config to
    enable the camera interface.

    ```
    sudo raspi-config
    ```

    Navigate to "Interfacing Options" ➤ "Camera" and
    enable it. Reboot if prompted.

4. Check Camera Connection: Verify that the camera is
    detected by running:

    ```
    vcgencmd get_camera
    ```

5. Update and Upgrade: Keep your Raspberry Pi up to
    date with the latest packages.

    ```
    sudo apt-get update
    sudo apt-get upgrade
    ```

6. Install Camera Software: Install the necessary
    software for working with the camera module. For
    example, use the picamera library for Python.

    ```
    sudo apt-get install python3-picamera
    ```

7. Capture Images: Write a simple Python script to capture images using the camera. Example using the picamera library:

```
from picamera import PiCamera
from time import sleep
camera = PiCamera()
camera.start_preview()
sleep(5)  # Adjust as needed
camera.capture('image.jpg')
camera.stop_preview()
```

Processing Videos in Raspberry Pi

When working with videos on Raspberry Pi, especially using the Raspberry Pi Camera Module or USB cameras, you'll follow a similar approach as with images, but with some modifications for video recording and processing. Following are the steps to get you started.

1. Use Python script to capture video:

```
from picamera import PiCamera
from time import sleep
camera = PiCamera()
camera.start_recording('video.h264')
sleep(10)  # Record for 10 seconds (adjust as needed)
camera.stop_recording()
```

2. Convert H.264 to MP4. The captured video is in H.264 format. You might want to convert it to MP4 for wider compatibility:

```
MP4Box -add video.h264 video.mp4
```

3. Streaming Video. You can also stream live video using tools like raspivid or by modifying your Python script:

```
from picamera import PiCamera
from time import sleep
camera = PiCamera()
camera.start_preview()
camera.start_recording('video.h264')
sleep(10)
camera.stop_recording()
camera.stop_preview()
```

4. Advanced Video Processing. If you're working with video processing, consider using libraries like OpenCV. Install OpenCV on your Raspberry Pi:

```
sudo apt-get install libopencv-dev python3-opencv
```

5. Example for OpenCV Video Processing. Read a video file and process frames using OpenCV:

```
import cv2
video_capture = cv2.VideoCapture('video.mp4')
while True:
    ret, frame = video_capture.read()
    # Your image processing code here
    cv2.imshow('Video', frame)
    if cv2.waitKey(1) & 0xFF == ord('q'):
        break
video_capture.release()
cv2.destroyAllWindows()
```

Case Study 11.1: Detecting Thread Quality of a Nut and Bolt

A vision system can significantly enhance the quality control process for nuts and bolts by providing detailed insights into the threads' quality and characteristics. Through the use of high-resolution cameras and sophisticated image processing algorithms, a vision system can capture and analyze various aspects of the threads, including thread pitch, depth, form, and surface finish. One of the key benefits of a vision system is its ability to detect defects that may not be visible to the naked eye. For example, it can identify incomplete threads, which can lead to improper assembly and reduced joint strength. It can also detect thread damage, such as nicks or burrs, that could compromise the integrity of the fastener. Additionally, a vision system can assess the overall quality of the threads, including their uniformity and consistency. By analyzing multiple threads across a sample of nuts and bolts, the system can detect variations in thread pitch or depth that may indicate manufacturing issues. Moreover, a vision system can provide quantitative data on thread dimensions and characteristics. This data can be used to ensure that the nuts and bolts meet the specified standards and tolerances. It can also be used for process optimization, allowing manufacturers to identify and correct issues in their production processes. Overall, a vision system offers a comprehensive and reliable method for evaluating the thread quality of nuts and bolts. Its ability to detect defects, assess thread quality, and provide quantitative data makes it an invaluable tool for ensuring the reliability and performance of fasteners in various applications.

In this case study, we will develop a vision system to check if a bolt has evenly spaced threads which is crucial to ensure the reliability and ease of installation of bolts. We begin by setting up a Pi camera interfaced to a Raspberry Pi board for capturing real-time video feed. This setup is illustrated in Figure 11-1. Once the camera is set up to capture the bolt image in its line of sight, we need to perform the initial configurations in the Raspberry Pi OS as discussed in Chapter 2. Then we need to install the *picamera* library using pip. Once these initial steps are taken care of, we can proceed to develop the code for capturing the video frames and determining the thread quality.

Figure 11-1. *Interfacing camera to Rasberry Pi board for capturing bolt image*

We will begin the code development by first creating a function for detecting the thread quality as follows. The operations performed by the function to determine the thread spacing in the bolt image are as follows:

1. Convert the input frames to grayscale.

2. Apply Gaussian blur using the *GausssianBlur()* function to reduce noise.

3. Apply thresholding using the *threshold()* function to get a binary image.

4. Contour Detection: Apply the *findContours()* function to find contours in the binary image that represent the threads of the nut.

5. Contour Filtering: Filter out contours that are too
    large or too small that are likely to be noise. This is
    done by using a lower as well as higher threshold
    on the contour area determined by applying the
    contourArea() function on the detected contours.

6. Center Calculation: For each valid contour, we
    calculate the center of the contour by finding
    its centroid. This is done by approximating the
    contours to polygons via the following steps:

    a. We first begin by determining a tolerance parameter *epsilon*
        for the contour approximation. This is done by setting this
        parameters to a small percentage (0.02) of the contour's
        perimeter, determined using the *arcLength()* function.

    b. The *approxPolyDP()* function is then used to approximate
        the contour to a polygon by using the tolerance parameter
        calculated in the previous step.

    c. Next, the moments of the approximated polygon are
        calculated using the *moments()* function.

    d. If the zeroth moment, which indicates the total pixel count,
        is not zero, then we calculate the x- and y-coordinates of
        the center of mass of the approximated polygon using the
        first-order moments *M["m10"]* and *M["m01"]*, divided by the
        zeroth moment *M["m00"]*.

7. Finally, we calculate the distance between adjacent thread centers and then calculate the average distance between threads. If the distances between threads are within a tolerance of 5 pixels from the average distance, then the threads are considered evenly spaced.

8. To display the results, as to whether the threads are evenly spaced or not, over the image, we use the *putText()* function.

This final image with the details of spacing as well as the status of the thread quality ('Good!' or 'Bad!') is returned by the function as illustrated in the following code.

```
import cv2
import numpy as np
from picamera import PiCamera
from picamera.array import PiRGBArray
def detect_thread_quality(image):
    gray = cv2.cvtColor(image, cv2.COLOR_BGR2GRAY)
    # Apply Gaussian blur to reduce noise
    blur = cv2.GaussianBlur(gray, (5, 5), 0)
    # Apply thresholding to get binary image
    _, thresh = cv2.threshold(blur, 200, 255, cv2.
    THRESH_BINARY)
    # Find contours
    contours, _ = cv2.findContours(thresh, cv2.RETR_TREE, cv2.
    CHAIN_APPROX_SIMPLE)
    # Filter out contours that are too large or too small
    valid_contours = []
    for contour in contours:
        area = cv2.contourArea(contour)
```

```
    if 100 < area < 1000:
        valid_contours.append(contour)
# Find the center of each thread
centers = []
for contour in valid_contours:
    # Approximate the contour to a polygon
    epsilon = 0.02 * cv2.arcLength(contour, True)
    approx = cv2.approxPolyDP(contour, epsilon, True)
    # Calculate the center of the contour
    M = cv2.moments(approx)
    if M["m00"] != 0:
        cx = int(M["m10"] / M["m00"])
        cy = int(M["m01"] / M["m00"])
        centers.append((cx, cy))
# Calculate the distance between adjacent centers
if len(centers) > 1:
    distances = [centers[i+1][0] - centers[i][0] for i in
    range(len(centers)-1)]
    avg_distance = sum(distances) / len(distances)
    is_evenly_spaced = all(abs(d - avg_distance) < 12 for d
    in distances)
    # Display if threads are evenly spaced based on average
    distance
    if is_evenly_spaced:
        cv2.putText(image, "Threads are evenly spaced",
        (20, 30), cv2.FONT_HERSHEY_SIMPLEX, 0.8, (0,
        255, 0), 2)
        status = 'Good!'
    else:
        cv2.putText(image, "Threads are not evenly spaced",
        (20, 30), cv2.FONT_HERSHEY_SIMPLEX, 0.8,
        (0, 0, 255), 2)
```

```
        status = 'Bad!'
    # Draw circles around the threads
    for center in centers:
        cv2.circle(image, center, 5, (0, 0, 255), -1)
    return status, image
```

In the next stage we are going to use the function to detect the thread quality from a bolt image in a video feed and display the result back in a GUI. For this purpose, we are going to reuse the GUI that we developed in Chapter 6 with some refinements suited for our use case as illustrated here. First, we import the *picamera* method from the picamera library that will allow us capture image using the Pi camera and also import the *PiRGBArray* method that will allow us to read the captured frames as raw numpy arrays. The GUI is comprised of two frames. The first frame consists of two video canvasses where the first canvas is used for displaying the frames captured with the Pi camera and the second canvas is used to display the processed frames returned by our function marked with the thread centers as well as the text containing the thread spacing details. The second frame, placed parallel to the first frame with the canvasses, consist of a label widget with the text *Thread Quality* and an entry widget to display the status of the thread quality received from our function. The resulting output as displayed in the GUI is shown in Figure 11-2.

```
from tkinter import *
from tkinter import filedialog
import cv2
from PIL import Image, ImageTk
import datetime
from picamera import PiCamera
from picamera.array import PiRGBArray
from ocr_det import ocr_det
# Create the main application window
```

```python
root = Tk()
root.title("Industrial Vision App")
root.geometry("1600x1000")
root.configure(bg="blue")
# Function to close the window
def close_window():
    root.destroy()
# Create labels
company_label = Label(root, text="KMAKGA Corporation Ltd",
                borderwidth=5, relief="ridge",
                font=("Arial Black", 24), fg="red",
                bg="dark blue")
company_label.grid(row=0, column=0, columnspan=4, padx= 30,
pady=0, sticky="ew")
version_label = Label(root, text="Version 1.0",bg="blue")
version_label.grid(row=1,column=2,padx=0,pady=0,sticky="e")
vision_label = Label(root, text="Vision System",
font=("Helvetica", 16,"bold"), fg="red", bg="blue")
vision_label.grid(row=2, column=0, columnspan=3, padx=0,
pady=10, sticky="ew")
# Create a frame to hold the canvases
frame = Frame(root, width=800, height=800, relief="ridge",
borderwidth=1,bg="blue")
frame.grid(row=3,column=0,padx=10,pady=0)
# Create canvases
video_canvas1 = Canvas(frame, borderwidth=2, width=500,
height=400, bg="blue")
video_canvas1.grid(row=3,column=0,padx=5,pady=5)
video_canvas2 = Canvas(frame, borderwidth=2, width=500,
height=400, bg="blue")
video_canvas2.grid(row=3,column=1,padx=5,pady=5)
```

```python
video_canvas1.create_text(80, 10, text="Video Feed",
font=("Helvetica", 10), anchor="ne")
video_canvas2.create_text(110, 10, text="Thread Image",
font=("Helvetica", 10), anchor="ne")
# Create a frame to display the thread quality
entry_frame = Frame(root, width=200, height=400, bg="blue")
entry = Text(entry_frame, borderwidth=2, relief="ridge",
height=1, width=10)
label = Label(entry_frame, text='Thread Quality',
font=("Helvetica", 18), fg="black", bg="blue")
label.grid(row=1, column=0, padx=5, pady=25, sticky="n")
entry.grid(row=1, column=1, padx=5, pady=25, sticky="w")
entry_frame.grid(row=3, column=1, padx=5, pady=5)
# create a close button
close_button = Button(root, width=15, height=2, borderwidth=2,
relief="ridge", text="Exit",  command=close_window)
close_button.grid(row=4, column=0, columnspan=2, padx=0,
pady=50, sticky="n")
# Function to update the video canvas with webcam feed
def update_video_canvas():
    for frame in camera.capture_continuous(cap, format='bgr',
    use_video_port=True):
        # Display original video in the first canvas
        orig_photo = ImageTk.PhotoImage(image = Image.
        fromarray(frame.array))  # Get frame data
        video_canvas1.create_image(0, 30, image=orig_photo,
        anchor=NW)
        video_canvas1.photo = orig_photo
        # Thread quality detection
        status, thread_dist_img = detect_thread_quality
        (frame.array)  # Get frame data
```

```
        thread_photo = ImageTk.PhotoImage(image = Image.
        fromarray(thread_dist_img))
        video_canvas2.create_image(0, 30, image=thread_photo,
        anchor=NW)
        video_canvas2.photo = thread_photo
        # Update the status to the text entry widget
        entry.delete(0.0, END)
        entry.insert(END, status)
        video_canvas1.after(10, update_video_canvas)
        # Schedule next update
        cap.truncate(0)
# Open the Pi cam
camera = PiCamera()
cap = PiRGBArray(camera)
# Call the update_video_canvas function to start displaying the
video feed
  update_video_canvas()
# Start the tkinter main loop
root.mainloop()
```

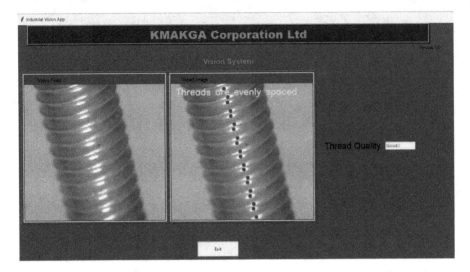

Figure 11-2. *Illustration of a thread quality detection system*

Case Study 11.2: Identifying Unmatched Components in a Set of Components

Identifying industrial components involves recognizing their characteristics, functions, and specifications. This skill is crucial for maintenance, repair, and replacement activities in industries such as manufacturing, automotive, and electronics. Here's how to identify OK and not OK parts in an industrial setting:

- Physical Inspection: Start by visually inspecting the component. Look for any signs of damage, wear, or corrosion. Check for any visible markings or labels that indicate the part number, manufacturer, or specifications.

- Measurements: Use precision measuring tools such as calipers, micrometers, or gauges to measure the dimensions of the component. Compare the measurements to the specifications provided by the manufacturer to ensure they are within tolerance limits.

- Functional Testing: If possible, test the component to ensure it functions correctly. This may involve connecting it to a test rig or system to verify its performance.

- Documentation: Refer to technical documentation such as manuals, datasheets, or schematics to identify the component and verify its specifications. Cross-reference the information with the physical characteristics of the component.

- Manufacturer Information: Look for any markings or labels that indicate the manufacturer of the component. This can help verify its authenticity and quality.

- Online Resources: Use online resources such as manufacturer websites, forums, or databases to research the component and find relevant information.

- Consultation: In case there is no clarity about the identification of a component, consult with colleagues, industry experts, or suppliers who may have experience with similar components.

Identifying OK and not OK parts in an industrial setting is crucial for maintaining operational efficiency, ensuring safety, and avoiding costly downtime. By following these guidelines and using the right tools and resources, industrial components can be accurately identified to make informed decisions about their maintenance and replacement.

Implementing an industrial vision system for identifying OK and not OK parts offers numerous advantages. Firstly, such systems provide a high level of accuracy, surpassing manual inspection methods and reducing errors. Secondly, they operate at high speeds, enhancing production efficiency and minimizing downtime. Thirdly, industrial vision systems ensure consistent results, applying the same inspection criteria to all parts. Additionally, while there may be initial setup costs, these systems can be cost-effective in the long term due to reduced labor expenses and increased operational efficiency. Moreover, these systems are flexible, easily adapting to inspect different parts or accommodate changes in production processes. They also enable data collection for analysis and process improvement. Furthermore, integrating vision systems with other industrial systems allows for a fully automated production line. By identifying defects early, these systems enhance product quality and reduce waste. Lastly, by automating the inspection process, industrial vision systems improve workplace safety by minimizing the need for manual inspection in hazardous environments.

In this case study, we will develop a system to identify unmatched components using a technique called template matching. We will begin by defining a function for identifying the unmatched components and then call this function inside the GUI code, as in our earlier use case, to apply the function on real-time video frames. The following code illustrates this function which takes the captured video frames along with the template images for OK and not OK images as input and produces an image with the status of each component marked on it along with a bounding box. The following are the steps involved in the code:

- Template Matching: Use *OpenCV's matchTemplate()*
  function to find the templates in each frame of the
  video. The input frame, the template image, and the
  template matching mode are provided as parameters to
  this function. In our example we use the *TM_CCOEFF_
  NORMED* which uses normalized cross correlation
  coefficient to measure the similarity between the
  captured frame and the template image.

- Finding Best Matches: The *where()* function in the
  numpy library is then used to locate the positions of
  the best matches for each template in each frame by
  comparing with a threshold value. This threshold value
  helps to filter out matches with a lower confidence level
  thereby reducing false positives. The above two steps
  are done twice with respect to the OK image and not
  OK image.

- Draw Rectangle: The *rectangle()* function is then used
  to create a bounding box around the detected areas for
  both the OK and not Ok images, and then the *putText()*
  function is used to label the areas as 'OK' or 'Not OK',
  respectively.

```
import cv2
import numpy as np
import cv2
import numpy as np
def component_id(frame, template_ok, template_not_ok):
    w_ok, h_ok = template_ok.shape[::-1]
    w_not_ok, h_not_ok = template_not_ok.shape[::-1]
    # Convert frame to grayscale
    gray_frame = cv2.cvtColor(frame, cv2.COLOR_BGR2GRAY)
```

```
  # Perform template matching for "OK" part
 res_ok = cv2.matchTemplate(gray_frame, template_ok, cv2.
TM_CCOEFF_NORMED)
   threshold_ok = 0.8
   loc_ok = np.where(res_ok >= threshold_ok)
   # Perform template matching for "Not OK" part
   res_not_ok = cv2.matchTemplate(gray_frame, template_not_ok,
   cv2.TM_CCOEFF_NORMED)
   threshold_not_ok = 0.8
   loc_not_ok = np.where(res_not_ok >= threshold_not_ok)
   # Draw rectangles for "OK" part
   for pt in zip(*loc_ok[::-1]):
       cv2.rectangle(frame, pt, (pt[0] + w_ok, pt[1] + h_ok),
       (0, 255, 0), 2)
       cv2.putText(frame, 'OK', pt, cv2.FONT_HERSHEY_SIMPLEX,
       0.5, (255, 255, 255), 2)
   # Draw rectangles for "Not OK" part
   for pt in zip(*loc_not_ok[::-1]):
       cv2.rectangle(frame, pt, (pt[0] + w_not_ok, pt[1] +
       h_not_ok), (0, 0, 255), 2)
       cv2.putText(frame, 'Not OK', pt, cv2.FONT_HERSHEY_
       SIMPLEX, 0.5, (255, 255, 255), 2)
   return   frame
```

The function will return the frame with each object in it surrounded by a bounding box and the corresponding label. The next step is to call the function from inside the GUI code to apply it on the frames captured by the webcam as illustrated in the following. The GUI consists of a single frame with two canvasses for displaying the frames from the original video and the output frames produced by the above function. The template functions, shown in Figure 11-3, are read using the *imread()*function within the code. Readers are encouraged to create button widgets to browse and select the template images as we did in Chapter 6. The GUI illustration of the system is shown in Figure 11-4.

```python
from tkinter import *
from tkinter import filedialog
import cv2
from PIL import Image, ImageTk
import datetime
from picamera import PiCamera
from picamera.array import PiRGBArray
from unmatched_part_detection import unmatched_part_detection
# Create the main application window
root = Tk()
root.title("Industrial Vision App")
root.geometry("1600x1000")
root.configure(bg="blue")
# Function to close the window
def close_window():
    root.destroy()
# Create labels
company_label = Label(root, text="KMAKGA Corporation Ltd",
                borderwidth=5, relief="ridge",
                font=("Arial Black", 24),fg="red",
                bg="dark blue")
company_label.grid(row=0,column=0,columnspan=4,padx=30,pady=0,
sticky="ew")
version_label = Label(root, text="Version 1.0",bg="blue")
version_label.grid(row=1,column=2,padx=0,pady=0,sticky="e")
vision_label = Label(root, text="Vision System",
font=("Helvetica", 16,"bold"), fg="red", bg="blue")
```

```
vision_label.grid(row=2, column=0, columnspan=3, padx=0,
pady=10, sticky="ew")
# Create a frame to hold the canvases
frame = Frame(root, width=800, height=800, relief="ridge",
borderwidth=1,bg="blue")
frame.grid(row=3,column=0,padx=10,pady=0)
# Create canvases
video_canvas1 = Canvas(frame, borderwidth=2, width=500,
height=400, bg="blue")
video_canvas1.grid(row=3,column=0,padx=5,pady=5)
video_canvas2 = Canvas(frame, borderwidth=2, width=500,
height=400, bg="blue")
video_canvas2.grid(row=3,column=1,padx=5,pady=5)
video_canvas1.create_text(80, 10, text="Video Feed",
font=("Helvetica", 10), anchor="ne")
video_canvas2.create_text(110, 10, text="Image with detected
parts", font=("Helvetica", 10), anchor="ne")
# create a close button
close_button = Button(root, width=15, height=2, borderwidth=2,
relief="ridge", text="Exit", command=close_window)
close_button.grid(row=4, column=0, columnspan=2, padx=0,
pady=50, sticky="n")
# Load the template images
template_ok = cv2.imread("template_ok.jpg")
template_not_ok = cv2.imread("template_not_ok.jpg")
# Function to update the video canvas with webcam feed
def update_video_canvas():
    for frame in camera.capture_continuous(cap, format='bgr',
    use_video_port=True):
        # Display original video in the first canvas
```

```
        orig_photo = ImageTk.PhotoImage(image= Image.
        fromarray(frame))
        video_canvas1.create_image(0, 30, image=orig_photo,
        anchor=NW)
        video_canvas1.photo = orig_photo
        # Matched parts detection
        parts_match_img = unmatched_part_detection(frame,
        template_ok, template_not_ok)
        parts_img = ImageTk.PhotoImage(image=  Image.
        fromarray(parts_match_img))
        video_canvas2.create_image(0, 30, image=parts_img,
        anchor=NW)
        video_canvas2.photo = parts_img
        video_canvas1.after(10, update_video_canvas)
         cap.truncate(0)
# Open the Pi cam
camera = PiCamera()
cap = PiRGBArray(camera)
# Call the update_video_canvas function to start displaying the
video feed
update_video_canvas()
# Start the tkinter main loop
root.mainloop()
```

(a) template_ok image   (b) template_not_ok image

Figure 11-3. *Template images*

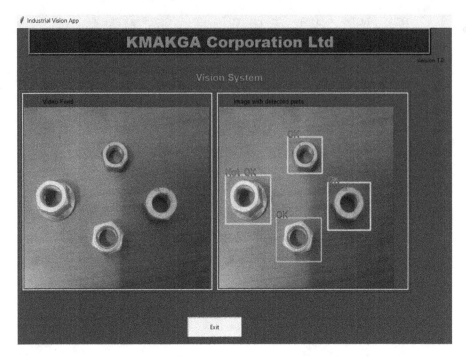

Figure 11-4. *Illustration of matched component detection*

Case Study 11.3: Thread Count Detection System

Quality control is very crucial in manufacturing industries where each component's integrity is critical to the overall functionality and safety of a product. Threaded fasteners, such as nuts and bolts, are an essential component in these sectors as they play a crucial role in joining different pieces together. To ensure their compatibility and dependability during assembly, nuts and bolts must have precise thread counts. In order to verify thread counts without the need for manual labor, computer vision technology can provide a more dependable and effective alternative. The system can quickly and precisely count the threads on nuts and bolts by integrating cameras and image processing algorithms.

In this section, let us discuss how to implement a vision system to ensure that the thread count in a bolt meets a predefined level. Let us first begin by defining a function *thread_count()* to compute the number of threads from a given bolt image, that takes an image and a threshold for the binary thresholding operation as inputs as illustrated in the following code. As we are not interested in the color information, the input image to the function is first converted to a grayscale image which is then inverted using the *bitwise_not()* function in the opencv library and fed into the *threshold()* function that we have discussed earlier in Chapter 5. The threshold value that we obtained as input to our *thread_count()* function is provided to this *threshold()* method. The pixels in the thresholded image are then inverted by subtracting from the maximum pixel value of 255 so that we get a black image of our bolt in a white background. Next, we extract the contours from the image using the *findContours()* method which can help to identify the distinct shapes formed by the threads in the image. The area of each contour is then determined using the *contourArea()* method, and this area can be used to filter out spurious contours formed by noise components in the image. Here we are using a threshold value for area as 4 which implies that a contour must have an area greater than 4 in order to be considered as a thread. The number of threads can therefore be determined by counting the number of contours with area greater than 4.

```
import cv2
def thread_count(img, thres):
    img_gray=cv2.cvtColor(img,cv2.COLOR_BGR2GRAY)
    inv_img=cv2.bitwise_not(img_gray)   #invert b&w colors
    res,thresh_img=cv2.threshold(inv_img, thres, 255, cv2.
    THRESH_BINARY_INV)
    thresh_img=255- thresh_img
```

```
contours,hierarchy=cv2.findContours(thresh_img, cv2.RETR_
TREE,cv2.CHAIN_APPROX_SIMPLE)
area = []
for i in range(len(contours)):
        area.append(cv2.contourArea(contours[i]))
count=len([num for num in area if num > 4])
return count, thresh_img
```

We can now call this function from inside our GUI code, illustrated as follows, to apply it on real-time frames captured from a video. As in our previous thread quality detection system, we have two video canvasses enclosed in a frame, one for displaying the capture video frames and the other for displaying the inverted frames after thresholding using the *thread_count()* function. Another frame consists of two labels: one label with the text *Thread count* followed by a text widget next to it for displaying the count and another label for displaying whether a fault is detected in the bolt image. We pass the captured frames to our *thread_count()* function which will produce two outputs: the count of the threads that is stored in the variable *sumt* and the inverted version of the thresholded image stored in the variable *thresh_img*. In our example, a threshold of 202 is provided to this function, but the value will vary depending upon the nature of the image. The original video frames are displayed in the first canvas, and the inverted frames are displayed in the second canvas.

A conditional statement is then used on the *sumt* variable to determine whether there is any fault in the bolt. We are using a threshold of 20 which implies that input bolt image should have at least 20 threads, the lack of which will be concluded as a faulty component. Therefore, we are passing the string "*No fault is detected*" to the text widget in the case of "*True*" condition and the string "*Fault detected*" in the case of "*False*" condition. To give the messages a distinguishing feature, we are displaying the result of "*True*" condition in green and that of "*False*" condition in red. Also we produce three beep sounds in case of detection of faulty components using the *beep*() method in the *winsound* library. We can configure the frequency and duration of the sound by adjusting the two input parameters to the *beep()* function. The two use cases are shown in Figures 11-5 and 11-6, respectively.

```
from tkinter import *
from tkinter import filedialog
import cv2
from PIL import Image, ImageTk
import time
from picamera import PiCamera
from picamera.array import PiRGBArray
from thread_count import thread_count
import winsound
# Create the main application window
root = Tk()
root.title("Industrial Vision App")
root.geometry("1600x1000")
root.configure(bg="blue")
# Function to close the window
def close_window():
    root.destroy()
# Create labels
company_label = Label(root, text="KMAKGA Corporation Ltd",
                borderwidth=5, relief="ridge",
                font=("Arial Black", 24),fg="red", bg="dark blue")
company_label.grid(row=0, column=0, columnspan=4, padx=30,
pady=0, sticky="ew")
version_label = Label(root, text="Version 1.0",bg="blue")
version_label.grid(row=1,column=2,padx=0,pady=0,sticky="e")
vision_label = Label(root, text="Vision System",
font=("Helvetica", 16,"bold"), fg="red", bg="blue")
```

```
vision_label.grid(row=2, column=0, columnspan=3, padx=0,
pady=10, sticky="ew")
# Create a frame to hold the canvases
frame = Frame(root, width=800, height=800, relief="ridge",
borderwidth=1, bg="blue")
frame.grid(row=3,column=0,padx=10,pady=0)
# Create canvases
video_canvas1 = Canvas(frame, borderwidth=2, width=500,
height=400, bg="blue")
video_canvas1.grid(row=3,column=0,padx=5,pady=5)
video_canvas2 = Canvas(frame, borderwidth=2, width=500,
height=400, bg="blue")
video_canvas2.grid(row=3,column=1,padx=5,pady=5)
video_canvas1.create_text(80, 10, text="Video Feed",
font=("Helvetica", 10), anchor="ne")
video_canvas2.create_text(110, 10, text="Thread Image",
font=("Helvetica", 10), anchor="ne")
# Create a frame to hold the configuration options
entry_frame = Frame(root, width = 200, height = 400, bg="blue")
label1 = Label(entry_frame, text='Thread Count',
font=("Helvetica", 18), fg="black", bg="blue")
entry = Text(entry_frame, borderwidth=2, relief="ridge",
height=10, width=40)
label2 = Label(entry_frame, text=' ', font=("Helvetica", 18),
fg="black", bg="blue")
label1.grid(row=0, column=0, padx=5, pady=25, sticky="n")
entry.grid(row=0, column=1, padx=5, pady=25, sticky="w")
label2.grid(row=3, column=0, columnspan=2, padx=5, pady=25,
sticky="n")
entry_frame.grid(row=3, column=1, padx=5, pady=5)
# create a close button
```

```
close_button = Button(root, width=15, height=2, borderwidth=2,
relief="ridge", text="Exit", command=close_window)
close_button.grid(row=4,column=0,columnspan=2,padx=0,pady=50,s
ticky="n")
# Function to update the video canvas with webcam feed
def update_video_canvas():
        for frame in camera.capture_continuous(cap,
        format='bgr', use_video_port=True):
        # Display original video in the first canvas
        orig_photo = ImageTk.PhotoImage(image = Image.
        fromarray(frame))
        video_canvas1.create_image(0, 30, image=orig_photo,
        anchor=NW)
        video_canvas1.photo = orig_photo
        # Thread detection
        sumt, thresh_img = thread_count(frame,202)
        thread_photo = ImageTk.PhotoImage(image = Image.
        fromarray(thresh_img))
        video_canvas2.create_image(0, 30, image = thread_photo,
        anchor=NW)
        video_canvas2.photo = thread_photo
    # Update thread fault status to text entry widget
    if sumt>=20:
        entry.delete(0.0, END)
        entry.insert(END, sumt)
        label2.config(text = "No fault is detected", fg =
        "green")
        label2.update()
    else:
        entry.delete(0.0, END)
        entry.insert(END, sumt)
```

```
        label2.config(text="Fault detected", fg="red")
        winsound.Beep(440, 500)
        winsound.Beep(440, 500)
        winsound.Beep(440, 500)
        video_canvas1.after(10, update_video_canvas)
        cap.truncate(0)
# Open the Pi cam
camera = PiCamera()
cap = PiRGBArray(camera)
# Call the update_video_canvas function to start displaying the
video feed
update_video_canvas()
# Start the tkinter main loop
root.mainloop()
```

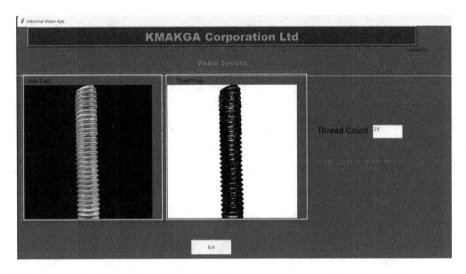

Figure 11-5. *Detection of a healthy component using thread count*

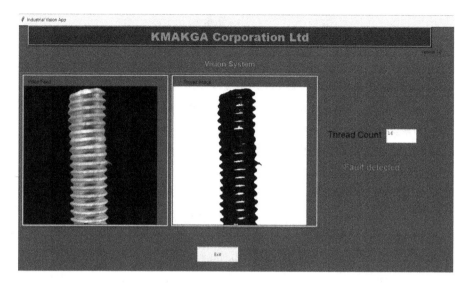

Figure 11-6. *Detection of a faulty component using thread count*

Case Study 11.4: OCR System for Text Extraction

We have already discussed about OCR systems in detail and have gone through different ways of implementing one in Chapter 9. In this section, let us take one of those methods and implement a proper OCR system that detects an image from a video feed, extracts the text from the image, and displays the result. We will use the EasyOCR Python library-based text extraction and also display the video feed from the camera along with the image labeled with the extracted text and the printed text all in a GUI which we built earlier in Chapter 6.

First, we will take the OCR code based on easyocr and convert it into a user-defined function that takes an image as input and returns the labeled image as well as the detected text as the output. This function is illustrated in the following code. The function, which we have named as *ocr_det*, takes an image represented by the variable *img* as the input and

313

returns the labeled image which is the image in the same variable with the bounding box as well as text labels marked on it and the detected text string represented by the variable *t*. Inside the function, the reader object is created using the *Reader()* method from the *easyocr* library and the *readtext()* method of the reader object is then used to detect the text from the image. The output of this method, represented by the variable *results*, will consist of a number of bounding boxes corresponding to different text objects in the image and the corresponding text strings. We iterate over this output to read and mark the text strings along with bounding boxes on the same input image. The additional component we have added here is the variable *t* which is initialized as an empty string before the loop. With each iteration, the corresponding text from the *results* variable is concatenated to this variable.

```python
import easyocr
import cv2
def ocr_det(img):
    # create a reader object and extract text from image
    reader = easyocr.Reader(['en'],gpu=False)
    results = reader.readtext(img,paragraph=True)
    # Create bounding box and display extracted text over
    the image
    t = ''
    for (bbox, text) in results:
        (tl, tr, br, bl) = bbox
        t += text  + '\n'
        tl = (int(tl[0]), int(tl[1]))
        tr = (int(tr[0]), int(tr[1]))
        br = (int(br[0]), int(br[1]))
        bl = (int(bl[0]), int(bl[1]))
        cv2.rectangle(img, tl, br, (0, 0, 255), 2)
```

314

```
cv2.putText(img, text, (tl[0], tl[1]-5),
            cv2.FONT_HERSHEY_PLAIN, 1,(0,0,255),2)
    return img, t
```

Now that we have written the code for OCR system with *easyocr* library as a user-defined function, the next step is to redesign the GUI to accommodate this use case. The following code illustrates our new GUI for OCR system. There are two frames in the GUI. The first frame consists of two video canvasses, one each for displaying the original video capturing an image and the image after text extraction marked with bounding boxes around the text areas and the corresponding text labels. The second frame consists of a label widget displaying the title for the text output and a text widget to display the actual text extracted from the image. To call the function *ocr_det* that we created earlier, we need to import the function from the code by using the filename that we used to save the code. Since the code in our case is saved with the same filename name as the function, we import the function as: *from ocr_det import ocr_det*. Once all the required libraries are imported and all the widgets are created, we then define a program to read frames from video capture object and then apply the *ocr_det* function to extract the text from the image. As discussed earlier, this function will return a labeled image with bounding box around the text areas with corresponding labels and the text string with all the extracted text. The original video frames are displayed in *video_canvas1* and the frames created by the function with the bounding boxes and labels are displayed in *video_canvas2*, and the text string is displayed in the text widget as illustrated in Figure 11-7.

```
from tkinter import *
from tkinter import filedialog
import cv2
from PIL import Image, ImageTk
import datetime
```

```
from picamera import PiCamera
from picamera.array import PiRGBArray
from ocr_det import ocr_det
# Create the main application window
root = Tk()
root.title("Industrial Vision App")
root.geometry("1600x1000")
root.configure(bg="blue")
# Function to close the window
def close_window():
    root.destroy()
# Create labels
company_label = Label(root, text="KMAKGA Corporation Ltd",
                borderwidth=5, relief="ridge",
                font=("Arial Black", 24),fg="red",
                bg="dark blue")
company_label.grid(row=0, column=0, columnspan=4, padx=30,
pady=0, sticky="ew")
version_label = Label(root, text="Version 1.0",bg="blue")
version_label.grid(row=1,column=2,padx=0,pady=0,sticky="e")
vision_label = Label(root, text="Vision System",
font=("Helvetica", 16,"bold"), fg="red", bg="blue")
vision_label.grid(row=2, column=0, columnspan=3, padx=0,
pady=10, sticky="ew")
# Create a frame to hold the canvases
frame = Frame(root, width=800, height=800, relief="ridge",
borderwidth=1, bg="blue")
frame.grid(row=3,column=0,padx=10,pady=0)
# Create canvases
video_canvas1 = Canvas(frame, borderwidth=2, width=500,
height=400, bg="blue")
```

```python
video_canvas1.grid(row=3,column=0,padx=5,pady=5)
video_canvas2 = Canvas(frame, borderwidth=2, width=500,
height=400, bg="blue")
video_canvas2.grid(row=3,column=1,padx=5,pady=5)
video_canvas1.create_text(80, 10, text="Video Feed",
font=("Helvetica", 10), anchor="ne")
video_canvas2.create_text(110, 10, text="Text detection",
font=("Helvetica", 10), anchor="ne")
# Create a frame to display the extracted text
entry_frame = Frame(root, width = 200, height = 400, bg="blue")
entry = Text(entry_frame, borderwidth=2, relief="ridge",
height=10, width=40)
label = Label(entry_frame, text='Detected Text',
font=("Helvetica", 18), fg="black", bg="blue")
label.grid(row=0, column=0, padx=5, pady=25, sticky="n")
entry.grid(row=1, column=0, padx=5, pady=25, sticky="w")
entry_frame.grid(row=3, column=1, padx=5, pady=5)
# create a close button
close_button = Button(root, width=15, height=2, borderwidth=2,
relief="ridge", text="Exit", command = close_window)
close_button.grid(row=4, column=0, columnspan=2, padx=0,
pady=50, sticky="n")
# Function to update the video canvas with webcam feed
def update_video_canvas():
    for frame in camera.capture_continuous(cap, format='bgr',
    use_video_port=True):
        # Display original video in the first canvas
        orig_photo = ImageTk.PhotoImage(image = Image.
        fromarray(frame))
        video_canvas1.create_image(0, 30, image=orig_photo,
        anchor=NW)
```

```
        video_canvas1.photo = orig_photo
        # Text detection using easyocr
        img, t = ocr_det(frame)
        text_photo = ImageTk.PhotoImage(image = Image.
        fromarray(img))
        video_canvas2.create_image(0, 30, image=text_photo,
        anchor=NW)
        video_canvas2.photo = text_photo
     # Update the detected text to the text entry widget
    entry.delete(0.0, END)
    entry.insert(END, t)
    video_canvas1.after(10, update_video_canvas)
    cap.truncate(0)
# Open the Pi cam
camera = PiCamera()
cap = PiRGBArray(camera)
# Call the update_video_canvas function to start displaying the
video feed
update_video_canvas()
# Start the tkinter main loop
root.mainloop()
```

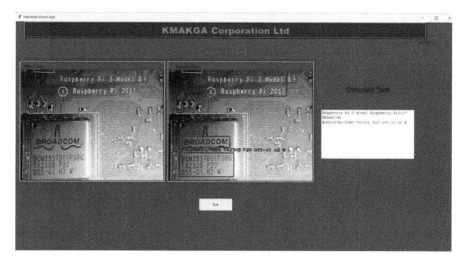

Figure 11-7. *Illustration of OCR detection system*

Summary

Congratulations, you have come to the end of the book! In this chapter, we have developed vision systems for four different industrial applications:

- Thread quality detection from nut/bolt images

- Unmatched components identification from an image consisting of multiple components

- Detection of thread counts in a given nut image

- Extraction of text from an electronic board using OCR technique

It is to be noted that all the systems developed in this chapter are tested in a simple room environment. Implementing the same systems in real industrial environment will have its own set of challenges. Nevertheless, you're encouraged to take the learning from this book and develop more such real-time vision systems.

319

Bibliography

[1] www.ibm.com/in-en/topics/computer-vision

[2] Kashif Shaheed et al., "A Systematic Review on
     Physiological-Based Biometric Recognition Systems:
     Current and Future Trends," Springer: Archives of
     Computational Methods in Engineering, 2021

[3] Younes Akbari et al., "Applications, databases
     and open computer vision research from drone
     videos and images: a survey," Springer: Artificial
     Intelligence Review, 2021

[4] https://automation-insights.blog/2021/03/10/
     machine-vision-5-simple-steps-to-choose-the-
     right-camera/

[5] Mugesh S, Hands-on ML Projects with OpenCV:
     Master computer vision and Machine Learning
     using OpenCV and Python, Kindle edition.

[6] James Chen, Learn OpenCV with Python by
     Examples: Implement Computer Vision Algorithms
     Provided by OpenCV with Python for Image
     Processing, Object Detection and Machine
     Learning, Kindle edition.

[7] Richard Szeliski, Computer Vision: Algorithms and
     Applications, Springer; 2011th edition.

© K. Mohaideen Abdul Kadhar and G. Anand 2024
K. Mohaideen Abdul Kadhar and G. Anand, *Industrial Vision Systems with Raspberry Pi*,
Maker Innovations Series, https://doi.org/10.1007/979-8-8688-0097-9

[8]   Reinhard Klette, Concise computer vision: an introduction into theory and algorithms, Springer-Verlag London, 2014.

[9]   E.R. Davies, Computer vision: principles, algorithms, applications, learning, 5th Edition Elseiver, - November 14, 2017.

[10]   Hartley, R., & Zisserman, A. (2003). Multiple View Geometry in Computer Vision. Cambridge University Press.

[11]   Shanmugamani, R. (2018). Deep Learning for Computer Vision. Packt Publishing.

[12]   Kaehler, A., & Bradski, G. (2016). Learning OpenCV 3: Computer Vision in C++ with the OpenCV Library. O'Reilly Media.

[13]   Solem, J. E. (2012). Programming Computer Vision with Python. O'Reilly Media.

[14]   Towards Data Science. Computer Vision. Retrieved from `https://towardsdatascience.com/tagged/computer-vision`

[15]   Rosebrock, A. PyImageSearch Blog. Retrieved from `https://www.pyimagesearch.com/blog/`

Index

A

Application programming
    interface (API)
    Azure compute
        vision, 240–247
    cloud-based services, 230
    definition, 230
    Google®, 231–240
Artificial intelligence (AI), 2, 7, 258
Artificial neural networks (ANNs),
    223, 261–264, 283
Azure Compute Vision
    deployment completion
        message, 243
    get_read_result() method, 245
    home page, 244
    keys and endpoint, 244
    Operation-Location URL
        string, 245
    physical infrastructure, 240
    portal home page, 241
    Python code, 245
    service configuration page, 242
    source code, 246–249
    steps, 241

B

Binary Large Objects (Blob)
    detection, 134–136
Binary Robust Independent
    Elementary Features
    (BRIEF), 181–185, 197

C

Camera Serial Interface (CSI)
    advantages, 27
    command line, 28
    interface, 27, 28
    module, 27
    OpenCV library, 31
    PiCamera module, 29
    Python library, 29
    source code, 29
    stream resulting, 31
    terminal window, 30
    USB ports, 30
Character user interface (CUI), 142
Charge-coupled device (CCD), 88
Cloud computing
    platform, 240

P, Q

GPSR Compliance
The European Union's (EU) General Product Safety Regulation (GPSR) is a set
of rules that requires consumer products to be safe and our obligations to
ensure this.

If you have any concerns about our products, you can contact us on

ProductSafety@springernature.com

In case Publisher is established outside the EU, the EU authorized
representative is:

Springer Nature Customer Service Center GmbH
Europaplatz 3
69115 Heidelberg, Germany